THE QURʾĀN AND KERYGMA

Themes in Qur'ānic Studies

Series Editors

Mustafa Shah
School of Oriental and African Studies, University of London

Abdul Hakim al-Matroudi
School of Oriental and African Studies, University of London

This series aims to introduce critical issues in the academic study of The Qur'ān and offers a variety of topics essential to providing an historical overview of The Qur'ān and the interrelated traditional teachings and beliefs which issue from it.

Published

Muslim Qur'ānic Interpretation Today
Media, Genealogies and Interpretive Communities
Johanna Pink

Philosophical Perspectives on Modern Qur'ānic Exegesis
Key Paradigms and Concepts
Massimo Campanini

Forthcoming

Prophets and Prophecy in the Qur'ān
Narratives of Divine Intervention in the Story of Humankind
Anthony H. Johns

Sufism and Scripture
A Historical Survey of Approaches to the Qur'ān in the Sufi Tradition
Harith Bin Ramli

The Qur'ān and its Concepts
Through the Lens of Scholarly Disciplines
Ulrika Mårtensson

THE QURʾĀN AND KERYGMA

BIBLICAL RECEPTIONS OF THE MUSLIM SCRIPTURE ACROSS A MILLENNIUM

Jeffrey Einboden

equinox

SHEFFIELD UK BRISTOL CT

Published by Equinox Publishing Ltd.

UK: Office 415, The Workstation, 15 Paternoster Row, Sheffield, South Yorkshire S1 2BX
USA: ISD, 70 Enterprise Drive, Bristol, CT 06010

www.equinoxpub.com

First published 2019

British Library Cataloguing-in-Publication Data
A catalogue record for this book is available from the British Library.

ISBN-13 978 1 78179 410 4 (hardback)
978 1 78179 411 1 (paperback)
978 1 78179 815 7 (ePDF)

Library of Congress Cataloging-in-Publication Data
Names: Einboden, Jeffrey, author.
Title: The Qur'ān and kerygma : biblical receptions of the Muslim scripture across a millennium / Jeffrey Einboden.
Description: Bristol, CT ; Sheffield, UK : Equinox, [2019] | Series: Themes in Qur'ānic studies | Includes bibliographical references and index. | Identifiers: LCCN 2018025066 (print) | LCCN 2018025878 (ebook) | ISBN 9781781798157 (ePDF) | ISBN 9781781794104 (hb) | ISBN 9781781794111 (pb)
Subjects: LCSH: Qur'an--Relation to the Bible. | Qur'an as literature. | Bible as literature. | Qur'an--Influence. | Comparative literature.
Classification: LCC BP134.B4 (ebook) | LCC BP134.B4 E35 2019 (print) | DDC 297.1/22609--dc23
LC record available at https://lccn.loc.gov/2018025066

Typeset by Advent Publishing Services, London

CONTENTS

Acknowledgements ix

INTRODUCTION 1

1
FROM AL-FĀTIḤA TO HALLELUJAH:
THE QUR'ĀNIC PSALTER OF ḤAFṢ AL-QŪṬĪ 9

2
'VERILY HAVE I FOUND ALLAH OFT-RETURNING':
THE QUR'ĀNIC POETICS OF SULAYMĀN AL-GHAZZĪ 35

3
'THE RELIGION OF THE MESSIAH IN MULTITUDES':
ECHOES OF THE QUR'ĀN ACROSS CHRISTIAN SCHISMS 56

4
'ADHERES TO THE ARABIC IDIOM':
LUDOVICO MARRACCI'S QUR'ĀNIC VULGATES 81

5
'BY ORIGIN AND LANGUAGE AN HEBREW':
THE GENESIS OF A JUDAIC QUR'ĀN 102

6
A 'TOTALLY TYPOLOGICAL' CHRISTIAN QUR'ĀN:
NORTHROP FRYE'S TRIPLE MIRROR 124

CODA: 'SYNTHESIS OF THE WORD' 144

Bibliography 148
Index 157

For my parents,

Pam and Ed

ACKNOWLEDGEMENTS

Concerned with textual encounters that cross multiple scriptural traditions, this study is itself multiple in its debts, aided by innumerable sources spanning several decades. My parents, Pam and Ed, to whom this study is dedicated, have set an example of love and wisdom that guides all my efforts, professional and personal. My wife, Hillary, and our children, Ezra and Eve, remain the gifts of my life for which I can never express sufficient gratitude.

Completed in Canada, and authored primarily in the US, *The Qur'ān and Kerygma* owes its material origins to colleagues and conferences in England, where I first came to read the Qur'ān in literary critical terms. During my doctoral work at the University of Cambridge in the early 2000s, I benefited immeasurably from the patient tutelage of Timothy Winter and Nadira Auty. In 2011 and 2013, Shawkat Toorawa facilitated my contribution to SOAS conferences on the Qur'ān in London, where I also met Todd Lawson, whose scholarship has fruitfully impacted this study, especially its sixth chapter. It is Mustafa Shah, also at SOAS, however, whose aid has been most crucial to *The Qur'ān and Kerygma.* Editor of the Equinox series Themes in Qur'ānic Studies to which this book is privileged to contribute, Mustafa's graciousness has proved essential to my efforts for many years, and *The Qur'ān and Kerygma* in particular would have been impossible without his encouragement, suggestions, and corrections. At Equinox, I am also grateful for anonymous peer-review feedback, as well as the superb editorial work of Amir Dastmalchian.

The Qur'ān and Kerygma owes inspiration also to Fr Sidney H. Griffith, and his pioneering scholarship on the early Christian Arabic canon; my thanks to Fr Isaac Slater for introducing me many years ago to Fr Sidney and his works. During the writing of *The Qur'ān and Kerygma,* parallel research projects have received essential support from many generous colleagues; I name with especial gratitude Jeff Barbeau, David Grafton, Timothy Marr, Walid Saleh, Asma Sayeed, Brian Yothers, and Eric Ziolkowski. I express my thanks also to Roma Kali who offered indispensable aid during my research at the Victoria University Library in Toronto, and to the library itself for permission to quote from their archival materials in Chapter 6.

Vital during these same years has been constant support from friends and family, including Becky, Steve, Avery, Josh, and Rachel; Syd and Lily;

Shelley and Mike; Andrew, Brad, James, Matt, Matthew, and Richard. Colleagues, students, and staff at Northern Illinois University have helped me in myriad ways as well, especially Betty Birner, who has not only encouraged my work, but enlivened it through regular conversations concerning both the Bible and the Qur'ān. At NIU, I am also deeply grateful to Melissa Adams-Campbell; Lara and Tim Crowley; Ryan Hibbett and Jessica Reyman; Amy Newman; Kathleen Renk; and Luz Van Cromphout.

To NIU I am also thankful for funding my final research during the summer of 2017, supporting my current stay in Toronto to complete *The Qur'ān and Kerygma*, where I write these last words of the book. Aptly, it was in Toronto that twenty years ago I worked towards my first degrees at York University, reading with gracious teachers who themselves had studied at the University of Toronto under Northrop Frye, whose words envelope this entire study.

Jeffrey Einboden
August 2017
University of Toronto

INTRODUCTION

> Ordinary rhetoric does not really proclaim: it gives an emotional tone to arguments and uses poetic figures to colour appeals to immediate action, but it seldom comes near the primary concern of 'How do I live a more abundant life?' This latter on the other hand is the central theme of all genuine kerygmatic, whether we find it in the Sermon on the Mount, the Deer Park Sermon of Buddha, the Koran, or in a secular book that revolutionizes our consciousness. In poetry anything can be juxtaposed, or implicitly identified with, anything else. Kerygma takes this a step further and says, 'You are what you identify with.' We are close to the kerygmatic whenever we meet the statement, as we do surprisingly often in contemporary writing, that it seems to be language that uses man rather than man that uses language.[1]

Published in 1990, *Words with Power: Being a Second Study of 'The Bible and Literature'* proved to be Northrop Frye's 'last big book', appearing just months before the Canadian critic's death in 1991.[2] A sequel, or 'second study', to his 1982 *The Great Code: The Bible and Literature*, the 1990 *Words with Power* culminated Frye's long career of publishing, but also his lifetime of pedagogy, arising from Frye's 'classic [...] lectures on the Bible and Literature' delivered over thirty years at Victoria College, University of Toronto.[3] And it is *Words with Power* from which the above selection derives, this full paragraph reflecting the interdisciplinary scope of Frye's engagements with 'The Bible and Literature', stretching from ancient scriptures to the modern 'secular', engaged with literature's 'poetic figures' as well as humanity's 'primary concern'. If plural in interest, Frye's above quotation is also catalysed by a single mode of expression, '*kerygma*' (κῆρυγμα), a Greek term typically translated as 'proclamation'.[4] Most often associated with the Gospels – with acts of Christian 'proclaiming', such as 'the Sermon on the Mount' – Frye's own definition of the 'kerygmatic' reaches well beyond the Christian scriptures, embracing ecumenically other sources, both religious and extra-religious, from a 'sermon' by the Buddha, to any 'secular book that revolutionizes our consciousness'. Amid these various verbal expressions, both specific and generic, Frye also lists an entire sacred canon, his catalogue including the title of a complete scripture: 'the Koran'. Mentioned briefly in his miscellany, the Muslim scripture seems peripheral to Frye's interests overall; and yet, his passing Qur'ānic allusion occupies a place that is surprisingly central. Despite its fleeting and parenthetical appearance, 'the Koran' forms the precise heart of Frye's paragraph, this two-word phrase exactly intersecting this *Words with Power* selection, the Muslim scripture emerging right in the middle of Frye's 'kerygmatic' discussion.[5]

The 'most cited literary critic and theorist in the world' during the years leading up to his last decade – the decade that spanned the publication of *Great Code* and *Words with Power* – Frye offers an apt opening to *The Qur'ān and Kerygma* in the above quotation from his 'last big book'. Not only does Frye set the titular terms for the present study but he also implicitly sets the 'primary concerns'.[6] Appealing to the Qur'ān while addressing Christian 'proclamation', Frye's paragraph is comparative in scope, and creative in emphasis; more importantly, however, it inadvertently situates the Muslim scripture at its structural centre, 'the Koran' emerging as the hidden interior to Frye's literary criticism of 'the genuine kerygmatic'. And, indeed, it is the Qur'ān's centrality to the Bible's literary afterlives that is explored in the present study. While the Qur'ān's biblical foregrounds have long been debated, including the Muslim scripture's complex relationship and response to the Judeo-Christian canon, this contentious subject has largely overshadowed a reciprocal interest that motivates *The Qur'ān and Kerygma*.[7] Rather than read the Muslim scripture in light of its biblical antecedents, the present study adopts the inverse approach, arguing that the Qur'ān has intersected innovative acts of biblical translation, composition, and commentary. As with Frye's paragraph, the Qur'ān seems marginal, and yet proves surprisingly central, to creative receptions and renditions of the Bible, enriching acts of authorship and interpretation that have contoured the legacy and language of Judeo-Christian 'kerygma'.

If Frye unintentionally performs the Qur'ān's forgotten centrality, his paragraph on the 'genuine keygmatic' from *Words with Power* also pinpoints the problematics of intentionality itself. 'We are close to the kerygmatic', Frye suggests, 'whenever we meet the statement [...] that it seems to be language that uses man rather than man that uses language.' Privileging the 'power' of 'language' – its ability to 'proclaim' both beyond and above authorial intent – Frye identifies another element central to *The Qur'ān and Kerygma*. Exploring the impact of Islamic idioms on non-Muslim authors and exegetes, the present study highlights the capacity of Qur'ānic 'language' to survive and to signify across cultural contexts and religious confessions, frequently in tension with the faith commitments of the very figures involved. While appeals to the Qur'ān by Western Christians such as Northrop Frye are typically framed in terms of 'orientalism' – implying dynamics of political power, arising from coercive histories of colonialism or imperialism – *The Qur'ān and Kerygma* instead explores the fertile endurance of Islamic expression within Christian contexts, with the Muslim scripture informing acts of biblical critique, creativity, and philology despite authorial intent and their expected 'uses'.[8] Although firmly committed to their own creeds, the non-Muslim authors featured in *The Qur'ān and Kerygma* produce writings which are syncretic in their linguistic and literary character, exemplifying not a 'religious pluralism' precisely, but sustaining instead 'what might be called a *kerygmatic pluralism*' – a phrase which I coined a dozen years ago when addressing J. W. Goethe's indebtedness to Sufi poetry.[9] Following Frye, *The Qur'ān and Kerygma*'s own 'primary concern' is verbal capacity, rather than cultural violence, investing significance not in the tendentious ambitions of 'man', but in literary trajectories of scriptural transmission, finding Qur'ānic 'words' conveyed 'with power' into novel environs of creative translations, adaptations, and interpretations of the Bible.

This concentration on language specifics also suggests another critical intervention that sustains *The Qur'ān and Kerygma*, namely, its privileging of the actual language of Muslim scripture, detecting diction most often associated with the Qur'ān emerging in biblical renditions and rhetoric. Unsurprisingly, the Qur'ān's impact on non-Muslim authors was most immediate on writers who shared this scripture's own original language. Surprisingly, however, the Qur'ān's role in shaping Christian Arabic literature has received insufficient notice, consistent with the broader scholarly 'neglect' suffered by this rich corpus of religious writings.[10] In recent decades, due to the scholarship of field pioneers such as Fr Sidney H. Griffith and Fr Samir Khalil Samir, as well as very recent efforts of scholars such as Samuel Noble and Alexander Treiger, Christian Arabic literature has gained new readers and garnered renewed attention – a trend which *The Qur'ān and Kerygma* aims to extend, dedicating its initial chapters to Christian Arabic translations and compositions especially indebted to Qur'ānic idioms.[11] Destabilising standard dichotomies of language and locale that frequently frame studies of Christian receptions of the Qur'ān, it is Ḥafṣ ibn Albar al-Qūṭī who stands at the opening to *The Qur'ān and Kerygma*, forming the focus of Chapter 1, which reads al-Qūṭī's ninth-century Arabic psalter rendered in his native Andalusia. Emerging from Europe, not the Middle East, this early instance of Christian Arabic literature is, Chapter 1 argues, decisively informed by Qur'ānic phraseology, with al-Qūṭī crafting a sacred text that synthesises Hebraic scripture, Christian authorship, and Islamic idioms. Shifting genres, from al-Qūṭī's biblical version to the versification of biblical themes, Chapter 2 adds subjectivity to the scriptural, examining the personal and spiritual poetics of the Palestinian bishop, Sulaymān al-Ghazzī. Christian in concern, yet Qur'ānic in character, al-Ghazzī's eleventh-century *Dīwān* is understood in Chapter 2 as complicating standard creedal distinctions; equally polemical and personal, the *qaṣā'id* (sg.

qasīda, i.e., 'ode') of al-Ghazzī are Christological and confessionary, and yet are also ironically sustained by recurrent appeals to Qurʾānic nomenclature and narratives.

Spanning opposing sides of the Mediterranean, the first two chapters of *The Qurʾān and Kerygma* set the scene for the more expansive Chapter 3, which reaches upward in coordinates and chronology, tracing a trajectory that straddles medieval Egypt, early modern England, and revolutionary New England. Opening again with Christian Arabic writings, Chapter 3 finds ecclesiastical authors in the East helping to convey the Qurʾān westward, with Islamic idioms encountered by British orientalists in editing and annotating Arabic historiographies by Christians such as Saʿīd ibn Baṭrīq, Severus ibn al-Muqaffaʿ, and Gregory Bar Hebraeus. Rather than easy syncretism, however, it is sectarianism that shapes Chapter 3, tracing the Qurʾān's emergence amid multiple Christian schisms, with the Muslim scripture impacting authors on contending sides of ecclesiastic controversies and political splits, from the Chalcedonian divide in the Christian East, to England's Civil War, to the Revolutionary War in America. Mediated by Christian Arabic sources, the Muslim scripture surfaces in editions published by pioneering Western Arabists, including Edward Pococke, Oxford's first Laudian Professor of Arabic, as well as the first voice invoked in Chapter 4, which opens with Pococke's influence on another Arabist negotiating Christian rendition and Qurʾānic rhetoric, namely, Ludovico Marracci. Transitioning from English Protestants in Chapter 3, it is the Pope's own confessor who is the focus of Chapter 4, which reads the Qurʾānic engagements that punctuate Marracci's career of Catholic apologetics. Celebrated for generating the last Latin translation of the Qurʾān – the 1698 *Alcorani Textus Universus* – Chapter 4 argues that Marracci's well-known rendition of the Muslim scripture into the Vulgate's vernacular is anticipated by another project earlier in his career: the three-volume *Biblia Sacra Arabica*, a complete translation of the Christian canon into Arabic which Marracci 'had also a hand in' producing.[12] Complementing the biblical character of Marracci's Qurʾānic translation, Chapter 4 is first to accent the Qurʾānic character of the *Biblia Sacra Arabica* – a 1671 translation that closes the circle of transmission initiated in Chapter 3, with Qurʾānic idioms no longer conveyed westward via Christian Arabic sources, but sent eastward in the pages of an Arabic Vulgate intended to 'propagate' Christianity in Muslim lands.

The final section of Chapter 4 turns to Marracci's afterlives, introducing the figure most immediately engaged by both the Italian's example and his errors: George Sale, London lawyer and English Arabist. As his predecessor, Sale not only renders the Qurʾān like Marracci, but also contributes to yet another Arabic translation of the Bible. However, unlike Marracci's *Alcoran*, Sale's 1734 English *Koran* will prove immensely influential, inspiring a range of fresh readings and renditions of the Muslim scripture, including its first translation into the very first biblical language: Hebrew. Surfacing at the end of Chapter 4, Sale's *Koran* forms the opening to Chapter 5, identified as the foreground to *al-Qōrān ō ha-Miqrā* – the pioneering Hebrew rendition of the Qur'ān by Hermann Reckendorf, published while lecturing on Semitic languages in Leipzig. Religiously discrete from previous Christian texts covered in *The Qur'ān and Kerygma*, Reckendorf's *al-Qōrān* comprises a Judaic translation that targets Jewish readers; published at the heart of Christian Europe, however, Reckendorf's *al-Qōrān* also intersects mid-century trends of biblical critique, both reflecting and resisting the philological and exegetical priorities of contemporary Christendom. Recalling the Arabic psalter of Ḥafṣ al-Qūṭī – which itself comprised a Christian translation of a Hebrew original via Islamic idioms – Reckendorf's publication of a Judaic Qur'ān in Christian Leipzig is shown in Chapter 5 to triangulate the three Abrahamic traditions, extending a complex trajectory of intra-scriptural exchange that reaches back to the beginning of *The Qur'ān and Kerygma*. Although unique in the nineteenth century, and still overlooked in the twenty-first, Reckendorf's rendition seems uniquely at home in the present study, deriving fresh definitions of biblical diction through Qur'ānic translation, with Judaic idioms and identities from both the Tanakh and the New Testament assuming new significance in the Hebrew *sūra*s of Reckendorf's *al-Qōrān*.

Following the focus of Chapter 5 on the forgotten translation of the Qur'ān into biblical idioms, it is the Qur'ān's hidden contributions to the 'Bible and Literature' which Chapter 6 considers, the concluding chapter of the present study dedicated to the Muslim scripture's impact on ordained United Church minister, and leading literary critic, Northrop Frye. Completing *The Qur'ān and Kerygma*'s northward and westward trajectory, as well as its progress up to the present day, Chapter 6 concludes in twentieth-century Canada, finding the Muslim scripture surfacing not only in Frye's widely distributed publications – such as *Words with Power*, quoted above – but also within venues more private, spanning Frye's pedagogical lectures and his personal marginalia. Implying Frye's intimate familiarity with the Qur'ān – a scripture cited to his students during classroom instruction and densely annotated when alone, with Frye's scribbles filling private copies of the Qur'ān now archived at the Victoria University Library, Toronto – Chapter 6 also situates the Muslim scripture as both a catalyst and complicating factor for Frye's literary approach to the Bible. Exemplifying for Frye aspects of the 'genuine kerygmatic', the Qur'ān also threatens to disrupt the closed coherency of the two testaments, occupying a third position that not only reinforces, but also reverses, the intentions of Frye's biblical criticism.

Returning to the problematics of intention and coherency in the final chapter, Chapter 6 of *The Qur'ān and Kerygma* also recalls the above quotation from Frye that stands at the opening to this Introduction, challenging the capacity of 'man' to control and to contain 'language' – a challenge that seems equally urgent for *The Qur'ān and Kerygma* itself. Literary in construct, as well as 'concern', the present study adopts a narrative style, tracing broad trajectories, both chronological and geographical. Unfolding westward in space, *The Qur'ān and Kerygma* draws a line forward too in time, spanning eleven centuries, between Ḥafṣ al-Qūṭī's renditions in the 880s and Northrop Frye's last writings in the 1980s. Aspiring to shape its contents into a chronicled sequence, the coherency intended by *The Qur'ān and Kerygma* is, however, anything but comprehensive, with innumerable alternate candidates for consideration falling outside this study's own intentions and limited 'uses'. Omitting sources for scrutiny that could equally exemplify the Qur'ān's impact on biblical legacies – sources, for instance, from the rich legacy of Coptic, Syriac, and Armenian literatures authored in the centuries following the advent of Islam – *The Qur'ān and Kerygma* offers only one possible path up through the 'kerygmatic pluralism' that punctuates the past millennium. Targeting textual case studies that seem exemplary, and yet are ironically often overlooked, it is the *literary* commitments articulated above that most determine this study's selections, concentrating on the verbal creativity of biblical writers as they appeal to the Qur'ān – an aesthetic priority that also accounts for the prominence of poetry in *The Qur'ān and Kerygma*. Celebrated for its semantic possibilities, deriving its 'power' from the capacious flexibility of 'language', poetry is itself an innately synthetic genre, comprising in Frye's formulation a type of literary speech in which 'anything can be juxtaposed, or implicitly identified with, anything else'. Exploring not only sacred verses but also the versifying of scriptures, while gesturing to the acclaimed 'poeticity' of Islamic revelation, *The Qur'ān and Kerygma* begins aptly with the Hebrew Bible's own most iconic book of poetry, finding no better place to open its initial chapter than a Christian's Qur'ānic rendition of the very first lines of Psalm 1.[13]

NOTES

1. Northrop Frye, *Words with Power: Being a Second Study of 'the Bible and Literature'*, ed. Michael Dolzani (Toronto: University of Toronto Press, 2016), p. 110.
2. For *Words with Power* as Frye's 'last big book', see Frye, *Words with Power*, p. viii.
3. This characterisation of Frye's 'classic […] lectures on the Bible and Literature' derives from Bob Rodgers, 'My Archetypal Quest', *The Educated Imagination: A Website Dedicated to Northrop Frye*, March 31, 2010, <https://macblog.

mcmaster.ca/fryeblog/2010/03/31/bob-rodgers-my-archetypal-quest>. Accessed 30 July 2019.

4. A term typically applied to Christian 'proclamation' or 'preaching', 'kerygma' ('κῆρυγμα') is itself a New Testamental term; see, for instance, Romans 16:25, which mentions the 'κήρυγμα Ἰησοῦ Χριστοῦ' ('the preaching of Jesus Christ'; King James Version, subsequently cited as 'KJV').
5. Frye's paragraph comprises 141 words; his phrase – 'the Koran' – comprises words 71 to 72 of this paragraph.
6. For Frye as the 'most cited literary critic and theorist in the world', see the Introduction to *Educating the Imagination: Northrop Frye, Past, Present, and Future*, ed. Alan Bewell, Neil ten Kortenaar, Germaine Warkentin (Montreal and Kingston: McGill-Queen's University Press, 2015), p. 3.
7. For a prominent recent study of the Qurʾān's biblical foregrounds, see, for instance, Gabriel S. Reynolds, *The Qurʾān and its Biblical Subtext* (London: Routledge, 2010).
8. In emphasising 'fertile' Islamic influence on non-Muslim authors and exegetes, rather than 'orientalism', *The Qurʾān and Kerygma* builds upon my 2014 *Islam and Romanticism*, which was 'interested primarily in cultural conversation, rather than political power' (see *Islam and Romanticism: Muslim Currents from Goethe to Emerson* (London: Oneworld, 2014), p. 5). Largely overlooked until Todd Lawson's recent scholarship (cited below in Chapter 6), Frye's own engagements with Islam in general, and the Qurʾān specifically, have received passing mention from Robert Bringhurst in his 'Reading between the Books: Northrop Frye and the Cartography of Literature', in *Educating the Imagination: Northrop Frye, Past, Present, and Future* (pp. 16–35), which notes that Frye 'was keen to read the Koran, in order to compare it against the Bible that he knew so well' (p. 28). Frye also has increasingly attracted notice from theorists and critics of orientalism; see, for instance, Ivan Kalmar, *Early Orientalism: Imagined Islam and the Notion of Sublime Power* (London: Routledge, 2012), p. 25, and Laetitia Nanquette, *Orientalism Versus Occidentalism: Literary and Cultural Imaging between France and Iran since the Islamic Revolution* (London: I. B. Tauris, 2016), pp. 16–17.
9. See Jeffrey Einboden, 'The Genesis of *Weltliteratur*: Goethe's *West-Ostlicher Divan* and Kerygmatic Pluralism', *Literature and Theology* 19:3 (2005): 238–250 (p. 246).
10. See Sidney H. Griffith, *The Church in the Shadow of the Mosque: Christians and Muslims in the World of Islam* (Princeton, NJ: Princeton University Press, 2010), p. 170, who emphasises 'the neglect that continues to plague the memory of the Christians of the world of Islam'. For a recent study that seeks to mitigate this neglect, see Clare Wilde's 2014 book concerning Qurʾānic engagements in 'early Christian Arabic texts', i.e., *Approaches to the Qurʾān in Early Christian Arabic Texts (750–1258 C.E.)* (Bethesda, MD: Academica Press, 2014) – a study which does not, however, treat the primary Arabic authors addressed in *The Qurʾān and Kerygma*, making no mention of Ḥafṣ al-Qūṭī, Sulaymān al-Ghazzī, Ibn Baṭrīq, or Ibn al-Muqaffaʿ, and including only one passing reference to Bar Hebraeus (p. 121).
11. For a formative contribution that includes the scholarship of both Sidney H. Griffith and Samir Khalil Samir see *Christian Arabic Apologetics during the Abbasid Period, 750–1258*, ed. Jørgen S. Nielsen and Samir Khalil Samir (Leiden: E. J. Brill, 1993); see also below for regular citation of individual works by Griffith.

Most notable among the recent efforts from Samuel Noble and Alexander Treiger is their collaboratively-edited volume *The Orthodox Church in the Arab World: 700–1700; An Anthology of Sources* (DeKalb, IL: Northern Illinois University Press, 2014), which is also cited further below.

12. For this assertion that Marracci 'had also a hand in' the 1671 *Biblia Sacra Arabica*, see T. Osborne et al. (eds.), *A New and General Biographical Dictionary: Containing an Historical and Critical Account of the Lives and Writings of the Most Eminent Persons in Every Nation; Particularly the British and Irish*, 12 vols. (London, 1761–1767), vol. 8, p. 249.
13. It is Thomas Hoffmann who has critiqued the Qur'ān's literary character in terms of 'poeticity'; see his *The Poetic Qur'ān*: Studies on *Qur'ānic* Poeticity (Wiesbaden: Harrassowitz, 2007) – a study which also makes passing references to Frye's literary criticism (see pp. 15 and 100).

1

FROM AL-FĀTIḤA TO HALLELUJAH: THE QURʾĀNIC PSALTER OF ḤAFṢ AL-QŪṬĪ

I

‘BUT HIS DESIRE IS IN THE *KITĀB ALLĀH*’

قد أفلح المرء الذي لم يذهب   في رأي أهل الجرم فعل المذنب
ولم يقم على سبيل الاثمة   ولا يكن يجلس بين الظلمة
في مقعد الإزراء والتداهي   لكن هواه في كتاب الله
كان، وفيه تاليا مرددا   نهاره وليله مجتهدا

He has succeeded who proceeds not
in the advice of sinful folk, immoral of act

and does not stand upon the sinners’ way
and does not sit amongst the unjust

upon the seat of contempt and cunning.
But his desire is in the *kitāb Allāh*

for he recites it repeatedly
day and night, diligently[1]

Psalm 1, lines 1–4, from
Ḥafṣ al-Qūṭī’s *Arabic psalter*

Despite their stylised diction and fashioned rhyme, these Arabic lines from ninth-century Spain are readily recognisable as the very first verses of Psalm 1. Establishing themes standard to the Psalms overall, these Arabic verses clearly convey the sense of their Hebraic source, promising success to the pious, while celebrating those who walk not in the ‘way’ of ‘sinners’. If authentic to its biblical original, however, the above translation may also sound oddly familiar to readers of the Qurʾān, with echoes of Islam’s scripture surfacing from its first words. The opening to this initial psalm itself overlaps Qurʾānic phraseology, leading with ‘*qad aflaḥa*’ (he has succeeded) – precisely the first words of verse 14 of Sūrat al-Aʿlā: ‘*qad aflaḥa man tazakkā*’ (‘He has succeeded who purifies himself’).[2] Shifting from its first words to its last, the above rendition of the introduction to Psalm 1 also ends with a word rich in Islamic resonance. At the very end of these Arabic verses, the devotee who searches the scriptures is described as 'diligent' (مجتهد ; *mujtahid*), a term frequently associated with Islamic jurisprudence (*fiqh*), denoting a jurist qualified to interpret 'primary sources'.[3]

These faint Islamic overtones in the introduction to Psalm 1 may seem a mere linguistic accident – the inadvertent result of rendering biblical poetry into ninth-century Arabic, a language inevitably contoured by Qur'ānic traditions. However, if unsurprising due to such historical contexts, these leading lines of Psalm 1 nevertheless offer an instructive precedent, hinting at a scriptural synthesis that shapes each of the primary texts treated in the present book, and especially its first chapter, which reads the pioneering Arabic psalter whose initial verses are excerpted above. Spanning several traditions within a single psalm, these quoted Arabic lines, rendered by Andalusian jurist Ḥafṣ ibn Albar al-Qūṭī (fl. 889), reflect the complex religious life and land from which they emerge. A Christian resident of medieval Córdoba, al-Qūṭī's rendered psalter represents one of the earliest and most extensive 'Mozarabic' texts produced in Muslim Spain; al-Qūṭī's Arabic achievement is not only rare, however, but has been rarely noticed. Beyond the full edition and French translation produced by Marie-Thérèse Urvoy in 1994, al-Qūṭī's Arabic psalms have received relatively little critical attention until very recently, with many details of al-Qūṭī's own life and labours remaining obscure.[4] And yet, although much uncertainty remains regarding al-Qūṭī, his Arabic psalter does, however, clearly mirror an era and area famed for interreligious encounter, reflecting Spain's so-called 'Golden Age' of Abrahamic exchange, known as 'La Convivencia'.[5] Celebrated for fertile contact between Muslims, Christians, and Jews, medieval Spain was also shaped, however, by intra-religious struggles, its foreground featuring discrete Christian traditions in contention. Al-Qūṭī's very name suggests such internecine history. Signifying 'the Goth', Ḥafṣ's patronymic – al-Qūṭī – recalls the Visigothic past of the Iberian peninsula, with Spain first occupied by Arian Goths before the ascendency of Trinitarian orthodoxy during the century before Islam's own arrival in 711.[6] If al-Qūṭī's very name recalls early Spain's intra-Christian sectarianism, his translation also anticipates Muslim Spain's role in bridging global divides, with the Iberian peninsula occupying a cultural pivot between East and West, as well as South and North, conveying Hellenic classics to northern Europe, with texts translated first from Greek to Arabic, and later, from Arabic to Latin.[7] Anticipating the hemispheric and continental straddles of the present study, unfolding from the Middle East to the far West, al-Qūṭī's psalter offers an apt origin for *The Qur'ān and Kerygma* in particular, not only arising from a territory and time uniquely impacted by cultural transfer, but also implying a discrete interplay of divergent cultures of language and textuality: biblical, Qur'ānic, as well as classical. Although al-Qūṭī's psalms reproduce fresh Semitic verses which are ultimately derived from a sister Semitic language – rendering ancient Hebrew into medieval Arabic – al-Qūṭī translates not directly from the Judaic psalter's original, but from a Roman intermediary, that is, St Jerome's Latin translations.[8] Straddling Hebraic source, Christian Vulgate, as well as the Islamic ethos innately arising from its Arabic, al-Qūṭī's psalter stands as a fruitful precedent for the present study, qualifying not only as the earliest text in its chronology, but also comprising a complex marriage of traditions that unfold and intertwine throughout *The Qur'ān and Kerygma*.

Amid its multiplicity of region and religion, a single phrase that seems especially emblematic emerges in the first four lines of al-Qūṭī's psalter, ironically unifying his rendition's diverse traditions. Returning to the initial lines of Psalm 1, as quoted above, a two-word expression in al-Qūṭī's third verse intersects the Islamically-evocative phrases at the opening and end of these lines – a two-word phrase that designates 'scripture' itself. The second half of al-Qūṭī's third line derives from the second verse of Psalm 1, which reads as follows, first in the original Hebrew, and second, in the Latin Vulgate:

כִּי אִם בְּתוֹרַת יְהוָה חֶפְצוֹ
but in the Torah of Jehovah is his delight[9]

sed in lege Domini voluntas eius
but in the law of the Lord is his desire[10]

Compared with these anterior texts, al-Qūṭī's Arabic seems an accurate, though inventive, substitute; rather than Hebrew 'Torah', or Latin 'law', the translation offered by al-Qūṭī adjusts and expands his psalmic source, altering the subject to be studied by the believer:

لكن هواه في كتاب الله
but his desire is in the *kitāb Allāh*

Recalling the scriptural, rather than legal, implication of the Hebrew '*tōrāh*' (תּוֹרָה), al-Qūṭī prefers to leave aside Jerome's 'law', replacing '*lege Domini*' with '*kitāb Allāh*' (the Book of God). Expressing the bibliographic implication of 'Torah' – this term potentially signifying the first five books of the Bible – al-Qūṭī's 'the Book of God' is faithful in a double sense, not only expressing accurately an aspect of his psalmic source, but also forming a flexible replacement that is potentially *full* of faiths, expansively suggesting multiple traditions in a single phrase.[11] Inter-scriptural in resonance, the generic 'Book of God' in al-Qūṭī's Arabic gestures to the biblical canon, helpfully embracing not only the Judaic 'Torah' of the original Psalm 1, but also equally applicable to the entire canon of al-Qūṭī's own Christianity. However, *kitāb Allāh* is additionally an Arabic phrase that evokes not only Judeo-Christian scripture, but also Islamic, qualifying as precisely the words the Qur'ān employs as its own title for itself, emerging in *āyāt* (sg. *āya*, i.e., verse) including 35:29:

> إِنَّ الَّذِينَ يَتْلُونَ كِتَابَ اللَّهِ وَأَقَامُوا الصَّلَاةَ وَأَنفَقُوا مِمَّا رَزَقْنَاهُمْ سِرًّا وَعَلَانِيَةً يَرْجُونَ تِجَارَةً لَّن تَبُورَ
>
> Surely those who recite the Book of God (*kitāb Allāh*) and perform the prayer, and expend of that We have provided them, secretly and in public, look for a commerce that comes not to naught.[12]

Considering its Qur'ānic associations, *kitāb Allāh* seems a somewhat ironic insertion into the opening of al-Qūṭī's psalter, with his first Christian description of the scripture to be studied coming equipped with Islamic resonance. However, the universal 'Book of God', with its subtle Islamic specifications, also marks an opening that anticipates the tensions navigated by the entirety of al-Qūṭī's Christian Arabic psalms. A scriptural introduction that spans dispensations, al-Qūṭī's rendition itself uneasily straddles ecumenical expressions as well as individual spiritual commitments, with al-Qūṭī's psalter comprising a Christian text that refigures Hebraic foregrounds via Qur'ānic phraseology, echoing a self-reference from Islam's scripture in the very opening to its first Psalm.

II

AL-QŪṬĪ'S OPENING AND 'THE OPENER'

The first Arabic lines of al-Qūṭī's first psalm anticipate, more broadly, his psalter's merging of multiple sacred traditions; however, this merger begins even before his first psalm opens, surfacing in al-Qūṭī's extended introduction to his psalter. A theoretical preface to his practical translation, al-Qūṭī's introduction is divided into discrete sections, offering a commentary that covers a wide topical range, from the psalms' verbal style to their interpretive history, emphasising especially the psalter's messianic meaning, appealing to sainted authorities, not only Paul and Augustine, but also Jerome – the translator whose Latin translations serve as al-Qūṭī's own source.[13] Even while surveying Christian contexts for the Hebrew Psalms, however, al-Qūṭī's introduction regularly recruits categories that seem rooted in the Qur'ān. This ecumenical overlap emerges from the opening sentence of al-Qūṭī's introduction, where the psalter's title is first mentioned; rather than label this biblical book with a term deriving from Hebrew, Greek, or Latin, al-Qūṭī instead designates the psalms as '*zabūr*' (زَبُور) – the Qur'ān's own term for the sacred text revealed to King David, first surfacing in the Muslim scripture's fourth chapter (v. 163).[14] It is not only their titular heading, however, but the psalms' body texts, which is anatomised Islamically in al-Qūṭī's introduction; in his Arabic, al-Qūṭī calls each psalm a '*sūra*' (سورة) and each psalmic line an '*āya*' (آية) – utilising these standard elements of Qur'ānic vocabulary for 'chapter' and 'verse', respectively.[15]

It is the interpretive core of his introduction, however, that prompts al-Qūṭī's more provocative appeals to Islamic terminology. Shifting from the psalms's headings to their hermeneutics, al-Qūṭī echoes Muslim traditions as he emphasises the messianic meaning that Christians see in the psalter. Drawing analogies between David (identified as the psalms's primary author) and Christ (identified as the psalms's primary subject), al-Qūṭī characterises the interpretation of the psalter as a type of '*ta'wīl*' (تأويل) – a term itself reminiscent of Qur'ānic traditions, suggesting 'a more mystical and esoteric sort of interpretation' of the Muslim scripture.[16] Indeed, it is *ta'wīl* that al-Qūṭī aptly invokes in passages such as the following from his introduction, which explicitly addresses an 'interior' approach to scriptural interpretation:

واعلم ان المزامير كلها قول ظاهر وباطن، وذلك قول وتأويل وقد فسره العلماء [...]

> And know that all psalms comprise communications either exoteric or esoteric, and that such communication and explanation (*ta'wīl*) have been exposited (*fassara*) by the scholars (*'ulamā'*).[17]

Situating the psalms within traditions of *ta'wīl*, al-Qūṭī first lists familiar categories, contrasting 'exoteric' and 'esoteric', invoking a binary between *ẓāhir* (ظاهر) and *bāṭin* (باطن) – an interpretive opposition especially prevalent within Sufi hermeneutics of the Qur'ān.[18] This exegetical dialectic anticipates al-Qūṭī's denoting the exegetes themselves as 'the *'ulamā'*' (العلماء), a traditional title for 'scholars' typical of Islam. Characterising biblical interpretation in standard terms of *tafsīr* – with biblical *'ulamā'*, such as St. Jerome, framed as a Christian *mufassir* – al-Qūṭī defines the exegetical authority and approach to the psalter with diction and dichotomies reminiscent of the Qur'ān's own interpretation.

Considering such Qur'ānic contexts in his psalter's preface, it is perhaps unsurprising that this same introduction concludes with al-Qūṭī's most climactic appeal to Islamic language. Ascending from mere human expertise to divine omniscience, al-Qūṭī closes his preface by progressing upward from textual interpretation to theological invocation. Outlining the organisation of the psalter itself, summarising its five-section structure, the final words of al-Qūṭī's preface departs from formal detail to invoke a doxological formula, his introduction's last words reading:

والله اعلم واحكم لا شريك له، وهو رب العرش العظيم تمت المصادر والحمد لله رب العالمين

> And Allah is most knowing, and most wise, there is no partner to Him. And He is the Lord of the Great Throne. (Thus) concludes the preliminaries, and praise be to Allah, Lord of the worlds.[19]

Packed with standard conventions, al-Qūṭī closes his preface with Arabic phrases that would seem entirely at home at the conclusion to a Qur'ānic *tafsīr*. From sapience to sovereignty, these lines open first by recognising God's omniscience – utilising the familiar elative *wa-Allāhu a'lam* (And Allah is more/most knowing) – before then appealing to God's majesty, praising Him as 'the Lord of the Great Throne' (*rabb al-'arsh al-aẓīm*): an epithet with clear precedents both in the Qur'ān and the prophetic *ḥadīth*, which also encourage God's remembrance utilising precisely this phrase.[20] Considering its Christian authorship, this emphatic echo of Islamic traditions is intriguing; more striking, however, is the phrase invoked immediately before, with al-Qūṭī celebrating God's singularity by asserting that 'there is no partner to Him' (*lā sharīka lah*) – a monotheistic confession with clear Muslim roots, original to Qur'ān 6:163, and regularly invoked as an Islamic rejection of plurality in the godhead.[21] Apparently unperturbed by the counter-Christian implications of such phrases, al-Qūṭī integrates into his introduction not only this creedal formula reminiscent of Islam, but also splinters of actual Islamic scripture, ending his preface with a Qur'ānic commonplace: *al-hamdu lillāhi rabb al-'ālamīn* (praise be to Allah, Lord of the worlds). Occurring first in the very first *āya* of the Muslim scripture after its opening doxology, al-Qūṭī elects to end his own introduction with the same phrase that inaugurates the Qur'ān, inserting a foundational verse from the Fātiḥa as the conclusion to his psalmic preface.[22] Inscribing Islam's 'Opener' into his own Arabic opening, al-Qūṭī closes his introduction with the very beginning of Islam's scripture, summarising his preface with a cross-kerygmatic appeal that sets the stage for the Qur'ānic psalter to come.

III

PSALMIC *ASMĀ'*

Ending with a fragment from the Qur'ān's first chapter, al-Qūṭī's introduction even earlier had integrated a clear echo from the foremost of all Qur'ānic formulae: the *basmala* – the benediction that prefaces all but one of the Qur'ān's 114 chapters. At the opening to a section that celebrates the psalter's 'recitation' (تلاوة ; *tilāwa*), asserting that the 'prophets' themselves 'prayed' the psalms, al-Qūṭī is prompted to break into praise; in the midst of his prosaic introduction, al-Qūṭī shifts stylistically, elevating his register to reach for poetic worship:

> فسبحان الله ما اعظم خطبه، واجل عجائبه التي (لا) تحصي، والطف مداخله واقرب وسائله،
> الرب القويم الرحمن الرحيم
>
> And glory be to Allah, how magnificent is His speech, and how sublime His wonders (in)numerable, and how gracious are His entrances, and how proximate are His ways of access, the Lord, the upright, the merciful, the compassionate[23]

Recalling standard conventions of devotion, it is the doxology that ends this exclamation that seems most striking; concluding his catalogue of superlative attributes, al-Qūṭī invokes Allah as *al-raḥmān al-raḥīm* (the merciful, the compassionate), precisely the divine names that form the Qurʾān's own doxology (In the name of Allah, the merciful, the compassionate). In recommending the psalter's recitation, it is instead the Qurʾān that is evoked, with al-Qūṭī's preface borrowing from the *basmala* assonant epithets for Allah, rehearsing the most recognisable names of 'mercy' from the Muslim scripture.

Merging the Qurʾān's opening with his psalter's introduction, al-Qūṭī's theoretical preface also anticipates his translation practice, his biblical poetry punctuated with appellations for Allah which are Islamically resonant. Indeed, the most obvious overlap between Qurʾānic diction and al-Qūṭī's own rendition is his regular appeal to '*al-asmāʾ al-ḥusnā*' – the ninety-nine 'most beautiful names' ascribed to God by Islamic traditions, catalogued primarily from the Qurʾān.[24] From the first pages of his Arabic psalter, it is these Islamic *asmāʾ* that emerge in al-Qūṭī's verses, invoking God with names from the ninety-nine such as '*qādir*' (capable); '*muṣawwir*' (fashioner); '*ʿazīz*' (powerful); '*khāliq*' (creator).[25] Echoing his introduction, however, it is the name '*al-raḥmān*' ('the merciful') that most regularly recalls the Qurʾān in al-Qūṭī's psalms – a name not only native to the *basmala*, but also the very title of Chapter 55 of the Qurʾān, that is, Sūrat al-Raḥmān. Appearing across multiple psalms, 'al-Raḥmān' surfaces in al-Qūṭī's rendition of Psalm 46, for instance, whose verses 10 to 11 read as follows:

قدولي الملك على الاجناس　　إلهنا خالق كل الناس
وجلس الرحمن ذو التقدس　　في عرشه المبارك المقدس

Verily the Sovereign reigns over the species
Our God, the Creator of all mankind

The Merciful, possessing sanctity, sits
upon His throne, blessed and holy[26]

Authentically psalmic in sense, God's sole 'sovereignty' in al-Qūṭī's translation yet recalls a range of Islamic precedents, these lines surrounding 'the merciful' with specifically Muslim signatures. Appealing to another of the 'ninety-nine names' – *khāliq*, (خالق ; creator) – al-Qūṭī also recounts the 'sitting' of al-Raḥmān upon his exalted *ʿarsh* (throne), a biblical image that subtly shifts towards Qur'ānic textuality, echoing *āyāt* such as Qur'ān 20:5:

الرَّحْمَنُ عَلَى الْعَرْشِ اسْتَوَى
al-Raḥmān sat Himself upon the *ʿarsh.*

Connecting precisely the two terms that are closely proximate in al-Qūṭī's own line 11, Qur'ān 20:5 itself aligns '*ʿarsh*' with '*al-raḥmān*', forming the first 'sovereign' source for al-Qūṭī's later Psalm 46, holding rhetorical sway over the Andalusian's Arabic rendition.[27]

If the Qur'ān's Sūra 55 – al-Raḥmān – is echoed in al-Qūṭī's appeal to 'the merciful', it is his own Psalm 55 that features an opposing epithet, appealing to God not as compassionate, but as 'the Compeller'. Invoking another of the *asmā' al-ḥusnā* near this psalm's opening, al-Qūṭī translates verse 5 of Psalm 55 as follows:

يا ايهـــا الجبـــار إنـــي ايمـــا　　　يوم فزعت انت لي فيه الرجاء

O, Thou, the Compeller (*al-jabbār*), verily I, on whatever
day that I fear, Thou art my hope[28]

Apostrophising God, Psalm 55 accents not divine *raḥma* but divine rigour, seeking refuge from enemies by appealing to Allah as '*al-jabbār*' (الجبار ; the Compeller), an epithet original to Qur'ān 59:23.[29] Motivated by 'fear' of his enemies, the psalmist here finds 'hopeful' comfort in God as 'the Compeller'; however, it is a holy 'fear of God' that emerges even earlier in al-Qūṭī's Psalm 33, whose verses 24 to 27 again emphasise divine force:

قريب الرب من الذين　　　هم بخوف الله خاشعين
وهو مسلم الأولاء ارواحه　　　ذليلة، اذلهـــا صلاحـــهم
ريب الهموم قد يكون يكثر　　　على التقـــي، والاله اكـــبر
ينجيه منهـــا كلهـــا وينصر

The Lord is close to those
who are humble in the fear of Allah

He is the saviour of those whose spirits
are submissive, made submissive by their righteousness

The doubt of distresses verily mounts
upon the God-fearing, but God is greater (*al-ilāh akbar*)

He delivers him from all of it, and supplies aid[30]

Spanning imminence and transcendence, these verses trace polarities of divine proximity and exaltation which seem Qur'ānic in texture. Not only is God 'near' – that is, '*qarīb*', an echo of Qur'ān 11:61 – but al-Qūṭī also designates Allah as '*akbar*' ('greater' or 'beyond'), constructing a Christian '*takbīr*' within his Arabic translation. In addition to divine distance and closeness, it is human piety that prompts al-Qūṭī's Qur'ānic borrowings, with believers pictured in 'fearful' (خاشعين ; *khāshi'īn*) and 'humble' (بخوف ; *bi-khawf*) obeisance – echoing *āyāt* such as Qur'ān 2:45 and 3:199.[31] Accorded majestic reverence, Allah merits here not only Muslim terms, however, but is Himself termed '*musallim*' (مسلم ; saviour). Rather than reminiscent of Islamic discourse, al-Qūṭī's '*musallim*' is instead cognate with '*islām*' itself, with this term denominating the Christian divine even as it shares the very same root that labels the Muslim religion (إسلام ; *islām* / مسلم ; *musallim*).[32]

The epithet '*musallim*' is recruited by al-Qūṭī not only to laud God as 'saviour' of 'spirits' in general, but also as 'saviour' of the individual 'self'. Returning to God's '*raḥma*', it is 'mercy' that forms the centrepiece to the psalmist's petition in Psalm 114:5–8, converted into Arabic by al-Qūṭī as:

ارغب يا رب, فكن مسلما　　نفسي عليها بالخلاص منعما
الرب هو راحم ذو عدل،　　الهنا ذو رحمة وفضل
الرب هو يحوز الصغار،　　اذللت لكن كان لي جار
يا نفسي فارجعي الى راحتك　　فالرب قد يحرزك من رحمتك

I am in longing, O Lord, so be (my) saviour
blessing my soul with salvation

The Lord, He is merciful, full of justice
our God, full of mercy and favour

The Lord, He is the one who holds the little ones
I was humiliated, but He was my protector

O my soul, return unto thy repose
for the Lord preserves thee out of mercy (for) thee[33]

Enlivened by assonance as well as rhyme, '*raḥma*' sustains the second verse above, which emphasises both 'mercy' and the 'merciful' ('*rāḥim*'), while also ascribing to Allah both '*ʿadl*' ('justice') and '*faḍl*' ('favour') – all terms which are Qur'ānically consistent.[34] However, it is the first-person envelope to this passage that seems especially evocative, these lines accenting the speaker's own 'soul' (*nafs*) at their opening and end. First pleading *for* his 'soul', asking God to be his 'saviour' (*musallim*), the psalmist offers a final petition *to* his 'soul' as well, voicing a command that echoes the Qur'ān, recalling a similar imperative to the '*nafs*' in Qur'ān 89:27–28. First below is the beginning of al-Qūṭī's last verse, and second, his apparent precedent from Sūra 89, with underlining added to emphasise the overlap of expressions:

يا نفسي فارجعي الى راحتك
(*yā nafsī fa-rjiʿī ilā rāḥatika*)
O my soul, return unto thy repose

(...) يَٰٓأَيَّتُهَا ٱلنَّفْسُ ٱلْمُطْمَئِنَّةُ ٱرْجِعِىٓ إِلَىٰ رَبِّكِ
yā ayyatuha al-nafsu al-muṭmaʾinna, irjiʿī ilā rabbika
O soul at peace, return unto thy Lord (...)[35]

Portraying the 'soul' as it 'returns' to divine 'peace', al-Qūṭī himself seemingly returns to the Qur'ān as his source, finding in the Muslim scripture not only serene 'repose', but a repository of expressions for the psalmist's sacred homecoming.

Ascribed adjectives both transcendent and immanent, both majestic and merciful, God's attributes occasionally span oppositions in the very same passage, with al-Qūṭī invoking contrasting epithets close together, both compelling and compassionate; not long after his echo of Sūra 89 in Psalm 114, for instance, al-Qūṭī offers the following verses as part of his Psalm 118:

عوني وترسي انت لي مقتدر، قولك قد رجوته منتظر
فجنبوني معشر الكفار، أحفظ عهدي ربي الجبار
ثبتني يا رب بحسب قولك، أحيا فلا تخزيني برحمك

رجائي الذي رجوت عندك

كن لي معاونا أكن مسلما وسرمدا بالعهد منك مغرما
أبغضت كل من عهودك عصى، إذ كل فكرهم كذوب ذو خطأ

My help and my shield, Thou art to me most powerful (*muqtadir*)
Thy word, I have hoped in it, expectant (*muntaẓir*)

Steer clear of me, ye troop of infidels (*al-kuffār*)
I keep my covenant with my Lord, the Compeller (*al-jabbār*)

Establish me, O Lord, according to Thy word
(that) I may live, and not be disgraced in Thy mercy

my hope, which I have hoped, is with Thee

Be Thou my helper, and I shall be safe (*musallam*)
And forever enamoured with the covenant of Thine

Thou hast despised all who have disobeyed Thy statutes
for all their thoughts are lies of sin[36]

Associating God again with 'mercy', it is '*muqtadir*' in the first verse above that also describes the divine, a term connoting 'most powerful' which qualifies as another of Allah's ninety-nine names, occurring in *āyāt* such as Qur'ān 18:45, 54:42, and 54:55.[37] Shifting from God's dominion to human dependence, the end of the first verse pairs '*muqtadir*' (مقتدر) with '*muntaẓir*' (منتظر) – which also echoes Qur'ānic precedents, appearing in the Muslim scripture to designate the pious who 'wait expectantly' for God's judgement.[38] Forming an Islamic envelope around this single verse, spanning divine and human, the remainder of the above passage bridges also between God and psalmist by applying to the latter a similar term previously applied to the former. Rather than God as '*Musallim*' ('saviour'), the psalmist identifies himself as '*musallam*' ('saved'), al-Qūṭī labelling his speaker as 'مسلم' – a term indistinguishable in its mere consonants from '*muslim*' (مسلم), with his biblical self-reference separated from Islamic adherence merely via vowels and diacritical marks.[39] Perhaps most resonant, however, is not the psalmist's own identification, but rather those against whom he identifies himself. Aptly established in oppositional rhyme with God's label as 'Compeller' (*al-jabbār*), al-Qūṭī names his enemies as '*al-kuffār*' (الكفار), a common Qur'ānic epithet for those who reject Allah.[40] Domesticating 'the disbelievers' for its own religious aims, al-Qūṭī recruits a Qur'ānic term that denotes non-Muslims to instead designate those *outside* the Christian communion, utilising diction that recalls the Muslim scripture, yet which also divert from Islamic intent. Opening up new avenues of identification, it is not al-Qūṭī's use of Islamic names, however, but his appeal to Islam's nemeses, such as *al-kuffār*, that helps link him to Qur'ānic traditions, with his Christian psalter merged with Muslim expressions in their shared objects of opposition.

IV

FROM *JAHANNAM* TO JESUS

ويعاتب الظالمين من الشعوب، ويذكر النار والكبريت الذي هو عذاب النار في جهنم.
(Psalm 10) condemns sinners (*al-ẓālimīn*) amongst the people, and makes remembrance of the fire and brimstone, which is the torment of the fire in *gehenna*.

from al-Qūṭī's introduction to Psalm 10[41]

Prefacing his poetic translation of Psalm 10 with prose commentary, al-Qūṭī offers the above description, interpreting this psalm as 'condemn[ing]' not the '*kuffār*', but '*al-ẓālimīn*' (الظالمين), perhaps the most common of Qur'ānic terms for 'sinners', occurring in nearly a hundred *āyāt*.[42] It is not only wayward people, however, but their place of wretchedness that seems reminiscent here of the Muslim scripture; specifying sin's consequences, al-Qūṭī offers names for the inferno that are equally Islamic. Portrayed first as 'the punishment of the fire' (*'adhāb al-nār*) – a phrase employed no less than eight times in the Qur'ān[43] – al-Qūṭī concludes his above introduction with *jahannam* (جهنم), a name for hell with biblical roots, but which also occurs seventy-seven times in the Muslim scripture.[44] Ending with this extreme locale, al-Qūṭī's final word descends to a lowly designation, even as the Qur'ān surfaces as a clear influence, forming the precedent for al-Qūṭī's psalmic vocabulary.

Although absent from his Hebrew source, 'hell' finds a regular place in al-Qūṭī's translation, conveyed into his psalter via acts of his Christian interpretation, but also his appeals to Islamic diction. Utilising not only generic phrases, but specific names from the Qur'ān, al-Qūṭī's version of the infernal underground in his psalter evidences Islamic foregrounds. Consider, for example, the Vulgate's '*confundantur impii taceant in inferno*' (let the wicked be ashamed, silenced in hell) – which al-Qūṭī renders in the twenty-ninth verse of his Psalm 30, a verse forecasting the impious 'descending down' into:

ســـــــــقـــــــــر،　　　　جزاء من بربه قد كفر

hell (*saqar*)
the recompense of him who, in his Lord, has disbelieved (*kafar*)[45]

Ironically set in rhyming apposition, al-Qūṭī pairs '*saqar*' with '*kafar*', synthesising in sound the abode of disbelievers (i.e., *saqar*) with their activity of disbelief (i.e., *kafar*). Most striking in this verse is not al-Qūṭī's poetic originality, but the proper placename he borrows, that is, '*saqar*' (سقر) –

a word not only utilised, but explicitly addressed, in the Qur'ān. A designation for 'hell', *saqar*'s definition is itself interrogated by the Muslim scripture, this infernal term highlighted as unfamiliar in the seventy-fourth chapter of the Qur'ān:

> ساصليه سقر وما أدراك ما سقر لا تبقي ولا تذر
>
> I shall surely roast him in *saqar*; and what will teach thee what is *saqar*? It spares not, neither leaves alone[46]

Mentioned in Sūra 74 even before its meaning is explained, '*saqar*' surfaces in the Qur'ān in conjunction with a question, prompting the parsing of hell's effects, defined as the place that 'spares not, neither leaves alone'. Offering not only the diction for Christian verses, the Qur'ān serves also as the dictionary for al-Qūṭī's vocabulary, standing as the original source for this later psalmic usage of '*saqar*', while also 'teaching' the significance of this same term.

Accounting for the final fate of disbelievers in his translation, it is the first disbeliever that al-Qūṭī also addresses, inserting Satan into his psalter. Unnamed in the Hebrew original, the Devil is ironically introduced into al-Qūṭī's Christian version via Islamic echoes, emerging for instance in the exegetical prologue which prefaces Psalm 90:

> تهليل مزمار داود. نبوة في الصالحين وفي المسيح الذي جربه ابليس. اخبرت النبوة ان لا بد الاباليس ان تمتحنه وتقايسه على ثلاثة اوجه: بالاكل والرغبة والكبرياء. وصوت البيعة على اعدائها من الجن الذين يوسوسون في منام الاداميين بالفكر الرديئة والخواطر السيئة
>
> A Davidic praise psalm. Prophecy regarding the righteous, and the Messiah, who was tempted by Iblīs. The prophecy recounts that the devils (*iblīs*es) surely subjected him to trial and gauged him via three means: with food, desire, and pride. And the Church's voice against her enemies amongst the *jinn* who temptingly whisper amid the slumber of mankind with vile thoughts and evil notions[47]

First announcing the main adversary to 'the Messiah', al-Qūṭī understands Psalm 90 as initially telling the trials of Christ, tempted not by 'Satan', however, but by 'Iblīs' – the Qur'ān's own 'proper name' for the Devil.[48] This interreligious characterisation of Satan is amplified as al-Qūṭī addresses secondary demons, with the devilish 'enemies' of 'the Church' designated by diction that is equally Islamic. Envisioning invisible creatures from the Qur'ān, al-Qūṭī inserts into the opening of his Psalm 90 'the *jinn*', infusing his Judaic source with these unseen entities named in the very title to the seventy-second chapter of the Qur'ān, Sūrat al-Jinn.[49] Telling of 'temptations' by such demonic forces, al-Qūṭī's text itself succumbs to inter-scriptural attraction, designating the Devil and his demons via Islamic idioms ('Iblīs', '*jinn*'), while also utilising a characteristic

Qur'ānic word for whispered seductions, identifying the *jinn*'s nocturnal appeals as '*yuwaswisūna*' (يوسوسون ; cf. the same verb utilised in Qur'ān 114:5).[50] Although barely perceptible – both nearly inaudible and entirely unseen – the *jinn* nevertheless concretely emerge in al-Qūṭī's introduction, surfacing in his psalter from an unseen Qur'ānic background.

Rendered into a Christian context, the gesture of Psalm 90 to 'the *jinn*' enriches an episode of the Messiah's own biography, reflecting al-Qūṭī's broader aim to trace Jesus's life in the psalms, from his birth to resurrection. Retreating from his satanic trials, it is Christ's nativity that al-Qūṭī locates in Psalm 109, offering the following exegetical introduction to his translation:

> مزمار داود. نبوة فيها ميلاد المسيح ابن مريم وملكه واسقفيته وامانته وجلوسه عن يمين الاب. والنبي يقول ان الكلمة متولدة من ذات الاب وان الابن خالق لا مخلوق
>
> Psalm of David. Prophecy in which is the birth of the Messiah, the son of Mary (*al-masīḥ ibn maryam*), and his kingdom, his episcopate, his trusteeship, and his sitting on the right hand of the Father. And the prophet says that the Word was begotten from the essence of the Father and that the Son is creator, not created[51]

A classic text of Christian worship, al-Qūṭī interprets Psalm 109 as recounting not only 'the birth of the Messiah', but also his sovereign reign, leading up even to his 'sitting on the right hand of the Father'. An overview of the essential elements of Christian orthodoxy, it is Qur'ānic phraseology, however, that informs al-Qūṭī's Christology, calling Jesus '*al-masīḥ ibn maryam*' (the Messiah, the son of Mary), a cognomen idiomatic of the Muslim scripture, recalling verses such as Qur'ān 3:45, which designates Jesus as '*al-masīḥ ʿīsā ibn maryam*' ('the Messiah Jesus, the son of Mary'). Emphasising the human genealogy of Jesus, al-Qūṭī pivots from this phrase to conclude the above with a striking assertion of Christ's divinity, even while invoking diction that is again Qur'ānically resonant, designating Jesus as 'creator, not created' (*khāliq lā makhlūq*). Shifting from his maternal origins, to his being 'begotten' by 'the Father', Christ is not only pictured as 'uncreated', but is characterised as 'creator' (*khāliq*) – al-Qūṭī ironically appealing to one of Allah's own ninety-nine names from the Qur'ān to define the divinity of Jesus.[52]

Crafting his own creative renditions, even while reading the uncreated 'Son' into his psalter, al-Qūṭī not only names the Messiah in his prose prefaces, but also in his poetic verses. Instead of an interpreted subject merely, Jesus becomes the actual substance of al-Qūṭī's Arabic translations, emerging in another psalm cherished for anticipating New Testament events: Psalm 50. In lines 14 to 18, al-Qūṭī's Psalm 50 is invested with messianic meaning not only implicitly, but explicitly, with the very name of Jesus spelled out in its verses, reading:

اخلق لي اللهم قلبا طاهرا، وجددن في الجوف مني قادرا
روحا يكون ثابت المقام، لا تغب عني وجهك المنعام
وروحك القدوس عني لا تزل، انك ربي من اليه يستهل
واردد الي فرح اليسوع، يسوعك المبارك المتبوع
مثبتا لي بروح قادر، مقتدرا لكل شيء قاهر

Make within me, O Allah, a clean heart
and renew within me, with power

a spirit that established of foundation
hide not from me Thy beneficent face

And let not Thy Holy Spirit depart from me
verily Thou, O my Lord, art He to Whom praise resounds

Return to me the joy of the Jesus (*al-yasū'*)
Thy Jesus, the blessed and obeyed

establishing me with a spirit powerful (*qādir*)
most powerfully (*muqtadiran*), unto all things victorious (*qāhir*)[53]

Appealing first to Allah for a 'clean heart' (*qalban ṭāhiran*), al-Qūṭī next renders the psalmist as supplicating to 'Thy Holy Spirit', before rounding out his Trinitarian translation by appealing to 'Jesus', inserting the very name of his Messiah into the penultimate verse above. Asking for the joy of 'the Jesus' (اليسوع ; al-Yasū'), al-Qūṭī inscribes the name of Christ twice into his verse 17, characterising him also as '*Thy* Jesus', who is not only 'blessed' (المبارك ; *al-mubārak*), but 'obeyed' (المتبوع ; *al-matbū'*).[54] Even as he inserts Christian confession into his Judaic translation, however, it is tropes and terms from Islam's scripture that surrounds al-Qūṭī's creed. Immediately after invoking Jesus's 'joy', it is the compelling power of the Qur'ān that ends the above selection, with the psalmist's security in the 'spirit' endowed with a series of God's *asmā'*, characterising Allah's infinite capacity with a triad of Qur'ānic epithets: '*qādir*' (powerful), '*muqtadir'* (most powerful), '*qāhir*' (victorious).[55] It is the final of these three, however, that seems most striking, emerging in an adapted echo of the end to many *āyāt*, with al-Qūṭī's final words above recalling final phrases of several Qur'ānic verses. For instance, compare al-Qūṭī's '[God is] unto all things victorious' (*li-kulli shay'in qāhir*) with the standard Qur'ānic phrase '[God is] powerful over all things' (*'alā kulli shay'in qadīr*).[56] Overlapping in assonance, even while replacing '*qāhir*' for '*qadīr*', al-Qūṭī confesses his own convictions in psalmic rendition as he revises Qur'ānic syntax within new surroundings. Amid his eisegetical insertion of 'Jesus' into the psalter – with Christ nominated, rather than annotated, within his Psalm 50 – al-Qūṭī also ensures that the Messiah is literally and linguistically enveloped by Qur'ānic echoes, with 'controlling' tropes such as '*qādir*' and '*qāhir*' forming a 'compelling' context for al-Qūṭī's own Christian beliefs.

VI

HALĀL HALLELUJAHS

As the psalter nears its conclusion, imperatives of praise become especially prominent, with numerous psalms opening with the familiar phrase '*hallelujah*' (הַלְלוּ-יָהּ ; 'praise *Jah*!') a command that is cognate with the very name of the Book of Psalms in Hebrew, that is, 'Təhillīm' (praises). This standard psalmic imperative initially becomes al-Qūṭī's concern in his own Psalm 105, as '*hallelujah*' emerges in this psalm's very first verse.[57] However, even before its opening lines, Psalm 105 is introduced by al-Qūṭī with another interpretative preface, which aptly starts with a gloss on '*hallelujah*' itself:

هللويا. شرحه لا اله الا الله

'*Hallelujah*'. Its interpretation is: 'there is no god but Allah'[58]

First transliterating the Hebrew '*hallelujah*' into Arabic – هللويا – al-Qūṭī then defines this fragment of foreign diction; rather than a simple command, however, al-Qūṭī defines '*hallelujah*' as a creedal declaration. No longer an imperative of praise, '*hallelujah*' is instead parsed as a doctrinal assertion – 'there is no god but Allah' – a monotheistic confession broadly consistent with Christianity, and yet Islamic in origin and association, this Arabic phrase forming the first half of the *shahāda* itself: the foundational 'witnessing' of the Muslim faith ('There is no god but Allah, and Muḥammad is Allah's messenger'). Equating a biblical genre with the genesis of extra-biblical belief, al-Qūṭī voices Islamic testimony to parse a pivotal psalmic term and type, reading the Hebrew '*hallelujah*' as embodying the essence of Muslim theology.[59]

The '*hallelujah*' imperative increasingly surfaces in the psalter's fifth book, which finds its own centrepiece in Psalm 118 – the longest of all the psalms, spanning more than 150 verses. Uniquely comprehensive, comprising twenty-two acrostic poems that cover the Hebrew 'alphabet […] in its entirety', Psalm 118 also stands as the culminating epitome of al-Qūṭī's Islamic indebtedness, exemplifying from its opening prose introduction his reach across scriptural expressions:[60]

هللويا، صوت البيعة الى ربها وصوتها للمؤمنين وصوتها للكفار الظالمين. وهي سورة...

> *Hallelujah*, the Church's call to her Lord, and her call to the believers, and her call to the disbelieving evil-doers, and it (Psalm 118) is a *sūra*…[61]

Already equated with the first half of the *shahāda*, it is '*hallelujah*' that aptly opens al-Qūṭī's introduction to Psalm 118, a psalm which he immediately identifies as a '*sūra*' (سورة) – this single term serving to bridge biblical and Qur'ānic genres. It is not only formal diction, but moral dichotomy, that recalls Islamic precedents, however, with Psalm 118 framed by al-Qūṭī as addressed to both 'believers' and 'disbelievers', comprising 'the Church's call' not only to '*al-mu'minīn*', but also to '*al-kuffār al-ẓālimīn*' – a phrase for 'sinners' that recalls *āyāt* such as Qur'ān 2:254.[62] Validating its credentials as a '*sūra*', Psalm 118 shifts from Islamic echoes in its preface to Qur'ānic quotations in its poetry, with al-Qūṭī offering the following for verses 34 to 36:

جنبني سبل كذب، واعطني	كتابك العدل، وفيه فاهدني
قد التزمت آيك الكريم،	لا تخزني يا سيدا رحيم
سبيل فرضك عليها اجري،	انك انت قد شرحت صدري

Avert me from the paths of lying, and bestow upon me
Thy righteous book, with which guide me

I have adhered to Thy noble sign
do not put me to shame, O Lord merciful (*raḥīm*)

Upon the way of Thy ordinance I trek
Verily Thou hast expanded my breast[63]

Surrounding these verses from Psalm 118 are various 'paths' (sg. *sabīl*, pl. *subul*), with the psalmist first petitioning to be kept from 'paths of deception', while finally invoking the 'path' of God's grace. It is not only divergent routes, however, but divine revelations, that are invoked here for direction, the psalmist requesting guidance from God's righteous 'book' in the initial line above. This appeal to Allah's '*kitāb*' in a Christian translation, however, is ironically articulated with a command reminiscent of the Qur'ān, the psalmist petitioning God to be 'guided' by his 'righteous book' with the imperative '*ihdinī*' (اهدني ; guide me!) – an echo of the very first directive addressed to Allah in the Fātiḥa (اهدنا ; *ihdinā*; guide us!; Qur'ān 1:6). It is not only al-Qūṭī's reference to scripture in general, but to scriptural verses in particular, that recalls the Qur'ān. In the second line of this selection, the psalmist promises to 'adhere' to God's '*āya*', a term for 'verse' whose Qur'ānic character is amplified by its adjective, this '*āya*' qualified as '*karīm*' ('noble'), a term customarily applied to the Qur'ān itself.[64] Amplifying the Islamic intonation of '*karīm*', however, is its assonance, set in rhyme with '*raḥīm*', with this most common Qur'ānic name for God concluding al-Qūṭī's second line. It is the final phrase of the third line above which perhaps is most striking; still appealing directly to Allah, the psalmist addresses God with these words of thanksgiving:

انك انت قد شرحت صدري
verily Thou hast expanded my breast[65]

Ending this verse with 'expansive' words, al-Qūṭī concurrently echoes, yet answers, the opening line to Sūrat al-Sharḥ (Qur'ān 94:1), where Allah Himself is quoted as inquiring:

أَلَمْ نَشْرَحْ لَكَ صَدْرَكَ
Did We not expand thy breast for thee?[66]

Reversing and replying to the above inquiry, al-Qūṭī's psalmist sets himself in dialogue with the Islamic divine, offering an affirmative Christian answer to this Qur'ānic question. Established in intimate conversation across scriptural canons, al-Qūṭī shows himself positively responsive to the Qur'ān in a double sense, not only appealing to the Muslim scripture as his source, but also confirming its own query, offering Psalm 118 as a biblical '*sūra*' that agreeably answers Sūrat al-Sharḥ.

Encouraged by the Qur'ān to 'expand' this core verse from Psalm 118, it is the call and response of this passage that anticipates later lines, such as verses 162 to 163 of this same psalm, which again centre on human duty towards the divine decree:

قد استغثتك بكل قلبي، لي فاستجب بما سألت ربي

احفظ عهدك بكل جذب

اياك قد دعوت سلمني اكن حافظا فرضك الحكم السنن

I sought Thy aid with my whole heart
answer me regarding that which I ask, my Lord

I shall keep Thy covenant with all rapture

Verily Thee did I petition, preserve me (*sallimnī*), I shall be a
keeper (*ḥāfiẓ*) of Thy ordinance, judgement (and) traditions (*al-sunan*)[67]

Voicing a plea for God 'to respond', as well as a pledge to uphold God's commission, al-Qūṭī's version conveys the covenantal relationship essential to the original Hebrew verses of Psalm 118. Unlike his Judaic source, however, overtones of Islam are subtly audible in al-Qūṭī's rendition, including the psalmist's petition to be 'saved' (*sallimnī*), another term cognate with '*Islām*' itself. Perhaps more intriguing is the speaker's commitment to 'keep' God's covenant, vowing himself to become a '*ḥāfiẓ*' (keeper, preserver) – a Qur'ānic term, customarily signifying a 'memoriser' of the Muslim scripture. Faintly assonating with his own name, the term '*ḥāfiẓ*' is applied by Ḥafṣ al-Qūṭī to the biblical psalmist; however, it is the Christian translator himself that also ambivalently becomes a '*ḥāfiẓ*', not only piously committed to 'keeping' God's 'covenant', but also 'retaining' Qur'ānic fragments in his own psalmic rendition.[68]

It is perhaps the last word of the above selection, however, that seems most Islamically resonant, with God's 'traditions' termed as '*sunan*' (سنن ; sg. '*sunna*') – an idiom most associated with Muslim praxis, designating an orthodoxy predicated on the 'Prophetic example'.[69] Refashioned as a Christian '*sunnī*' in Psalm 118, al-Qūṭī's speaker pursues 'paths' that cross multiple sacred 'traditions'; however, only one psalm earlier, this same speaker had built up similar structures of synthesis. Cherished by Christians for its forecasting of 'messianic meaning', Psalm 117 also reaches back to Judaism's temple foundations, with verses 22 to 24 and 27 to 28 reading in al-Qūṭī's renditions as follows:[70]

الصخرة التي البناة احتقروا، هي برأس الركن صارت فابصروا
من لدن السيد هذا صنع، فصار في أعيننا مستشبع
ها ان ذا اليوم الذي قد فعله ذو العزة الرب فكل الحمدله
الله ربنا لنا لقد ظهر، فبالغصون عيدوا ذات الزهر
حتى الى قرن عزيز الهيكل محراب ربنا الاعز الأفضل

The stone which the builders despised
it has become the head of the corner, thus witness!

From our Lord is this done
and it has become in our eyes a saturation

Behold, this is the day that He has made
the Lord of might, and all praise to Him

Allah, our Lord, to us manifested
thus with blooming boughs, celebrate the feast

Even unto the exalted horns of the Temple
the *miḥrāb* of our Lord, the most powerful, most graceful[71]

It is the first verse of this psalmic selection that is most cherished by Christians, quoted prophetically and autobiographically by Jesus in the New Testament; speaking to his disciples after entering Jerusalem and cleansing the Temple, Christ cites this same psalm, identifying himself as the 'stone which the builders rejected' who will ultimately become the 'head of the corner'.[72] This first verse quoted from Psalm 117 above is not, however, its only architectural allusion, with the final verse of this selection returning to temple imagery; rather than merely 'the stone', it is the entire sacred structure that is referenced in this last line, alluding specifically to 'the temple' (الهيكل ; *al-haykal*). Building from single 'stone' to the entire 'sanctuary', this templar envelope to al-Qūṭī's selection also suggests obverse poles in his rendition. Opening with a Hebrew verse on the 'stone' that is later quoted in Christian scripture, the temple that emerges by the end of this passage is instead Islamic in construction, integrating within its interior a '*miḥrāb*' (محراب) – a term typically suggesting a mosque's 'niche' which marks the direction of Mecca.[73] Erecting this 'prayer niche' within a passage that concerns the central space of early Jewish worship – the temple – al-Qūṭī's rendition of Psalm 117 spans messianic 'rock' and Muslim '*miḥrāb*', first drawing dimensions that seem Christian in conceit, yet whose broad eastward embrace is Islamically orientated. Constructing a psalmic sanctuary that features Christ as its 'cornerstone', and yet whose idioms point towards Qur'ānic traditions, al-Qūṭī outlines a space that aptly encloses the diverse subjects and strategies of the present chapter, and offers it a fittingly concrete conclusion. It is in this hybrid 'temple', assembled from a triad of traditions – Judaic, Christian, Islamic – that al-Qūṭī seems most often to reside, an Andalusian poet whose biblical translation upholds the columns of his own faith, and yet inscribes into its walled interior linguistic lines that are Qur'ānic in origin, synthesising a masonry of scriptural mixture, a 'saturated' compound that remains a wonder to 'witness'.

NOTES

1. Ḥafṣ al-Qūṭī, *Le Psautier Mozarabe de Hafs Le Goth*, ed. and trans. Marie-Thérèse Urvoy (Toulouse: Presses Universitaires du Mirail, 1994), p. 21, hereafter cited as 'al-Qūṭī, *Psautier*'. This edition features al-Qūṭī's Arabic original and Urvoy's French translation on discrete facing pages, but which yet share the same pagination. The present chapter provides my own English translations of al-Qūṭī's Arabic verses; however, I have benefited immensely from the French provided by Urvoy in her edition in crafting my versions of al-Qūṭī. In this, and subsequent, chapters, I retain the numbering system for the psalms as utilised by authors such as al-Qūṭī, deriving from the Vulgate or the Septuagint. Arabic selections throughout *The Qur'ān and Kerygma* reflect primary sources quoted, unless otherwise noted, despite these sources occasionally departing from normative orthography (e.g., failure to include the hamza, especially in early modern printed editions).

2. Translations from the Qur'ān provided throughout this study frequently follow A. J. Arberry, (trans.), *The Koran Interpreted* (New York: George Allen & Unwin Ltd, 1955)). This rendition of Qur'ān 87:14, however, is my own (Arberry provides 'Prosperous is he who has cleansed himself'). This idiom from Sūra 87 (i.e., *aflaḥa man*) is also invoked by al-Qūṭī at the very end of his 143-verse poetic preface to his translation (al-Qūṭī, *Psautier*, p. 22) – i.e., his *urjūza* – which closes with precisely this phrase immediately before his Psalm 1 begins with the similar usage of '*qad aflaḥa*'. For this same phrase, also see Qur'ān 23:1.
3. For '*mujtahid*' and its usage in *fiqh* to denote a jurist 'possessing the qualifications to independently derive legal rulings from the primary sources', see Aaron Spevack, *The Archetypal Sunnī* Scholar: *Law, Theology, and Mysticism in the Synthesis of Al-Bājūrī* (Albany, NY: State University of New York Press, 2014), p. 167.
4. For Marie-Thérèse Urvoy's edition, see note 1 above, which comprises the most substantive treatment of al-Qūṭī; however, Urvoy's scholarship in 1994 was itself anticipated by D. M. Dunlop, who authored some of the earliest exploratory articles on al-Qūṭī, including his 'Ḥafṣ B. Albar—the Last of the Goths?', *Journal of the Royal Asiatic Society of Great Britain & Ireland* 86 (1954): 137–151. More recently, al-Qūṭī has increasingly merited mention in studies of Muslim Spain, as well as full essays and articles; see respectively, for instance, Janina M. Safran's *Defining Boundaries in Al-Andalus: Muslims, Christians, and Jews in Islamic Iberia* (Ithaca: Cornell University Press, 2015), pp. 101–102 and Augustine Casiday's '"The Sweetest Music That Falls Upon the Ear": Translating and Interpreting the Psalter in Christian Andalucia' in *Meditations of the Heart: The Psalms in Christian Thought and Practice; Essays in Honour of Andrew Louth*, ed. Andreas Andreopoulos, A. M. Casiday, Carol Harrison, and Andrew Louth (Turnhout: Brepols, 2011), pp. 225–242. Appearing even as the present study was completed, and thereby not considered in my own treatment, was the most recent study authored by leading authority on al-Qūṭī, Pieter van Koningsveld, whose *The Arabic Psalter of Hafs Ibn Albar al-Qûtî: Prolegomena for a Critical Edition* appeared late in 2016 (published by Aurora, Leiden).
5. For al-Qūṭī's uncertain origins and identity, as well as the problems of securing definite information regarding his biography, see Casiday's 'The Sweetest Music That Falls Upon the Ear', which even notes that '[i]n the the mid-Nineteenth Century, Hafs was presented as a Jewish translator' (p. 231). See also David James, *Early Islamic Spain: The History of Ibn al-Qūṭīya* (London: Routledge, 2011), p. 55, which emphasises al-Qūṭī's role as jurist. Even the date of al-Qūṭī's death is in dispute. Some studies reference 889 CE for al-Qūṭī's death, such as Lejla Demiri's 2013 *Muslim Exegesis of the Bible in Medieval Cairo: Najm al-Dīn al-Ṭūfī*'s (d. *716 = 1316) Commentary on the Christian Scriptures; a Critical Edition and Annotated Translation with an Introduction* (Leiden: Brill), p. 30. However, 889 CE may instead signal merely the date of al-Qūṭī's completion of his psalter. In Yousef Casewit's 'A Muslim Scholar of the Bible: Prooftexts from Genesis and Matthew in the Qur'an Commentary of Ibn Barrajān of Seville (d. 536/1141)', *Journal of Qur'anic Studies* 18:1 (2016): 1–48, the date 889 CE is attributed to *both* al-Qūṭī's death as well his psalter's completion (pp. 1 and 2 respectively). Although often celebrated, the authenticity of Spain's *La Convivencia* has been recently critiqued by Darío Fernández-Morera in his monograph *The*

Myth of the Andalusian Paradise: Muslims, Christians, and Jews Under Islamic Rule in Medieval Spain (Wilmington, Delaware: ISI Books, 2016).

6. The patrionymic 'al-Qūṭī' as a signal of 'Hispano-Gothic heritage' is discussed by Charles L. Tieszen in his *Christian Identity amid Islam in Medieval Spain* (Leiden: Brill, 2013), even invoking Ḥafṣ al-Qūṭī himself (p. 108). For the early establishment of Arianism in Spain, see R. W. Mathisen, 'Barbarian "Arian" Clergy, Church Organization, and Church Practices' in *Arianism: Roman Heresy and Barbarian Creed*, ed. Guido M. Berndt and Roland Steinacher (London: Routledge, 2016), pp. 145–192 (p. 162).
7. Surveying Spain's translation campaigns, Charles Burnett's 'The Translating Activity in Medieval Spain', in *The Legacy of Muslim Spain*, ed. Salma Khadra Jayyusi (Leiden & New York: E. J. Brill, 1992), pp. 1036–1058, is one of the few treatments of these campaigns of translation that also includes brief mention of Ḥafṣ al-Qūṭī (named in passing on page 1037). Al-Qūṭī is also named once in the more recent overview by Julio-César Santoyo – i.e., 'Revisiting the History of Medieval Translation in the Iberian Peninsula' in *The Routledge Companion to Iberian Studies*, ed. Javier Munoz-Basols, Morales M. Delgado, and Laura Lonsdale (Florence: Taylor and Francis, 2017), pp. 93–104 – but with the erroneous date of 989 ascribed to his psalter (p. 95).
8. Jerome is mentioned specifically by al-Qūṭī in his preface to his psalter (al-Qūṭī, *Psautier*, pp. 8–9), as well as in his extended *urjūza*. While Jerome is associated with the Latin 'Vulgate' – a term and text I use for comparison with al-Qūṭī – it is likely that al-Qūṭī accessed multiple Latin translations by Jerome. See Arie Schippers, 'Medieval Opinions on the Difficulty of Translating the Psalms: Some Remarks on Ḥafṣ al-Qūṭī's Psalms in Arabic *Rajaz* Metre', in *Give Ear to My Words: Psalms and Other Poetry in and around the Hebrew Bible*, ed. Janet Dyk and Nico A. Uchelen (Amsterdam: Societas Hebraica Amstelodamensis, 1996), pp. 219–226, which notes, following Urvoy, that 'Ḥafṣ' translation is not directly based upon the Hebrew, but upon translations into Latin by Saint Jerome (347–420), and possibly on a mixture of three of his translations, the *Psalterium Romanum* (composed 384), the *Psalterium Gallicanum* (composed in Palestine in 389–90) and *Psalterium ex hebraico* (composed from 390–391)' (p. 223). See also Casiday, 'The Sweetest Music That Falls Upon the Ear', which observes that al-Qūṭī 'in all likelihood availed himself of several of St Jerome's Latin translations' (p. 233).
9. I offer an overly exact paraphrase of the opening to this Hebrew verse; the KJV of this same material reads: 'But his delight *is* in the law of the LORD'.
10. Although it is not certain which of Jerome's Latin versions al-Qūṭī follows for his Psalm 1 (see note 8 above), I offer here this psalmic quote from the standard critical edition of the *Vulgate* (see Swift Edgar and Angela M. Kinney (eds.), *The Vulgate Bible*, *vol. 3*, ed. (Cambridge: Harvard University Press, 2010), p. 150).
11. Replacing Jerome's '*lege*' with 'كتاب', al-Qūṭī's rendition gestures to the extra-jurisprudential significance of the Hebrew 'תּוֹרָה', which suggests not 'law' merely, but has been the traditional title of the first five books of the Bible.
12. The translation of this partial quotation from Qur'ān 35:29 is sourced from Arberry's *Koran*, with my added insertion of the transliteration (i.e., '*kitāb Allāh*').
13. Al-Qūṭī's 'Prologue' (as his psalter's prose introduction is entitled by Urvoy), spans pages 1–13 in her edition; for the naming of these three figures, see al-Qūṭī, *Psautier*, pp. 2, 6 and 8–9, respectively.

14. The term '*zabūr*' (زَبُور) appears at the very opening to al-Qūṭī's psalter introduction (al-Qūṭī, *Psautier*, p. 1). Although Qur'ān 4:163 features '*zabūr*', this term appears with a definite article a single time in the Qur'ān as well, i.e., 21:105. A cognate form – *al-zubur* (الزُّبُر) – appears in verses such as Qur'ān 3:184.
15. Both '*sūra*' (and its plural '*suwar*'), as well as '*āyāt*', occur on page 12 of al-Qūṭī, *Psautier*.
16. William C. Chittick, *The Sufi Path of Knowledge: Ibn al-'Arabi's Metaphysics of Imagination* (Albany , NY: State University of New York, 2009), p. 199.
17. Al-Qūṭī, *Psautier*, p. 5.
18. For a recent treatment of the '*ẓāhir–bāṭin* (exoteric–esoteric) dichotomy', see Maryam Moazzen, 'A Garden beyond the Garden: 'Ayn al-Quḍāt Hamadānī's Perspective on Paradise' in *Roads to Paradise: Eschatology and Concepts of the Hereafter in Islam*, ed. Sebastian Günther, Todd Lawson, and Christian Mauder, 2 vols. (Leiden: Brill, 2016), vol. 1, pp. 566–578 (p. 571).
19. Al-Qūṭī, *Psautier*, p. 13.
20. For this precise phrase – *wa-huwa rabb al-'arsh al-'aẓīm* – which Arberry renders as 'He is the Lord of the Mighty Throne', see Qur'ān 9:129. For a relevant prophetic *ḥadīth*, related by 'Abd Allāh b. Ja'far, see Sara Sviri, 'Words of Power and the Power of Words: Mystical Linguistics in the Works of al-Hakim al-Tirmidhi', *Jerusalem Studies in Arabic and Islam* 27 (2002): 204–244 (p. 237).
21. A Qur'ānic phrase, as well as a term commonly featured in doxologies introducing Muslim discourse, *lā sharīka lah* is also included in a Dome of the Rock inscription; see S. D. Goitein *Studies in Islamic History and Institutions* (Leiden: E. J. Brill, 1968), p. 139.
22. The verse *al-hamdu lillāhi rabb al-'ālamīn* qualifies as the second *āya* of the Fātiḥa, with only the *basmala* preceding it in the Qur'ān. For the phrase '*rabb al-'ālamīn*' as used by another Christian Arabic author – Ibn al-Muqaffa' – see Chapter 3, note 20, below.
23. Al-Qūṭī, Psautier, p. 7. Urvoy's edition does not include '*lā*' ('لا'); however, her accompanying French rendition – i.e., '*innombrables*', which is reflected in my own '(in)numerable' – suggests that the Arabic original should be read with negation.
24. For '*al-asmā' al-ḥusnā*', see *Encyclopedia of Islamic Civilization and Religion*, ed. Ian Netton (Abingdon, UK: Routledge, 2008), p. 95.
25. These *asmā'* appear in al-Qūṭī, *Psautier*, on the following pages respectively: '*qādir*', p. 80; '*muṣawwir*', p. 152; ''*azīz*', p. 81; '*khāliq*', p. 106.
26. Al-Qūṭī, *Psautier*, p. 82.
27. This translation of Qur'ān 20:5 follows Arberry, who offers 'the All-compassionate sat Himself upon the Throne'; however, see also Chapter 4 below, which addresses another psalm translator's echo of this same Qur'ānic trope, utilising a cognate form of the verb '*istawā*' (استَوَى ; sat [Himself]).
28. Al-Qūṭī, *Psautier*, p. 93.
29. The definite *al-jabbār* (الجبار) appears only once in the Qur'ān, i.e., 59:23; however, the indefinite *jabbār* (جبار) – signifying 'a tyrant' – occurs in multiple *āyāt*, including Qur'ān 11:59.
30. Al-Qūṭī, *Psautier*, p. 62.
31. The form *khāshi'īn* (خاشعين) occurs also in Qur'ān 42:45; however, in this *āya*, it applies not to the pious, but those 'exposed [to the fire]'.

32. I follow the vowelling of Urvoy's edition, which supplies a *tashdīd* for the *lām* of 'مسلم' ('*musallim*'), thereby helping to distinguish this term from the word '*muslim*' itself (i.e., 'مسلم') – a connection which I also emphasise below in another context. In her edition, Urvoy renders the nominal phrase 'وهو مسلم' instead as '*Il sauve*' (He saves).
33. Al-Qūṭī, *Psautier*, p. 183. As Urvoy recognises in her footnotes, *raḥmatika* (رحمتك) signifies literally '*dans ta miséricorde*'; however, to render this verb in conformity with its context, she offers '*(Sa) miséricorde pour toi*', which also informs my English translation.
34. For *Allāh* and *ʿadl* in the Qurʾān, see 16:90 (*inna Allāha yaʾmuru bil-ʿadl*). More common in the Qurʾān is *faḍl*, frequently attributed to Allah with *dhū* (ذُو), just as it appears in al-Qūṭī's translation ('*dhū…faḍl*); see, for instance, Qurʾān 2:251: '*wa-lākinn Allāha dhū faḍlin ʿalā al-ʿālamīn*'.
35. It is Arberry's English that I supply here to render this partial quote from Qurʾān 89:27–28.
36. Al-Qūṭī, *Psautier*, pp. 192–93.
37. In her own notes to this psalm, Urvoy herself recognises that both '*muqtadir*' and '*jabbār*' are '*nom divin islamique*' (Al-Qūṭī, *Psautier*, pp. 192 and 193).
38. For this participle, see Qurʾān 7:71, which ends with the Prophet Hūd's declaration that: '*innī maʿakum min al-muntaẓirīn*' (I shall be with you watching and waiting [*muntaẓirīn*]; Arberry's translation, with transliteration added).
39. The vowelling of Urvoy's edition again suggests al-Qūṭī's 'مسلم' to be '*musallam*', with a *tashdīd* on this term's *lām*; Urvoy also renders this term as '*sauf*' (al-Qūṭī, *Psautier*, p. 193).
40. The term *al-kuffār* (الكفار), with its definite article, occurs more than a dozen times in the Qurʾān to designate the 'disbelievers'; for its first Qurʾānic occurrence, see 5:57.
41. Al-Qūṭī, *Psautier*, p. 32.
42. This enumeration includes not only the oblique form '*al-ẓālimīn*', but also the nominative of this same participle, i.e., '*al-ẓālimūn*'.
43. For Qurʾānic occurrences of '*ʿadhāb al-nār*', see 2:126; 2:201; 3:16; 3:191; 8:14; 32:20; 34:42; 59:3.
44. See Feras Hamza, 'Temporary Hellfire Punishment and the Making of Sunni Orthodoxy' in *Roads to Paradise*, vol. 1, pp. 371–406; Hamza notes 'that the early exegetical tradition took *jahannam* as *the* name of hell, especially since of the 111 references to hellfire, *jahannam* occurs 77 times' (p. 374).
45. Al-Qūṭī, *Psautier*, p. 57. For this quotation from the Vulgate, see Edgar and Kinney (eds.), *The Vulgate Bible*, *vol. 3*, p. 225; this translation, adapted also from the English on p. 225, is slightly altered to match more closely the original Latin of this verse, with 'silenced' added to render '*taceant*'.
46. This quotation from Qurʾān 74:26–28 is rendered by Arberry; however, I alter his translation of 'سقر' from 'Sakar' to my '*saqar*' for the sake of consistency with standard transliteration. For other Qurʾānic occurrences of '*saqar*', see 54:48 and 74:42.
47. Al-Qūṭī, *Psautier*, p. 145.
48. This quotation regarding 'Iblīs' derives from *The Qur'an: An Encyclopedia*, ed. Oliver Leaman, p. 179.
49. Although comprising the title of Chapter 72, 'the *jinn*' are first mentioned in Qurʾān 6:100. Characteristic of the Qurʾān, the *jinn* yet also claim pre-Islamic

origins; see Christopher M. Moreman, *Beyond the Threshold: Afterlife Beliefs and Experience in World Religions* (Lanham, MD: Rowman & Littlefield, 2010), p. 80.

50. Compare, in particular, the last verses of the Qur'ān, which also utilise the same imperfect form of '*waswasa*', but in the singular (*alladhīna yuwaswisu fī ṣudūri al-nās*; Qur'ān 114:5) – a usage which surfaces immediately before the final verse of the Qur'ān (i.e., 114:6), which itself mentions the *jinn* (*min al-jinnati wa'l-nās*).
51. Al-Qūṭī, *Psautier*, p. 177.
52. See note 25 above, for al-Qūṭī's usage of '*khāliq*'. Al-Qūṭī's description of Jesus as '*khāliq lā makhlūq*' seems especially to be directed against Christologies with Arian tendencies, which would indeed consider the 'Son' to be 'created'.
53. Al-Qūṭī, *Psautier*, p. 88.
54. Al-Qūṭī's invocation of the name of Jesus cleverly recalls the original of Psalm 51:14, with his '*yasū'ka*' (يسوعك) forming an Arabic cognate to the Hebrew source's '*yishə'ekha*' (יִשְׁעֶךָ ; Thy salvation).
55. For '*qādir*', '*muqtadir*', and '*qāhir*' as applied to Allah in the Qur'ān, see, for example, the following verses respectively 6:37, 18:45, and 6:18.
56. This Arabic phrase first occurs in Qur'ān 2:20, but also recurs in dozens of subsequent *āyāt*.
57. For 'Psalms 104–106' as 'the first of the Hallelujah psalms', see William L. Holladay, *The Psalms Through Three Thousand Years: Prayerbook of a Cloud of Witnesses* (Minneapolis: Fortress Press, 2000), p. 79.
58. Al-Qūṭī, *Psautier*, p. 167; Urvoy herself recognises in a footnote that *lā ilāha illa Allāh* comprises a '*Formule islamique*'.
59. Al-Qūṭī's interpretation of the transliterated Hebrew term 'هللويا' is especially apt considering its similarity to the authentically Arabic term '*tahlīl*' (تهليل) – which is indeed occasionally used to signify the recitation of '*lā ilāha illa Allāh*' (see Hans Wehr, *A Dictionary of Modern Written Arabic*, ed. J. Milton Cowan (Wiesbaden: Otto Harrassowitz, 1961), p. 1030). Although striking, al-Qūṭī's appropriation is not unique; see Griffith, *The Church in the Shadow of the Mosque*, p. 58, which quotes an even earlier Arabic Christian text that reflects the adoption of *lā ilāha illa Allāh*. Griffith additionally explains that 'it appears [...] that some contemporaneous Arabic-speaking Christians were making the first phrase of the Islamic *shahāda* their own; that they did so at all is a measure of their enculturation into the world of Islam'.
60. See Jeremy L. Smith, *Verse and Voice in Byrd's Song Collections of 1588 and 1589* (Woodbridge UK: Boydell Press, 2016), p. 24.
61. Al-Qūṭī, *Psautier*, p. 186. Al-Qūṭī concludes his introduction to this psalm by noting its acrostic character, with the primary manuscript utilised by Urvoy listing in particular '*alif, jīm, dāl*'.
62. See Qur'ān 2:254, for words similar to the two employed by al-Qūṭī utilised in tandem in the phrase '*al-kāfirūna humu al-ẓālimūna*'.
63. Al-Qūṭī, *Psautier*, pp. 187–188. In her French rendition, Urvoy replaces '*kitābuka al-'adl*' with '*Ton juste livre*', but also notes that this phrase comprises a '*Terme musulman*', without, however, highlighting the more pronounced Islamic echoes in this same psalm as rendered by al-Qūṭī.
64. The tradition of applying the adjective '*karīm*' to 'the Qur'ān' claims origins within the scripture itself; see, for instance, Qur'ān 56:77, i.e., '*innahu la-qur'ānun karīm*'.

65. Al-Qūṭī, *Psautier*, p. 188.
66. This is Arberry's rendition of Qur'ān 94:1, although his edition does not include a question mark after 'thee' which I here supply.
67. Al-Qūṭī, *Psautier*, p. 194.
68. A participle signifying one who 'retains, keeps, or guards', '*ḥāfiẓ*' is also the title of a 'memoriser' (of the Qur'ān, or alternately, the *ḥadīth*); however, in the Qur'ān itself, '*ḥāfiẓ*' is also applied to Allah Himself (see 12:64, i.e., '*fa-Allāhu khayrun ḥāfiẓan*').
69. For '*sunna*' as the 'Prophetic example', see Mohammed Moussa, *Politics of the Islamic Tradition: The Thought of Muhammad al-Ghazali* (London: Routledge, 2016), p. 10.
70. For the 'messianic meaning' of Psalm 118 (Psalm 117 in al-Qūṭī's numbering), and its connection to the First Temple, see James H. Charlesworth, 'Jesus and the Temple' in *Jesus and Temple: Textual and Archaeological Explorations*, ed. James H. Charlesworth (Minneapolis, MN: Fortress Press, 2014), pp. 145–181 (p. 170).
71. Al-Qūṭī, *Psautier*, p. 185. Al-Qūṭī's usage '*mustashbi'*' (مستشبع) is curious; Urvoy renders this term '*pour les combler*', which corresponds with my 'saturation' above.
72. These quotations derive from Matthew 21:42 in the KJV.
73. Urvoy herself adds a note in her edition, recognising simply that '*miḥrāb*' (محراب) is '*vocabulaire musulman*' (al-Qūṭī, *Psautier*, p. 185).

2

'VERILY HAVE I FOUND ALLAH OFT-RETURNING': THE QUR'ĀNIC POETICS OF SULAYMĀN AL-GHAZZĪ

I

JESUS'S *SHARĪʿA*

Closing with the Messiah's *miḥrāb*, the last chapter's concluding treatment of al-Qūṭī's Psalm 117 anticipates yet another conclusion, reaching forward to the final *qaṣīda* in the poetry collection of Sulaymān al-Ghazzī, 'the first Arab poet whose *dīwān* deals exclusively with Christian concerns'.[1] Born around 940, al-Ghazzī began his life in the same century that witnessed the death of al-Qūṭī. These two Christian Arabic authors share not only biographical time, however, but also build a similar sacred space, with the concluding *qaṣīda* of al-Ghazzī's poetic corpus featuring the very same architecture established in al-Qūṭī's Psalm 117. After versifying moral imperatives from the Gospel of Matthew, al-Ghazzī's final *qaṣīda* broadens to consider God's communications, conveying His bibliographic message to mankind:[2]

هكذا قيل في النبوة لما   وضع الله للعباد كتابا
أوضح الحق في الشريعة إيسو   ع وعلى بقدسه المحرابا

Thus is it said in the prophecy when
Allah established for the servants a book (*kitāb*)

Jesus elucidated the truth in the *sharīʿa*
and elevated in his sanctuary the *miḥrāb*[3]

Recalling al-Qūṭī's psalter by invoking Allah's *kitāb* in his first line above, it is al-Ghazzī's second line that seems especially reminiscent of al-Qūṭī, locating a *qibla* in the midst of Christian sacred space. At the heart of his sanctuary, Jesus places a prayer niche, with a *miḥrāb* erected within the Messiah's own shrine.[4] Even before this end to his second line, however, al-Ghazzī echoes al-Qūṭī by utilising a term evocative of Muslim praxis. Although al-Qūṭī associated Christ with the '*sunna*', al-Ghazzī aligns Jesus with another jurisprudential term suggestive of Islam. Asserting that the Messiah 'elucidated' spiritual 'truth' (*al-ḥaqq*) al-Qūṭī defines Jesus's doctrine via a word now synonymous with Islamic law, discovering the Messiah's message implied in the *sharī'a* (الشريعة).[5]

Charting prophecy's progress, with Allah's *kitāb* passed to His servants, al-Ghazzī outlines a brief economy of biblical revelation that is yet redolent of Islam, paralleling al-Qūṭī's own poetic employment of Qur'ānic idioms. Sharing a literary 'niche', these two Christian poets each 'elevate' a '*miḥrāb*' in their verses that points bi-directionally, forming a single *locus* that links two scriptural traditions, while also bridging the here and the hereafter – a portal of prayer that spans not only dispensations, but dimensions, reaching eastward to Islam, as well as upward to the divine. If sharing specific imagery, however, the disparities between al-Ghazzī and al-Qūṭī are perhaps just as striking; erecting the same sacred space in their poetic lines, these near contemporaries are also spatially separated, arising from opposing sides of the Mediterranean. Authoring verses which are Christian in creed, yet Qur'ānic in texture, al-Ghazzī flourished far from al-Qūṭī's Andalusia, native not to Europe, but the Middle East, as his name suggests (with 'al-Ghazzī' meaning 'of Gaza').[6] Palestinian in origin, and rising to the rank of Orthodox bishop, al-Ghazzī is also unlike al-Qūṭī in the scope of his extant writings, expressing piety not only in his religious poetry, but also in theological prose, penning disquisitions on primary Christian concerns, including 'the Cross' itself.[7] These external splits in genealogy and genre are complemented by the internal perspectives discretely exhibited in the poetics of al-Qūṭī and al-Ghazzī. Pivoting forward in time from Chapter 1, Chapter 2 transitions also away from translation, moving inwards from al-Qūṭī's biblical rendition to the autobiographical intimacy of al-Ghazzī's poetry. In his Arabic psalter, al-Qūṭī had covertly infused his own interests into lines of Christian scripture; rather than rendering a universal canon, al-Ghazzī's verses directly reflect individual sentiment and spiritual experience, innovating poetry that articulates first-person passions, producing 'haunting poems of grief and religious fervor which often evoke memories of the Holy Land and pilgrimage to the biblical *loca sancta*', as Sidney H. Griffith has described.[8]

Spanning these opposing perspectives in Christian poetics – universal text vs. individual context – the writings of al-Qūṭī and al-Ghazzī are ironically united in their Islamic engagements, with both poets consistently and creatively appealing to Qur'ānic precedents. Due to the texts they produce, however, their inter-scriptural borrowings assume divergent significances. The audacious character of al-Qūṭī's Qur'ānic appeals derives partly from the canonical text which is his source, daring to import Islamic vocabulary into biblical rendition. As the following chapter explores, however, the achievement of al-Ghazzī's ecumenical appeal arises partly from its subjectivity, producing 'remarkably personal' verses, in Samuel Noble's words, that express a private Christian identity through Qur'ānic expressions.[9] Rather than being deferred through a third position – à la al-Qūṭī and his translation of the psalmist's texts – the Islamic usages that emerge in al-Ghazzī's verses seem more immediate and idiomatic, not merely reflecting a general inter-scriptural environment, but also a personal willingness to inscribe Qur'ānic fragments into his own Christian autobiography, with al-Ghazzī's spiritual life unfolding surprisingly amid Islamic lines.

II

AUTOBIOGRAPHIC *ASMĀ'*

It is from the final *qaṣīda* in al-Ghazzī's edited *Dīwān* that his above appeal to 'the *sharī'a*' of 'Jesus' originates; however, even after the conclusion to this last *qaṣīda*, al-Ghazzī's *Dīwān* continues briefly, its modern edition including an appendix that offers an additional poetic piece: a 'prayer' voiced by al-Ghazzī in Arabic '*saja'*'. Opening with the following lines, this appended prayer epitomises the intimate character of al-Ghazzī's pious artistry, petitioning God in the first-person:

اللهم إني اسألك،
يا نور الأنوار, وعالم الأسرار، وكاشف الأضرار،
الملك الجبار، ذا العزة والوقار،
منزل الأمطار، ومحصي نبات الأشجار،
واضع الأرض في القرار، وجاعل الشمس لضياء النهار،

O Allah, verily I implore Thee
O Light of Lights, Knower of Secrets, and Reliever of Hardships
The King, the Compeller, He Who possesses might and majesty
Who sends down the rains, and tallies the sprouts of the trees
And establishes the earth in the fixed place, and makes the sun to illumine the day[10]

Cataloguing God's graces, from celestial to terrestrial, al-Ghazzī's last line seems especially evocative of Qur'ānic imagery, praising Allah for 'establishing the earth in the fixed place (*al-qarār*)' – a phrase that is itself previously established in *āyāt* such as Qur'ān 40:64, which also speaks of God 'ma[king] for you the earth a fixed place (*qarār*)'.[11] Ending with this earthy echo of the Qur'ān, it is the middle line of al-Ghazzī's selection that ascends to heavenly heights, invoking in a single line two of the divine *asmā'*. Recalling labels used by al-Qūṭī, al-Ghazzī appeals to God as 'al-Malik' and 'al-Jabbār' – two of the 'ninety-names' that appear together in *āyāt* such as Qur'ān 59:23.[12] It is, however, the very end of this same line that features Qur'ānic diction more uncommon, and yet more idiomatic; celebrating Allah as 'possessing' not only 'might' but 'majesty', al-Ghazzī's latter term – 'al-Waqār' (الوقار) – finds its precedent in Sūra 71, whose thirteenth *āya* inquires:

مَا لَكُمْ لَا تَرْجُونَ لِلَّهِ وَقَارًا
What ails you, that you look not in God for majesty (*waqār*)[13]

Appearing in Qur'ān 71:13 as one of Allah's attributes, '*waqār*' appears only once in the Muslim scripture, comprising one of the Qur'ān's *hapax legomena*.[14] Rather than merely regular Qur'ānic terms, it is such rare usages as *waqār* that aids al-Ghazzī as he ascribes 'grandeur' to God, his Christian *Dīwān* demonstrating familiarity not only with the typical, but also the atypical, terms of the Qur'ān, even while lauding God Himself as inimitable 'Light'.

Although focused on divine transcendence, and cataloguing God's acts of creation, this selection opens with immanence and intimacy, concentrating on the individual speaker's own creativity, framing this poetic prayer as highly personal, with al-Ghazzī inserting his 'I' immediately after invoking Allah (إني ; verily I). This close proximity between divine *asmā'* and human self-reference informs the entirety of al-Ghazzī's *Dīwān*, with the poet's own identity consistently paralleled by Qur'ānic appeals, not only at the opening to his verse compositions, but also at their conclusion. Consider, for instance, the very close to al-Ghazzī's brief sixty-seventh *qaṣīda*, whose final verse includes the author's own petition for forgiveness:

وأثاب من قال القصيدة   غافر الذنب المقدم
And let Him reward the one who spoke the *qaṣīda*
the Forgiver of Sins, the Expeditor[15]

At the end of this final line, the Lord is labelled lastly by al-Ghazzī in his sixty-seventh *qaṣīda* as '*al-muqaddim*' (the Expeditor) – yet another of Allah's ninety-nine *asmā'*.[16] It is al-Ghazzī's two-word term for God, however, that seems most significant: '*ghāfir al-dhanb*' (the Forgiver of Sins), a phrase that not only recalls the title of the Qur'ān's fortieth chapter, Sūrat Ghāfir, but that also overlaps precisely with this *sūra*'s third *āya*, which itself begins:

غَافِرِ الذَّنْبِ وَقَابِلِ التَّوْبِ
Forgiver of Sins, Accepter of Penitence

Concluding his *qaṣīda* by recalling the start of a *sūra*, al-Ghazzī's Qur'ānic appeal to Allah seems all the more impactful as it emerges in the very same line that includes his own self-reference. Even as the poet identifies himself as a pious supplicant, he ascribes to God a Qur'ānic signature, with the same Christian voice that 'speaks' this '*qaṣīda*' claiming refuge with the 'Forgiver' whose holy name overlaps with Sūrat Ghāfir.

If uniquely personal, al-Ghazzī's usage of such phraseology in his sixty-seventh *qaṣīda* is far from unique in his *Dīwān*, with this Christian collection frequently featuring divine names from the Qur'ān. God is invoked by al-Ghazzī, for example, with single *asmā'* including *malik*, *muqtadir*, *muṣawwir*, and *al-bāri'*.[17] He is also qualified, however, with entire phrases familiar to Islamic discourse, such as the standard doxology *subaḥāna wa ta'ālā* (most holy and most high), and, more intriguingly, with *rabb al-bayt* (Lord of the House) – a two-word fragment that is not only Qur'ānic, but which also recalls pre-Islamic Arabia, with al-Ghazzī quoting in his Christian verses this echo of Meccan antiquity, in which Allah was lauded as 'Lord' of the 'Ka'ba' – that is, 'the house' (*al-bayt*).[18] Invoking names essential to Islam, al-Ghazzī not only integrates *asmā'* implicitly into his *qaṣā'id*, however, but inserts explicit meditations on the *asmā'* into individual poems, highlighting the power of God's labels in lines such as the following from Qaṣīda 78:

إن الإله القديـــم الحـي متحـد　　لذاته، لا كاســـمانا اساميـــكا

أبديت خلق السما والأرض مقتدرا

Verily God, the pre-eternal, the ever-living, is unified
of His essence, not like our names are Thy names

Thou hast manifested the creation of the heavens and the earth omnipotently[19]

As seen previously, al-Ghazzī again invokes God with Islamic nomenclature, employing nominatives such as '*al-ḥayy*' (the ever-living), as well as the accusative '*muqtadiran*'; (omnipotently), which recalls this same term's form in Qur'ān 18:45.[20] The Islamic origins for these labels invite especial attention as al-Ghazzī himself asserts in these lines the distinctive nature of divine 'names'. Shifting from third person to second, al-Ghazzī's initial line above begins with Qur'ānic epithets such as 'al-Ḥayy' before apostrophising God directly, declaring that 'Thy names' are unlike 'our names' – not only an intriguing shift in person and number (i.e., *iltifāt*), but a pronominal shift that insists on the concrete divide between 'Thee' and 'us'.[21] Ironically, even while recognising the incommensurability of the divine and human –

between the 'names' for God and man – al-Ghazzī himself blurs distinctions between scriptural expressions, bridging the gulf between his own biblical poetics and Qur'ānic idioms.

Featuring Islamic *asmā'* that form not only the content, but also the concerns, of his Christian verses, the ironies of al-Ghazzī's names for God are amplified further in his eighth *qaṣīda*, which begins with the following fascinating lines:

ألف تألف لامها بالهاء　　لوجود إسم جل في الأسماء
اسم عددناه ثلاثة احرف　　باللفظ، والتوحيد في المعناء

An 'A', its 'L' joins to the 'H'
to instantiate a name, sublime amongst names

A name which we enumerate as three of letter
in outward expression, but it is oneness in inner meaning[22]

Again isolating Allah's name above all others, al-Ghazzī yet complicates the 'sublime' singularity of this highest of *asmā'*, investing the very term for 'God' in Arabic with meaning that is immense, but also multiple. In the three basic 'letters' of this singular 'name' – that is, 'A', 'L', 'H' (*alif*, *lām*, *hā'*) – al-Ghazzī discerns a dichotomy between plurality and singularity, while implying also the very dichotomy that divides Christianity from Islam.[23] Rather than read the *a-l-h* root of Allah as monotheistic merely, al-Ghazzī emphasises that this name is not only 'one' in 'meaning', but also 'three' in 'letter'. Triple in symbol, yet signifying *tawḥīd* (oneness). the Arabic etymology of 'Allah' offers al-Ghazzī a linguistic link between traditions, with God's most exalted name negotiating religious difference. Investing the *word* 'God' with theological import, al-Ghazzī adopts a logocentric approach that reflects his Christian commitments. And yet, in his plural reading of the singular divine, al-Ghazzī suggests that the 'inner meaning' of the Trinitarian name itself is *tawḥīd* – a statement that serenely ascribes supreme significance to the same 'oneness' proclaimed by the Qur'ān, even while applying to the Christian Trinity a term typically designating the sole divinity of Allah (توحيد ; *tawḥīd*).[24]

III

THE *JĀNN* AND THE MAGDALENE

Synthesising theological traditions in God's transcendent 'name', the *asmā'* of Allah also aid al-Ghazzī in syncing discrete scriptural narratives, recruiting Qur'ānic idioms to versify stories essential to Christian revelation. The most sustained retelling of a single biblical episode in al-Ghazzī's *Dīwān* opens his second *qaṣīda*, which is itself based on the Bible's second book. Rendering events from Exodus 3, this *qaṣīda* recounts Allah's address to Moses from the 'burning bush':

قال تعالى: قدميك اخلعهما فالقدس ما يصلح بالنعل يطا
وامض الى شعبي بمصر إنني رأتهم تتهدوا تحت الشقا
فقال موسى: من أقل أرسلني؟

He said – exalted be He – make bare thy two feet
for it is not permitted to tread with sandals upon 'the holy'

Go to My people in Egypt, for verily have I
seen them sighing under hardship

Then Moses said: who shall I say that sent me?[25]

In the first words of the first verse above, al-Ghazzī invokes God with a familiar 'exalted' epithet, recalling Islamic conventions with '*qāla ta'ālā*' (He said, exalted be He) – a standard substitute for 'Allah', a formula appearing frequently, for example, in *tafsīr* traditions.[26] Opening with this nominal replacement for 'God', al-Ghazzī also anticipates his *qaṣīda*'s own concern with 'naming', retelling the first Exodus encounter between Allah and Moses, in which the latter asks 'who shall I say that sent me?'. Ironically, however, in versifying this biblical inquiry concerning divine identity, al-Ghazzī appeals to extra-biblical idioms of divine speech, interweaving Qur'ānic strands into this Exodus account. As recognised by Neophytos Edelby in the footnotes to his edition of the *Dīwān*, several overlaps with various *sūra*s emerge in al-Ghazzī's diction; for example, this Christian poem employs Qur'ānic idioms such as '*ikhla'* [...] *al-na'l*' (remove [thy] sandal), recalling Sūrat Ṭā Hā's twelfth verse, which voices a similar imperative, that is, '*fakhla' na'layk*' ('so remove thy two sandals'). The Qur'ānic character of al-Ghazzī's version of Exodus amplifies, however, as his second *qaṣīda* continues; after Moses asks Allah concerning an *āya* (آية; sign) to convince the Israelites of his authority, God responds as follows in al-Ghazzī's next verses:

أجابه: كفك أرددها الى إبطك تعد بيضا على لون النشا
ثم أعدها مرة ترجع الى كيانها من غير سؤ يختشى
ألق العصا في الأرض تسع حية

(God) responded to him: thy hand, retract it into
thy armpit, it shall revert to whiteness, the colour of starch

Then bring it back once more, it shall return to
its natural state without harm to be feared

Throw the staff on the earth, (it shall become a) fast-moving serpent[27]

Again echoing the Qur'ān with phrases such as *ghayr sū'* (without harm; cf. Qur'ān 28:32), it is al-Ghazzī's last line above that seems most intriguing, not merely integrating Qur'ānic vocabulary, but outlining a Qur'ānic version of Exodus events. Versifying God's imperative to 'cast down' Moses's 'staff', al-Ghazzī invokes targeted language from Qur'ān 20:20, the former appearing in the lefthand column and the latter in the righthand column of Table 2.1.

al-Ghazzī, Qaṣīda 2:9	**Qur'ān 20:20**
ألق العصا في الأرض تسع حية	فَأَلْقَاهَا فَإِذَا هِيَ حَيَّةٌ تَسْعَىٰ
Throw the staff on the earth, (it shall become a) fast-moving serpent	He threw it down, and – lo and behold! it became a serpent fast-moving

Table 2.1. A comparison of a verse from al-Ghazzī's second *qaṣīda* with a verse from the Qur'ān.

Retelling the shift of Moses's staff into a 'swift' serpent, al-Ghazzī's Christian poetry itself swiftly shifts into Qur'ānic exposition, as Edelby has again acknowleged.[28] Borrowing not only Islamic diction, but also detail, al-Ghazzī fleetingly departs from the Bible, reforming his verses instead from a Qur'ānic phrase – that is, '*ḥayyatun tas'ā*' (serpent, fast-moving) – a phrase which has no analogue in Exodus.[29] Considering the Qur'ānic texture of his biblical retelling, it is especially apt that Moses in al-Ghazzī's account queries God concerning an '*āya*' ('sign' or 'verse') – a term that subtly assumes its double significance in the above lines, suggesting not only the miraculous 'sign(s)' that Allah grants to Moses, but also the 'verse(s)' that al-Ghazzī himself receives from the Qur'ān as he crafts his Arabic account of Exodus.

For Christians, the miracles given to Moses are, of course, anticipations of the ultimate 'signs' performed by the Messiah – a typological link between Old Testament and New Testament that al-Ghazzī often implies in his verses.[30] Indeed, even before his second *qaṣīda*'s retelling of Moses's miracles, al-Ghazzī's first *qaṣīda* clarifies this continuity, cataloguing God's graceful interventions into sacred history, stretching from biblical beginnings and culminating in the Gospels. Transitioning between testaments, a coherency emerges across the biblical canon not only in the consistency of God's 'signs and wonders', but also in al-Ghazzī's regular appeal to Qur'ānic *āyāt* (signs/verses) as he retells elements from both the Judaic and Christian scriptures. Versifying acts of providence from the Hebrew Bible, al-Ghazzī's initial *qaṣīda* ultimately reaches up to Christ's own miracles, mentioning Gospel moments such as Jesus's 'changing' of 'water [into] wine', his 'walking on water', and his casting out a demonic legion from Mary Magdalene.[31] It is this latter miracle, however, that accrues Islamically-resonant language in al-Ghazzī's account, with the fifty-eighth verse of his first *qaṣīda* sounding as much Qur'ānic as it does Christian:

وهو الذي ضرب الجان الالى علقوا　　　بالمجدلية، رب الانس والجان

And (Jesus) is the one who struck the *jānn*, those stuck in
the Magdalene, the Lord of man and *jānn*[32]

Although it is 'devils' that afflict the woman in the Gospel's account, for al-Ghazzī it is instead '*al-jānn*' (الجان ; collective plural of *jinn*) that Jesus 'strikes'. Recalling the appearance of these invisible creatures in al-Qūṭī's psalter, al-Ghazzī envisions '*al-jānn*' and 'the Magdalene' within the same scriptural corpus, as well as the same bodily corpus, with Christ expelling these Qur'ānic identities that are possessing Mary's person. However, it is not the first, but the second, mention of the *jinn* in al-Ghazzī's verse that seems most 'striking'. Credited with their exorcism, Christ is also characterised by al-Ghazzī as the 'Lord of man and *jānn*' – a phrase that is familiar once again from the Muslim scripture, recalling several *āyāt* which pair together precisely humanity and the *jinn*, mentioned in tandem as Allah's creatures.[33] Portraying Jesus as the *jinn*'s 'Lord', al-Ghazzī's verse not only borrows a Qur'ānic epithet, but also shifts its subject, attributing to Christ the same sovereignty over 'man and *jinn*' that is exclusively Allah's domain in the Muslim scripture.

Translating 'devils' into '*jinn*', even as Jesus miraculously heals 'the Magdalene', it is the 'Devil' himself who is translated as al-Ghazzī depicts Christianity's core miracle: the resurrection. Rather than merely the Messiah, it is Jesus's prime antagonist that acquires Qur'ānic diction in al-Ghazzī's *Dīwān*, with Satan accruing an Islamic signature in the second line of the following passage from Qaṣīda 12 (lines 29–30):

هذا المسيح بموته نحيا اذا　　　متنا وحاز جسومنا النؤوسا
في ثالث اليوم الإله أقامنا　　　فيه، وأسقط ضدنا إبليسا

This Messiah, in his death, we live, when
we die, and our bodies attain the sarcophagus

On the third day, God raised us up
in him, and he overthrew our antagonist, Iblīs[34]

Celebrating his faith's foundational event – the rising of Jesus three days after his death – al-Ghazzī surrounds this essential metamorphosis with quite another conversion, rebranding the Devil himself with an idiom original to Islam. In al-Ghazzī's poetic retelling, the enemy 'conquered' by Christ is called 'Iblīs', this Qur'ānic label emerging at the end of the second line above, aptly situated in rhyme with the end of the first line's *na'wūs* (نؤوس ; sarcophagus). Associated with death and himself defeated, the Devil shares not only sound, but significance, with the fatal locus from which 'we' are resurrected, al-Ghazzī aligning 'Iblīs' with '*na'wūs*'. Gaining ascendency via al-Ghazzī's verses, even as the 'adversary' himself is 'overthrown', Satan's Qur'ānic name emerges as stylistically central to this Christian account of the resurrection, with 'Iblīs' forming the end of the actual verse from which new life and a new poetic line springs from the sarcophogus.[35]

IV

QUR'ĀNIC HOURI IN THE CHRISTIAN HEREAFTER?

A universal resurrection is heralded by Christ's specific 'rising' in al-Ghazzī's twelfth *qaṣīda*, with Jesus's return from the dead implying 'our' own eternal 'life'. This broader eschatological concern emerges frequently throughout al-Ghazzī's *qaṣīda*s; versifying the otherworldly consequences of worldly beliefs and behaviour, al-Ghazzī's sixty-fifth *qaṣīda*, for instance, forecasts the discrete futures that await both 'believers' and 'unbelievers':

والمؤمنون به في البعث يجتمعوا ليأخذوا ما أعد الله من نعم
عن اليمين يقوموا في كرامته متوجين بتيجان على اللمم
والكافرون وأهل الشر يطردهم الى عذاب أليم طرد منتقم

And the believers will be gathered together in the resurrection (*al-ba'th*)
so that they may receive what Allah has promised of blessings

On the right they will stand in His beneficence
crowned with crowns upon [their] locks

And the disbelievers and the evil folk, He will drive them
to a painful punishment, a driving of retribution[36]

Establishing an opposition common to the Qur'ān, these verses contrast *al-mu'minūn* (the believers) with *al-kāfirūn* (the unbelievers) – words inverse in meaning, yet set in rhymed parallel, opening alternate lines in the above passage.[37] Consistent with a Qur'ānic perspective, these contrastive terms also acquire an Islamic identity via the adjectives and attributes that surround them in al-Ghazzī's verses. Leading line 1, for example, the 'gathering' of 'the believers' in the afterlife is labelled '*al-ba'th*' (البعث) – literally, 'the sending forth' – an apocalyptic idiom that recalls *āyāt* such as Qur'ān 22:5.[38] Perhaps more familiar is the phrase that designates the fate of 'the unbelievers', who are 'driven' down to a place of 'punishment', which is identified as '*'adhāb alīm*', two words which are highly typical of the Qur'ān, appearing together in dozens of *āyāt*.[39]

Denominating the otherworld with diction from another tradition, al-Ghazzī amplifies his Islamic idioms as his *Dīwān* details the precise hereafter 'promises' made to believers and unbelievers. Utilising the very verb above that 'drove' (طرد; *ṭ-r-d*) the damned into hell, al-Ghazzī's seventy-first *qaṣīda* again depicts this same penalty, with the evildoers 'drive[n]' to a 'punishment [of] fire'.[40] However, these same lines also specify further heavenly rewards, echoing the Qur'ān's own manifold image of the blissful abode:

ويعطي لأبراره منعما   جنان الخلود بجناتهن
ويطرد أشراره للعذاب   الى النار تضرم نيرانهن
فلا شيء يشبه أفراحهن   ولا شيء يشبه أحزانهن

To His righteous will be given blessedly
gardens of eternity amongst their gardens

And His evildoers will drive onward to the punishment
into the fire, ignited with their flames

And there is nothing like to their joys
and there is nothing like to their sorrows[41]

Instead of 'believers' merely, the blessed are here identified as '*abrār*' (أبرار; righteous) – a term typical of the Qur'ān's portrait of paradise, appearing in several *sūra*s.[42] More specifically, however, it is Sūra 55 – al-Raḥmān – that seems to inform al-Ghazzī's compound conception of heaven. Recalling the promise of Sūrat al-Raḥmān of multiple gardens above gardens, al-Ghazzī's own verses depict a pastoral plurality, envisioning paradise not as a single garden, but 'gardens of eternity amongst their gardens'.[43] Although incommensurable in its pleasure and pain – possessing joys and sorrows that are unlike anything else – al-Ghazzī's hereafter is ironically very much like Qur'ānic parallels, overlapping another scripture's expressions to describe experiences which are themselves inimitable.

Merging the multiple and the incomparable, al-Ghazzī's portrait of paradise occasionally strays into the polemical, not only describing the delights of heaven in Islamic terms, but also anxiously distinguishing these paradisal joys from Islamic precedents. Addressing the believers directly with '*yā mu'minūn!*', al-Ghazzī's lines 19 to 21 of his Qaṣīda 31 again versify the afterlife, but refute, not recommend, the heavenly rewards described in the Qur'ān:

لا تطمعوا أن يوم البعث يطعمكم   من الفواكه أثمارا وأعنابا

ولا يزوجكم حورا فيعجبكم   جمالهن على الفردوس إعجابا

إن المعاد لدار ما ترون بها   من المطاعم والملبوس جلبابا

Do not hope that on the day of resurrection (*al-ba'th*) that you shall be fed
from fruits, neither harvest yields, nor grapes

You will not be given in marriage to heavenly virgins (*ḥūr*), thus astonishing you
with their beauty within paradise as a wonder

Verily the afterlife is an abode in which you will not see
places to eat, nor clothes for garments[44]

Describing the rewards of the day of resurrection (*yawm al-ba'th*; cf. Qur'ān 30:56), al-Ghazzī again echoes Islamic diction to portray the paradisal; here, however, Qur'ānic elements and identities are not embraced, but denied. In his appeal to celestial 'fruits' (الفواكه ; *al-fawākih*), for instance, al-Ghazzī echoes *sūra*s such as 23, 37, and 77, but only to clear his own Christian paradise of such provender. With clever wordplay, al-Ghazzī conjoins, as well as contradicts, heavenly hopes and the mere eating of fruits, admonishing Christian readers in his second line that they should *not* 'hope' (طمع ; *tama'*) 'to eat' (طعم ; *ta'am*) from a harvest in heaven.[45] Invoking Islamic images in opposition, the element that al-Ghazzī seems most anxious to reject, however, is the *ḥūr* ('heavenly virgins' or 'houris'), who occupy the entirety of his third verse above. Promised to the Muslim faithful in multiple Qur'ānic passages, the *ḥūr* are evacuated from heaven as given by al-Ghazzī, who empties the blissful abode of all corporeality, including not only houris, but also clothing and consumables.[46] Intriguingly, however, the *ḥūr* are not only denied, but also detailed, by al-Ghazzī, with the latter half of his third line accenting their aesthetic wonder. Even while banishing the sensual from paradise, the astounding beauty of the *ḥūr* persists in al-Ghazzī's poetry, his artistry still profiting from their perfection, even as it denies the *ḥūr* a place in heaven. Refusing to endorse marriage in the next world, al-Ghazzī's own earthly verses yet remain wedded to paradisal imagery offered by Islamic sources; seeking to separate out his own Christian eschatology, al-Ghazzī ironically embraces Qur'ānic idioms in opposition, producing poetic lines that are still sustained by the same 'fruits' cropped from a vision of heaven he rejects.

V

'EXALTED BE GOD ABOVE WHAT THEY SAY'

Explicitly agonistic, these verses from Qaṣīda 31 are rare in, rather than representative of, al-Ghazzī's *Dīwān*, which tends to be more personal than polemical, implicitly echoing the Qur'ān in lines that intimately confess al-Ghazzī's own spiritual commitments. Such intersections between Christian interiority and Qur'ānic allusions emerge often at the very opening to al-Ghazzī's poems. Indeed, Qaṣīda 31 itself – whose lines 19 to 21 are treated immediately above, rejecting the Qur'ānic '*ḥūr*' – itself features the following first two lines:

تـوبـوا فإنــي وجـدت الله توابا   ومن ترجــاه للغفـران مـا خـابا
يا مؤمنون بإيسوع المسيح، ثقوا   بالله، فـهو عليــكم أشــفق الآبا

Repent, for verily have I found Allah Oft-Returning
and he whose hope is dedicated to the Forgiver is not disappointed

O believers in Jesus the Messiah, trust in
Allah, for He, to you, is most solicitous as a Father[47]

First urging readers to 'repent' (توبوا ; *tūbū*; lit., 'turn ye all'), al-Ghazzī's plural imperative is followed by the singular and self-reflective 'I found'. Admonishing initially his whole audience to 'turn' to God, it is al-Ghazzī who himself turns inward, offering his own testimony of Allah, 'finding' Him to be '*tawwāb*' ('Oft-Returning'). Framed as an individual experience, this Christian piety itself reflects a Qur'ānic precedent, however, with al-Ghazzī's own 'finding' itself to be found previously in Qur'ān 4:64 – a verse that surrounds Allah with the very same human action ('to find') as well as divine epithet ('Oft-Returning'), predicting that if 'wrong doers' had asked for forgiveness then:

لَوَجَدُوا اللَّهَ تَوَّابًا رَحِيمًا
they would have found Allah indeed Oft-returning, Most Merciful[48]

Expressed in the intimate first-person, al-Ghazzī's declaration – 'Verily have I found Allah Oft-Returning' – itself turns out to be borrowed second-hand, his subjective experience originating in a Qur'ānic subjunctive, making individual and concrete a conditional *āya* concerning those who 'would have found Allah indeed Oft-Returning'. Intriguingly, however, al-Ghazzī's Qur'ānic confession in his first line is complicated by his second, which recognises God again as a source of trust, but also associates Allah with extra-Islamic terms. Opening once more with a plural appeal, calling to all 'believers' in 'the Messiah', al-Ghazzī's second line also again 'turns' towards the intimate, privileging not the individual, however, but the familial, appealing to 'Allah' as 'Father' (*ābā*). Introducing his thirty-first *qaṣīda* with lines that complexly span scriptures, al-Ghazzī's initial line echoes the Qur'ān in the first person, while his second line closes with a markedly Christian epithet, characterising 'God' as a caring parent – an introduction that itself is compound in genealogy, generated from multiple scriptural sources, even as it ends by proclaiming a singular paternity in God the 'Father'.

Intimately turning towards the 'Oft-Returning' in his Qaṣīda 31, al-Ghazzī also dramatises other acts of divine intimacy, his thirteenth *qaṣīda* appealing to Islam for expressions, and an exclamation, as al-Ghazzī recounts the resurrection of Lazarus in lines 7 to 12:

فقلن له: يا رب أنت تقيمه، وأمرك في كل الخليقة ماضيا
أجاب: بهذا تؤمنا وتصدقا؟ فقلن: نعم يا رب، والطرف باكيا
فقال: أروني موضع القبر، إنني أتيت لتجديد الحياة مناديا
وقد كان محيي الميت يعرف قبره، ولكن ليوري ضعف جسم ترابيا
فنادى بباب القبر: عازر رد لي فجاوبه: لبيك, والصوت عاليا
فقال: اكشفوا عنه برفق...

Thus they said to (Jesus): O Lord, Thou shalt raise (Lazarus)
thy command is effective throughout all of creation

He answered: in this do you two believe and trust?
then they said: 'yes, O Lord', with weeping eyes

Then he said: 'Show me the place of his tomb, for I
have come calling to the renewal of life'

Verily the quickener of the dead was aware of his tomb
but so that he might appear in the weakness of the earthy body

Then he called at the door of the tomb, 'Lazarus, return to me!'
And he responded: 'at your service!' (*labbayk*) with a loud voice

Then he said: 'Unveil him with kindness...'[49]

Narrating an episode from John 11, al-Ghazzī initially reimagines Jesus's conversation with Lazarus's sisters – Mary and Martha – not only versifying their exchange, but also adding exegesis, inserting a gloss on this Gospel account.[50] Asking to be led to Lazarus's tomb in the fourth line above, Jesus's request compels al-Ghazzī to interject, confirming that Christ already knew the answer to his own question. It is the name by which Jesus is called in this same line, however, that seems most significant, al-Ghazzī specifying Christ as 'the quickener of the dead' – '*muḥyī al-mayyit*' (محيي الميت) – an alliterative epithet that echoes Qur'ān 30:50, where a nearly-identical name is applied to Allah Himself:

إِنَّ ذَٰلِكَ لَمُحْيِ ٱلْمَوْتَىٰ وَهُوَ عَلَىٰ كُلِّ شَيْءٍ قَدِيرٌ
surely He is the quickener of the dead (*muḥyī al-mawtā*),
and He is powerful over everything[51]

Merging divine identities, Christian and Qur'ānic, al-Ghazzī adapts an epithet from the Muslim scripture for the Messiah – an adaptation that anticipates al-Ghazzī's next line as well, where Lazarus vocally responds after his resurrection, calling out to Christ: '*labbayk*' (لبيك ; lit., 'at your service!' or, more simply, 'here I am!').[52] Although consistent with this context, expressing a meaning faithful to this Gospel moment, Lazarus's cry of '*labbayk*' also oddly situates him as a *ḥajjī*, with Lazarus's term qualifying as the precise exclamation expressed by Muslim pilgrims as they approach the Ka'ba. Still wrapped in burial vestments, Lazarus voices the '*labbayk*' as he approaches his own Lord; clothed in a literal *iḥrām* – his funeral shroud, from which he needs to be 'gently unveiled' – Lazarus is aptly portrayed by al-Ghazzī as he pursues a holy pilgrimage towards 'the One who makes alive the dead'.[53]

Translated from death to life, Lazarus also rises via an act of scriptural translation, with al-Ghazzī infusing Islamic nomenclature into biblical narrative. Substituting one sacred idiom for another in his poetic practice, al-Ghazzī occasionally makes this substitution process itself the subject of his poetry; consider, for instance, Qaṣīda 26, which apologises for the Christian faith against Jewish objections:

كذب القائلون فيها محالا   وتعالى الإلـه عما يقولوا
فات ما فات من شريعة موسى،   شرع إيسوع للشعوب بديل

The speakers lie absurdly against (the Word of God)
and exalted be God above what they say!

Moses's law (*sharī'a*) has been superseded
(by) Jesus's laws (*shuru'*), a substitute for the nations[54]

Superseding the foregoing dispensation, al-Ghazzī suggests Christianity supplants Mosaic law, the latter displaced by a new doctrine, Jesus's teaching forming the true 'substitute' (بديل ; *badīl*). A standard claim of supersessionism, al-Ghazzī's theological commitment acquires fresh irony, however, due to the language of its expression, utilising Islamic vocabulary to trace this trade of biblical traditions. Although reaching back to the previous Abrahamic religion – Judaism – it is the subsequent religion of Abraham that supports al-Ghazzī's confession, with Muslim idioms enriching his claims for Christian ascendency. In 'substituting' the Messiah for Moses, it is 'the *sharīʿa*' (شريعة , pl. شرع) that al-Ghazzī associates with biblical unfolding, appealing to a term essential to traditions of Islamic jurisprudence even as Jesus supersedes Judaic 'law'. As this present chapter nears its end, the *sharīʿa* of Jesus fittingly returns, first noted in the last *qaṣīda* of al-Ghazzī's *Dīwān* quoted at the very beginning to Chapter 2 above. However, here in al-Ghazzī's twenty-sixth *qaṣīda*, he invokes more than merely an Islamic association, advancing instead apologetics that are Qur'ānic in character. Defending his own creed, arguing for Christ's divinity contra Jewish doctrines, it is al-Ghazzī's first line above that seems most audacious; describing those who deny 'the Word of God' – '*kalimat Allāh*' – al-Ghazzī rejects the refusers of Christian truth, dismissing them with the phrase:

وتعالى الإله عما يقولوا
and exalted be God above that they say!

This Christian critique of 'disbelievers' itself forms a quotation, paralleling the Qur'ān's own condemnation of those who speak inappropriately concerning Allah, echoing statements such as the following from Qur'ān 17:43, which clear God from that which 'they say':

وَتَعَالَىٰ عَمَّا يَقُولُونَ
and exalted be He above that they say![55]

Not only a common phrase in the Qur'ān, this exclamation – 'exalted be He above that they say' – is commonly expressed *against* Christians, critiquing claims of Christ's divinity; for example, a similar usage occurs in Qur'ān 6:100, which exalts Allah far 'above' those who ascribe sons or daughters to Him.[56] Recruited by al-Ghazzī to champion precisely the claims critiqued in the Qur'ān, his *qaṣīda* adapts this expression to mean exactly the opposite of his Islamic source, with this exclamation of Muslim monotheism invoked to confirm the Messiah's divinity. Even as his *qaṣīda*'s content claims a religious substitution – with Christian '*sharīʿa*' supplanting Judaic – the form and phraseology of al-Ghazzī's verses imply quite another act of supplanting, with Qur'ānic speech appropriated for Christian apology. Aptly, considering the personal character of al-Ghazzī's *qaṣāʾid*, this substitution is itself centred in the replacement of person, with the 'they' of the Qur'ān's original – 'exalted be He above that they say!' – adjusted to denote others in its new Christian context. Pitting himself against all those who reject his own creed, al-Ghazzī contends against the 'they' who disbelieve Christ's divinity, even while employing Qur'ānic nomenclature that originally resisted Christian belief. Although the Qur'ān's own verses critique a 'they' willing to recognise plurality in the godhead, a reversed 'they' is critiqued in the same phrase as utilised by al-Ghazzī, referring now to those who refuse to recognise the second person of the Trinity. Speaking his own tradition anew even as he reflects his own personal perspective, al-Ghazzī is able to reinvent audaciously the very person of a Qur'ānic verb, with '*yaqulūn*' – 'they say' – no longer opposing Christians such as himself, but instead critiquing all those who oppose Christianity, with this phrase of *tawḥīd* emerging as a vehicle for Trinitarianism, the Muslim scripture giving ironic voice to al-Ghazzī's Christian *sharī'a* that advocates the worshipping of 'the Word of God'.

NOTES

1. For this quotation, and for an overview of Sulaymān al-Ghazzī's life and literary labours, see Samuel Noble, 'Sulaymān al-Ghazzī' in *Christian–Muslim Relations 600–1500*, ed. David Thomas, 2010. <http://dx.doi.org/10.1163/1877-8054_cmri_COM_25138>. Accessed 30 July 2019.
2. The Gospel of Matthew ('*Injīl Matā'*) is explicitly cited in line 30 of this *qaṣīda* – i.e., Qaṣīda 79. See Sulaymān al-Ghazzī, *Sulaymān al-Ghazzī*: *Shā'ir* wa-*Kātib Masīḥī Malakī*, ed. Neophytos Edelby, 3 vols. (Jūniya, Lebanon: al-Maktabat al-Būlusiyya, 1984–1986), vol. 2, p. 407. This three volume edition of al-Ghazzī's works, edited by Neophytos Edelby, features the *Dīwān* as its second volume, subsequently cited simply as 'al-Ghazzī, *Dīwān*'.
3. Al-Ghazzī, *Dīwān*, p. 407. The name 'Īsū'' (Jesus) straddles the divide in the second line of the above quotation.
4. Unless otherwise noted, I am unaware of previous criticism or translations of the poetic lines treated in this chapter. See Griffith, *The Church in the Shadow of the Mosque*, p. 170, who notes that 'none of his [i.e., al-Ghazzī's] works has been translated into a modern western language'. Since Griffith's study, Samuel Noble contributed a vital chapter on al-Ghazzī to his edited collection with Alexander Treiger (i.e., pp. 160–170 of *The Orthodox Church in the Arab World, 700–1700: An Anthology of Sources*) which also includes the English rendition of two of al-Ghazzī's *qaṣā'id*.
5. Customarily equated with 'Islamic law', '*sharī'a*' is itself mentioned in Qur'ān 45:18; unsurprisingly, however, this term is complex in its historical usages, with 'law' seeming an inadequate equivalent (for this recognition, see also Wael Hallaq, *Sharī'a*: Theory, *Practice*, *Transformations* (Cambridge: Cambridge University Press, 2012), p. 3). Although associated with Islam, and, indeed, even occasionally considered 'exactly synonymous with Islam' (as Tariq Ramadan observes in

his Chapter 4 of *Islam: The Essentials*, trans. Fred Reed (London: Pelican, 2017)), '*sharīʿa*' is a term that was historically applied to biblical traditions, invoked by Christian Arabic writers such as al-Ghazzī (see also Chapter 3 below for another such Christian usage).

6. As Noble recognises in his *Christian–Muslim Relations 600–1500* entry, '[t]here are no sources for his [al-Ghazzī's] biography apart from what can be gleaned from the contents of the Dīwān and his prose writings', which thereby leaves much uncertain in his life (Noble himself lists al-Ghazzī's year and place of birth as 'probably about 940' and 'possibly Gaza or elsewhere in Palestine').
7. For al-Ghazzī's prose treatise *Fī al-Ṣalīb* ('On the Cross'), see al-Ghazzī, *Sulaymān al-Ghazzī: Shāʿir* wa-*Kātib Masīḥī Malakī*, ed. Edelby, vol. 3, pp. 102–114.
8. Griffith, *The Church in the Shadow of the Mosque*, p. 170; this appraisal of al-Ghazzī's poetry is also partially quoted by Noble in his al-Ghazzī contribution to *The Orthodox Church in the Arab World, 700–1700*, p. 162.
9. This quotation derives from the opening to Noble's *Christian–Muslim Relations 600–1500* entry; the intimacy of al-Ghazzī's verses is usually associated with the 'grief' mentioned by Griffith, arising from the loss of his son. The present chapter, however, will instead emphasise not the familial, but the spiritual intimacy of al-Ghazzī's Qur'ānic appeals in his Christian poems.
10. It is Edelby's introduction to this appended al-Ghazzī prayer that describes it as *musajjaʿ* (مسجع ; composed in *sajʿa*); see al-Ghazzī, *Dīwān*, p. 409. This quotation that opens al-Ghazzī's prayer is to be found on *Dīwān*, p. 411.
11. This is quoted from Arberry's *Koran* translation, with the opening to this *āya* reading in his rendition: 'It is God who made for you the earth a fixed place and heaven for an edifice'.
12. See, in Arberry's translation, 'He is God; there is no god but He. He is the King (*al-malik*), the All-holy, the All-peaceable, the All-faithful, the All-preserver, the All-mighty, the All-compeller (*al-jabbār*), the All-sublime. Glory be to God, above that they associate!'.
13. This rendition of Qur'ān 71:13 derives from Arberry, with its word order adjusted to more strictly match the original; Arberry offers 'What ails you, that you look not for majesty in God'.
14. Although the root *wa-qa-ra* occurs multiple times in the Qur'ān, '*al-waqār*' is unique to 71:13.
15. Al-Ghazzī, *Dīwān*, p. 356. In Edelby's edition, *al-qaṣīda* (القصيدة) is broken up over the line break.
16. This represents Arberry's rendition from Qur'ān 40:3, which also informs my translation of al-Ghazzī's '*ghāfir al-dhanb*' as 'Forgiver of sins'. For '*al-muqaddim*' as one of the ninety-nine names, see *Encyclopedia*, ed. Netton, p. 95.
17. For these divine names, see respectively al-Ghazzī, *Dīwān*, '*malik*' (p. 345); '*muqtadir*' (p. 135); '*muṣṣawir*' (p. 410); and '*bāriʾ*' (p. 352).
18. For '*subḥāna taʿālā*', which occurs in the second line of al-Ghazzī's forty-seventh *qaṣīda*, see *Dīwān*, p. 273. The phrase '*rabb al-bayt*' is used by al-Ghazzī at the very opening to his eleventh *qaṣīda* (*Dīwān*, p. 99). In his introduction to this *qaṣīda*, Edelby notes that al-Ghazzī's poem likens 'reason' to a 'house', and identifies Allah as the 'Lord of this house' (*Dīwān*, p. 99). For Allah as 'a god recognised by the Meccans as *rabb al-bait*', see Jacques Waardenburg, 'Towards a Periodization of Earliest Islam according to its Relations with Other Religions'

in *The Qur'an: Style and Contents*, ed. Andrew Rippin (Farnham, UK: Ashgate, 2011), pp. 93–116 (p. 94).

19. Al-Ghazzī, *Dīwān*, p. 402.
20. While God is described as '*muqtadir*' in other *āyāt* – including two instances of this term in Sūra 54 – it is Qur'ān 18:45 that applies this idiom to Allah in the accusative, i.e., '*muqtadiran*'
21. For *iltifāt* – the 'shifts of person, number, and tense in discourse' – as one of the Qur'ān's stylistic features, see Mustansir Mir, 'Language' in *The Blackwell Companion to the Qur'ān*, ed. Andrew Rippin (Malden, MA: Blackwell Publishing 2008), pp. 88–106 (pp. 94–5), and M. A. S. Abdel Haleem, 'Grammatical shifts for rhetorical purposes: "Iltifat" and related features in the Qur'ān', *Bulletin of the School of Oriental and African Studies* 55:3 (1992): 407–432.
22. Al-Ghazzī, *Dīwān*, p. 83.
23. Edelby emphasises in his introduction to this *qaṣīda* that al-Ghazzī's lines detects in Allah's name the 'mystery of divine oneness (*tawḥīd*) in the trinity' (al-Ghazzī, *Dīwān*, p. 83).
24. Al-Ghazzī's reading of Christian truth into the very letters of Allah's name recalls a parallel, yet more audacious and well-known, Christian act of interpretation undertaken by Paul of Antioch, who reads the *muqaṭṭa'āt* of the second chapter of the Qur'ān as signifying 'the Christ'. For Paul, Sūrat al-Baqara's '*a-l-m*' (الم) comprise the first letters of *al-masīḥ* (المسيح); this interpretation, also upheld by an 'anonymous monk of Jerusalem', is treated in Clare Wilde's 'Early Christian Arabic Texts: Evidence for Non-'Uthmānic Qur'ān Codices, or Early Approaches to the Qur'ān?' in *New Perspectives on the Qur'ān: The Qur'ān in its Historical Context 2*, ed. Gabriel S. Reynolds (London: Routledge, 2011), pp. 358–371 (p. 369), as well as the second chapter to her *Approaches to the Qur'ān in Early Christian Arabic Texts (750–1258 C.E.)*, pp. 57–104.
25. Al-Ghazzī, *Dīwān*, p. 36.
26. The term '*ta'ālā*' (تعالى) is, of course, Qur'ānic. However, for the full phrase '*qāla ta'ālā*' in *tafsīr* literature, and its commentary traditions see, for instance, al-Ṭabarī, *Daqāiq Lughat al-Qur'ān fī Tafsīr Ibn Jarīr al-Ṭabarī*, ed. 'Abd al-Raḥmān 'Umayra (Beirut: 'Ālam al-Kutub, 1992), vol. 1, p. 309.
27. Al-Ghazzī, *Dīwān*, p. 36. It is on this same page that Edelby cites specific *āyāt* – Qur'ān 20:12 and 28:32 – to parallel al-Ghazzī's 'remove [thy] sandal', and 'without harm' respectively.
28. See al-Ghazzī, *Dīwān*, p. 36, for Edelby's ninth footnote, where he briefly notes 'the Qur'ān 20:19–20' as a precedent for al-Ghazzī's account of Moses's casting his staff, and its transformation into a 'fast-moving serpent'. The above translation from Qur'ān 20:20 derives from *The Qur'an: A New Translation*, trans. M. A. S. Abdel Haleem (Oxford: Oxford University Press, 2011), with one alteration. While Abdel Haleem's translation features 'a fast-moving serpent', I shift the adjective here to emphasise the Qur'ān's own order of words (i.e., providing instead 'a serpent fast-moving').
29. In neither of the two Exodus passages that speak of the 'serpent' into which Moses's staff turns (Exodus 4:3 and Exodus 7:9–17) is the serpent itself described as 'fast moving' (as it is in the accounts provided by both the Qur'ān and al-Ghazzī's *Dīwān*).

30. Edelby emphasises in his introduction to al-Ghazzī's second *qaṣīda* the links between the 'New Testament' and the 'Old Testament' drawn by al-Ghazzī, as well as his privileging the former over the latter (see al-Ghazzī, *Dīwān*, p. 35).
31. For these miracles, see respectively al-Ghazzī, *Dīwān*, p. 32 (line 59); p. 33 (line 62); and p. 32 (line 58).
32. Al-Ghazzī, *Dīwān*, p. 32.
33. The very final verse of the Qur'ān is comprised simply of these two categories of God's creatures, i.e., '*min al-jinnati wa'l-nās*' (from *jinn* and men).
34. Al-Ghazzī, *Dīwān*, p. 106.
35. Annotating line 29, Edelby explains the meaning of its idiosyncratic second half, noting that this verse concerns the consigning of 'our bodies' to 'sarcophagi' after our death (see al-Ghazzī, *Dīwān*, p. 106).
36. Al-Ghazzī, *Dīwān*, p. 351.
37. For '*al-mu'minūn*' set in opposition with '*al-kāfirūn*', see Qur'ān 3:28.
38. For an additional occurrence of '*al-ba'th*', see Qur'ān 30:56.
39. For the first and last occurrence of '*adhābun 'alīm*' in the Qur'ān, see 2:10 and 84:24.
40. Al-Ghazzī, *Dīwān*, p. 370.
41. Al-Ghazzī, *Dīwān*, p. 370; these lines represent 15–17 of Qaṣīda 71.
42. Qur'ānic instances of '*al-abrār*' in paradise are to be found, for instance, in 76:5, 82:13, and 83:18.
43. The plurality of paradise in Sūrat al-Raḥmān is enriched by this chapter's dual forms; see, for instance, Qur'ān 55:62: '*wa-min dūnihimā jannatān*' (And besides these shall be two gardens; Arberry's translation).
44. Al-Ghazzī, *Dīwān*, pp. 206–207.
45. Al-Ghazzī's wordplay derives from his use of the same root letters differently ordered in two discrete words (i.e., *jinās al-mukhālif*).
46. This indirect critique of Islam seems to be characteristic of al-Ghazzī's style, informing not only his poetry, but his prose. Samuel Noble has noted in his appraisal of al-Ghazzī's prose treatises that '[t]hese works are primarily apologetic and concerned with the defense of Melkite orthodoxy against ancient and contemporary Christological heresies. Although Sulaymān never mentions Islam by name, much of the apologetic content clearly has an eye towards Islam, especially in his defenses of the Trinity, the Incarnation, and the cross'; see Samuel Noble, 'Prose theological treatises', in *Christian Muslim Relations: A Bibliographical History. Volume 2, 900–1050*, ed. David Thomas and Alex Mallett (Leiden: Brill, 2010), pp. 619–623 (p. 620).
47. Al-Ghazzī, *Dīwān*, p. 205.
48. Arberry renders the end of this verse as 'they would have found God turns, All-compassionate'; however, it is Yusuf Ali that renders '*tawwāban*' (تَوَّابًا) as 'Oft-returning', which I employ above (see his *Koran: An English Interpretation of the Holy Quran with Full Arabic Text* (Lahore: Muhammad Ashraf, 1992)).
49. Al-Ghazzī, *Dīwān*, p. 164.
50. Adapting this John 11 episode, al-Ghazzī's assertion that Jesus was already familiar with the tomb of Lazarus is not included in the Gospel account; however, this sentiment does recall John 6:6 ('And this he said to prove him: for he himself knew what he would do'; KJV translation).
51. This represents Arberry's rendition; I also invoke his 'quickener of the dead' in translating al-Ghazzī's similar Arabic phrase, i.e., '*muḥyī al-mayyit*'.

52. These alternate translations appear as part of the entry for '*labbayk*' (لبيك) in Manfred Ullmann's *Wörterbuch der klassischen arabischen Sprache, Vol. II/1* (Wiesbaden: Otto Harrassowitz Verlag, 1983), p. 182.
53. This formulation is Mark Seifrid's, paraphrased from Romans 4:17; see Mark Seifrid, *The Second Letter to the Corinthians* (Grand Rapids: Eerdmans, 2014), p. 251.
54. Al-Ghazzī, *Dīwān*, p. 180.
55. My version of this phrase derives partly from Arberry, who renders this phrase in his *Koran* as 'High indeed be He exalted above that they say!'.
56. The parallel phrase in Qur'ān 6:100 employs the same assertion of divine sublimity ('exalted be He above'), but offers an alternate final verb, i.e. '*wa-ta'ālā 'ammā yaṣifūn*' ('High be He exalted above what they describe!'; Arberry's translation).

3

‘THE RELIGION OF THE MESSIAH IN MULTITUDES’: ECHOES OF THE QURʾĀN ACROSS CHRISTIAN SCHISMS

I

A BISHOP’S *SHARĪʿA*

> فلما مات صير بعده هرقل بطريرك على الاسكندرية واصلح عشرين اسقفا . فواحد من هؤلاء
> الاساقفة اسمه اومانيوس خالف الشريعة
>
> And when he (Demetrius) died, Heracles was made after him patriarch over Alexandria, and ordained twenty bishops. And one of these bishops was named Ammonius, who transgressed the *sharīʿa*
>
> from Saʿīd ibn Baṭrīq’s *String of Gems*[1]

Born in 940, Sulaymān al-Ghazzī began life in the same year that marks the life’s end of fellow Orthodox author and prominent ecclesiast in nearby Alexandria: Saʿīd ibn Baṭrīq (c. 877–940). Commonly called by his Greek label – ‘Eutychius’ – the overlap of Saʿīd’s death in Egypt and Sulaymān’s birth in Palestine reflects broader commonalities in their literary careers and contributions. Spending his last years serving as Melkite patriarch of Alexandria, Saʿīd ibn Baṭrīq shares with Sulaymān al-Ghazzī a primary place in the Christian Arabic canon, pioneering not its poetry, but historiography, penning the first major chronicle in Arabic by a Christian. Entitled *String of Gems* (*Naẓm al-Jawhar*), Ibn Baṭrīq’s ‘universal history’ is ambitious, offering an account of the whole world, beginning from ‘creation’ itself.[2] As the above quotation from his *String of Gems* suggests, however, Ibn Baṭrīq’s concern was not merely global, but also local; especially interested in the Christian past of his homeland, Ibn Baṭrīq highlights figures from the Egyptian Church, including ‘Heracles’, who served in the land’s highest ecclesiastical office during the pivotal third century.[3] Turning attention to his beloved Alexandria, however, Ibn Baṭrīq’s memorial to his own patriarchal predecessor features another overlap with his near contemporary in neighbouring Palestine. Recalling the two *qaṣāʾid* of Sulaymān al-Ghazzī that bracket the last chapter, Ibn Baṭrīq’s selection that opens the present chapter features another Christian appeal to the *sharīʿa*. Paralleling al-Ghazzī's poetry, Ibn Baṭrīq's prose maps a Christian orthodoxy that invokes terminology with Islamic associations – a parallel that reflects broader inter-scriptural engagements that are shared by both of these pioneers of Christian Arabic literature.[4]

Native to nearby patriarchates, while associated with contending genres – poetry and prose – this mutual appeal to 'the *sharīʿa*' by al-Ghazzī and Ibn Baṭrīq also hints at a critical difference dividing both their medieval lives and their modern legacies. While the *sharīʿa* is invoked by Saʿīd to imply a Christian consensus, expressing his community's shared commitment to 'divine law', Ibn Baṭrīq's usage instead describes the ouster of 'Ammonius', the Egyptian bishop who is labelled a schismatic, condemned for 'transgress[ing]' the '*sharīʿa*'.[5] Although a term of religious adherence, '*sharīʿa*' allows Ibn Baṭrīq to define religious 'transgression', with Ammonius's Christian heresy ironically denominated by an idiom now most often associated with Islam. A single word amid his 'universal' *String of Gems*, Ibn Baṭrīq's historical appeal to 'the *sharīʿa*' also reflects the Christian strife that shapes his own career, recalling ecclesial disunion in Egypt that still engulfs Ibn Baṭrīq's tenth-century life in Muslim Alexandria. While al-Ghazzī's life will stretch up to the cusp of the 'Great Schism' – the 1054 divorce between Catholicism and Orthodoxy – Ibn Baṭrīq's own literary career intersects a more immediate schism, not between Catholic West and Byzantine East, but between churches in Egypt, Chalcedonian and non-Chalcedonian. An adherent of the former, Ibn Baṭrīq's writings resist his Christian compatriots who belong to the latter, contending against Egyptian miaphysites – that is, members of what is typically known as the Coptic Church. Beginning long before his birth, and echoing through the centuries that have followed his death, Ibn Baṭrīq's investment in Egypt's domestic religious divides is reflected especially in his pioneering Arabic chronicle, *String of Gems*, a text informed by not only Islamic traditions but also by intra-Christian polemics. Even as he appeals to Qur'ānic idioms, Ibn Baṭrīq advances a critique of fellow Christians in Egypt, defending his Chalcedonianism against non-Chalcedonianism, contributing to the formation of a 'heresiographical milieu' – a phrase coined by Sidney H. Griffith, whose scholarship has authoritatively explored such intra-Christian struggles in 'the World of Islam'.[6]

Intersecting these historical overlaps and oppositions, a final distinction between al-Ghazzī and Ibn Baṭrīq emerges in their later afterlives, with these contemporary pioneers of Christian Arabic literature giving rise to inverse legacies. Straddling the Orthodox–Catholic divide in 1054, separating Christian East and West, al-Ghazzī's life and labours will be largely lost to memory on both sides of the Great Schism, eluding critical recuperation until the twentieth century.[7] Alternately, Ibn Baṭrīq's career, marked by ecclesiastic ruptures in Egypt, will enjoy an afterlife both extended and ecumenical, his *String of Gems* read and remembered from East to West, received by Christians from diverse and discrete communions. Shaped by Egyptian rifts, Ibn Baṭrīq's history yet echoes across area and era, imported from medieval Alexandria into early modern England, even reaching readers in America during the Revolution. Indeed, the brief selection from *String of Gems* quoted above is sourced not from forgotten medieval manuscripts recently recovered, but from early modern editions of Ibn Baṭrīq's writings. The first published iteration of *String of Gems* appeared in London nearly a half millennium ago, printed during the pivotal year 1642 – the very year that sparked 'revolution' in the British Isles, with Ibn Baṭrīq's words surfacing in England even as its own religious and political schisms led to the English Civil War.[8] Sharing an indebtedness to Islamic idioms, Ibn Baṭrīq's Arabic prose diverges from al-Ghazzī's poetry by eluding later obscurity, impacting intra-religious strifes to come, with Ibn Baṭrīq's Qur'ānic vocabulary ironically punctuating future Christian schisms. Arising from environs defined by Muslim–Christian encounter, and helping to launch Christian Arabic literature, Ibn Baṭrīq's writings themselves not only map a split between Chalcedonian adherents and their opponents in Egypt, but also echo forward and westward, re-emerging amid other national splits, from England to America. Indeed, the long legacy of Ibn Baṭrīq's Christian writings exemplifies a facet of Qur'ānic reception in the West often overlooked.[9] While early European engagement with Islam is typically conceived as 'orientalism', plagued by interreligious bias, the Qur'ān also surfaces in the West via the intra-religious recovery of Eastern ecclesiasts. As Christian Arabic authorship advances from the medieval Middle East to early modern Europe, the idioms of Muslim scripture also unexpectedly reach Western readers, imported under the cover of Christian ecumenicism. And it is pioneers of Christian Arabic such as Ibn Baṭrīq, the present chapter suggests, that help thread such 'strings' of cross-scriptural expression, inadvertently introducing Islamic diction into fresh environs of political revolution and religious rupture, with the Qur'ān conveyed far westward in the writings of Eastern Christians themselves involved in domestic schisms.

II

SCHISMS OF *SHAYṬĀN*

Intersecting Christian schisms at home in tenth-century Egypt, while impacting Christian divisions to come, Ibn Baṭrīq's historiography itself reaches back to begin with the first religious schism, recounting humanity's own original split: 'the Fall' of Adam and Eve. On its initial page, Ibn Baṭrīq's *String of Gems* opens with an account of 'creation' that is quickly followed by mankind's first rupture, with the temptation of Adam and Eve soon subverting the world's original purity and paradisal order.[10] Broadly biblical, sourced primarily from the first chapters of Genesis, Ibn Baṭrīq's account also implicitly reaches beyond the bounds of Christian tradition, internalising Islamic vocabulary while retelling humanity's expulsion and exile from Eden:

> ان الله عز وجل خلق الدنيا بما فيها وآدم وحواء في ستة ايام وكان خلق آدم في اليوم السادس. وبارك الله في اليوم السابع لان فيه اكمل الله الخلق وادخل آدم وحواء في الفردوس . وامرهما ان يأكلا من جميع الاشجار ما خلا شجرة المعرفة فلا يأكلا منها. فوسوس الشيطان لحواء فخالفت ما امرها الله تعالى به فأكلت من الشجرة واطعمت آدم منها . فلما عصيا ربهما اخرجهما من الجنة
>
> Verily Allah – mighty and sublime – created the world, what is in it, as well as Adam and Eve, in six days, and He created Adam on the sixth day. Allah blessed the seventh day, for in it did Allah complete the creation, and entered Adam and Eve into paradise, and commanded these two that they eat from all of the trees, except the tree of knowledge from which they were not to eat. And Shayṭān (Satan) whispered a temptation to Eve, and she transgressed what Allah – exalted be He! – commanded her, and she ate from the tree, and gave Adam to eat also from it, and when they had disobeyed their Lord, He ejected the two of them out of the garden[11]

Recounted in recognisable detail, the content of this Christian account of creation, and the fall of man, seems unsurprising. However, Ibn Baṭrīq's summary of Genesis is punctuated by Islamic fragments, spanning divine honorifics and demonic adjectives. Even in advance of creation, Allah's own name is accompanied by a familiar doxology – 'mighty and sublime' (*ʿazza wa-jall*) – a convention common not to the Qur'ān, but to Muslim discourse more broadly, beginning with the Ḥadīth itself.[12] Perhaps more striking than these epithets for God is the outcome of Satan's actions. In Ibn Baṭrīq's account, the Devil's temptation of the first two humans leads God to 'eject the two of them (*akhrajahumā*) out of the garden', which seems faintly reminiscent of the Qur'ān, recalling verses such as 2:36 that employs the same verbal and pronoun form:

فَأَزَلَّهُمَا الشَّيْطَانُ عَنْهَا فَأَخْرَجَهُمَا مِمَّا كَانَا فِيهِ

Then Shayṭān caused the two of them to slip (from *al-janna*)
and ejected the two of them (*akhrajahumā*) out of that they were in[13]

This Qur'ānic verb of exile finds its complement in Satan's seductive verbalising as described by Ibn Baṭrīq, with an Islamic texture emerging in his Devil's 'whispered' temptation:

فوسوس الشيطان لحواء فخالفت ما امرها الله تعالى به
Then Satan whispered (*fa-waswasa al-shayṭān*) to Eve,
and she transgressed what Allah – exalted be He! – commanded her[14]

Closing with an honorific for Allah common to the Qurʾān – ‘exalted be He’ (تعالى) – it is Satan’s speech act that seems most redolent of the Muslim scripture, inviting comparison with *āyāt* such as Qurʾān 20:120:

فَوَسْوَسَ إِلَيْهِ الشَّيْطَانُ قَالَ يَا آدَمُ هَلْ أَدُلُّكَ عَلَىٰ شَجَرَةِ الْخُلْدِ
Then Satan whispered to him (*fa-waswasa ilayhi al-shayṭān*)
saying, ‘Adam, shall I point thee to the Tree of Eternity’…[15]

Inverse in gender, with Genesis prompting Ibn Baṭrīq to identify not ‘Adam’ but ‘Eve’ as the target of temptation, it is Satan’s subtle ‘*waswasa*’ that amplifies the link between these two Edenic accounts. According to Ibn Baṭrīq, at the very moment that Eve herself becomes a ‘transgressor’ from ‘what Allah has ordered’, an Islamic idiom resounds in Satan’s ‘whisper’ (*waswasa*), with this Christian retelling quietly accepting Qurʾānic influence even as it traces the successful temptation of mankind.

Although opening with ‘creation’, framing itself as ‘universal’, Ibn Baṭrīq’s *String of Gems* will advance a perspective that is nevertheless particular, reflecting not passive disinterest, but a defense of its author’s own doctrine. Cosmic in span, yet sectarian in view, Ibn Baṭrīq’s ‘work aims to uphold and promote Chalcedonian orthodoxy’ in the face of ‘other Christian sects’, especially his fellow Egyptian Christians, the miaphysite Copts, as first mentioned above.[16] Such partisanship, however, itself would prompt controversy, soon catalysing the authorship of Ibn Baṭrīq’s compatriot, and Coptic opponent, Severus ibn al-Muqaffaʿ (d. after 987). Recalling the career of Ibn Baṭrīq himself, Ibn al-Muqaffaʿ qualifies not only as a prominent Egyptian writer and ecclesiast, but also as a pioneer of Christian Arabic, emerging as ‘one of the first Coptic authors to write exclusively in Arabic’.[17] Miaphysite leader in Muslim Upper Egypt, pastoring fellow Copts as Bishop of Ashmunein, Ibn al-Muqaffaʿ will also engage in polemics, offering an ‘apologetic literary response’ to *String of Gems*, seeking to refute Ibn Baṭrīq’s championing of his Chalcedonianism.[18] Contesting each other, upholding divergent confessions, Ibn al-Muqaffaʿ nevertheless shares with Ibn Baṭrīq not only a precedence in Christian Arabic, but also a surprising indebtedness to Qurʾānic traditions, incorporating idioms that ‘see[m] overwhelmingly Islamic’.[19] Ironically, Ibn al-Muqaffaʿ’s ‘Islamic’ diction surfaces especially in his own intra-Christian critique of Ibn Baṭrīq, that is, Ibn al-Muqaffaʿ’s *Kitāb al-Majāmiʿ* (‘Book of the Councils’), which Stephen J. Davis has rightly recognised as ‘extensive[ly]’ utilising ‘Islamic terminology’.[20] An Arabic chronicle concerning the Christian ‘Councils’, Ibn al-Muqaffaʿ’s *al-Majāmiʿ* follows Ibn Baṭrīq’s own history, authored not only in the wake of *String of Gems*, but also equally straddling local and 'universal' interests. If sharing genres, however, Ibn al-Muqaffaʿ's history is harshly critical of Ibn Baṭrīq, seeming so set against *String of Gems* that it is regularly known under the polemical title *Réfutation de Saʿīd ibn Batriq*.[21] Eponymously termed a 'refutation', repulsing his Egyptian predecessor and fellow pioneer of Christian Arabic, Ibn al-Muqaffaʿ's *Kitāb al-Majāmiʿ* is not only sectarian in concern, but also seeks to trace the origins of all spiritual schism. Rather than retreat merely as far as Adam's temptation – as Ibn Baṭrīq's *String of Gems*, quoted above – Ibn al-Muqaffaʿ's chronicle reaches back even further, returning to the fall before 'the Fall': the rebellion of Satan himself. Recounting this first act of disobedience, with Satan rejecting the divine decree, Ibn al-Muqaffaʿ is ironically led into covert alignment with his own Egyptian adversary – Ibn Baṭrīq – by again invoking Islamic language in his Christian historiography very near to the opening of the *Kitāb al-Majāmiʿ*:

> فصار شيطانا عظيما وسمى ابليس وسموا الملائكة الساقطين معه شياطين وقد قال بعض الناس ان الشيطان انما سقط من السما لانه لم يرض بالسجود لادم وليس هو كذلك لان اشعيا النبي يقول في نبوته لم يسقط كوكب الفجر الا لانه فكر وقال انصب لي كرسيا على نجوم السما واجلس على السحب واتشبه بالعلي وكان سقوطه من قبل ان يخلق ادم

> ...(the Devil) became a great *shayṭān*, and was named 'Iblīs', and the fallen angels were named with him '*shayāṭīn*'. Some people have said that Satan only fell from heaven because he was not willing to perform *sujūd* to Adam. But this is not so, for the Prophet Isaiah declares in his prophecy that the star of the morning did not fall except that he thought, and declared, 'I will lift up for my self a throne above the stars of heaven, and sit upon the clouds, and I will be like to the Most High'. And thus (Satan's) fall was before Adam was created...[22]

It is again an act of naming that prompts Qur'ānic precedents to surface in this Christian historiography. Opening his passage with intriguing passives, Ibn al-Muqaffaʿ records the labels acquired by Satan and his host, without, however, gesturing to the source of their fallen names – a circumlocution that subtly evades this account's Islamic debts. The Devil himself 'was named Iblīs', Ibn al-Muqaffaʿ suggests, while his fellow rebels 'were named *shayāṭīn*' – utilising two terms common not to biblical, but Islamic, traditions.[23] Refraining from supplying a specific reference, Ibn al-Muqaffaʿ's passage soon turns from Islamic dependence to debating Islam, disputing the Qur'ān's own account for why Satan fell. Vaguely credited to 'some people', the Qur'ānic cause for Satan's rebellion – his refusal to prostrate (*sujūd*) to Adam (cf. Qur'ān 2:34) – is itself denied by Ibn al-Muqaffaʿ, who instead appeals to biblical sources, citing 'Isaiah' specifically, to suggest that Satan's 'fall was before Adam was created'.[24] Passively unrecognised, yet actively resisted, the Muslim scripture supplies the labels utilised by Ibn al-Muqaffaʿ, but also stands as the authority that he refuses to follow. Although made possible by Qur'ānic names, it is the Qur'ānic narrative against which Ibn al-Muqaffaʿ contends, implicitly accepting Islam's etymologies, while rejecting the aetiology of *Shayṭān*'s own schism.

It is not merely Iblīs's insurrection in heaven, however, but mankind's own revolt that Ibn al-Muqaffaʿ outlines, pinpointing the same paradisal lapse that is recounted by Ibn Baṭrīq in his *String of Gems*. Consistently seeking to surpass Ibn Baṭrīq, however, Ibn al-Muqaffaʿ's *Kitāb al-Majāmiʿ* will later allude not only to 'the Fall', but also its effects, framing the consequences of man's exile in explicitly Islamic terms:

> [...] فلما زل ابونا ادم وتعدى الى ما لم يومر به وخالف الخالق تبارك اسمه اطاع ابليس اللعين الحسود المحتال على بنيه [...] فعاقبه الله عز وجل على خيانته فان اخرجه الى عالم الكون والفساد [...] فصار بنوه من بعده في مثل حاله ولم يدع العدو المحال حالا من الشر والا انزلها بهم وصار كالمالك لهم والرييس عليهم فصرفهم في محبة عبادة الاوثان وجحود نعم الرحمان
>
> [...] and when our father Adam slipped, and violated that which he was ordered not to do, and transgressed against the creator (*khālafa al-khāliq*) – blessed be His name! – he obeyed Iblīs, the cursed, the envier, the beguiler of his sons. [...] But Allah, mighty and sublime, punished him for his treason, and then He expelled him into a world of incidence and iniquity. [...] And his sons after him came themselves to be in like condition, with the fraudulent enemy never leaving aside any vice except that he brought it down upon them. And (Iblīs) became like their king and leader over them, turning them to the love of worshipping idols, and to denying the favours of the merciful (*al-raḥmān*)[25]

For Ibn al-Muqaffaʿ, it is 'the Fall' that renders the first human a '*mukhālif*', applying the very same verb to Adam that Ibn Baṭrīq had attributed to Eve, that is, '*khālafa*' (خالف ; transgressed). This verb of violation is, however, invoked with ironic assonance, Ibn al-Muqaffaʿ placing in proximity two terms similar in sound, but inverse in significance; in Ibn al-Muqaffaʿ's Arabic, 'the creator' assonates with Adam's 'transgression', with '*khālafa*' followed by '*al-khāliq*' – one of the ninety-nine names for Allah, whose Islamic resonance is also reinforced by the phrase that follows it: '*tabārak ismuh*' (blessed be His name), echoing *āyāt* such as Qur'ān 55:78.[26] After this pun, pairing Adam's disobedience with Allah's divine name, Ibn al-Muqaffaʿ also invokes Islamic labels for Allah's adversary; named again 'Iblīs', Satan is also ascribed attributes reminiscent of Muslim prophecy, including *al-ḥasūd* (الحسود ; the envier) and *al-ʿadū* (العدو ; the enemy) (cf. Qur'ān 113:5 and 2:168), as well as *al-laʿīn* (اللعين ; the cursed) another epithet for Iblīs common in Muslim sources.[27] It is the divine name invoked by Ibn al-Muqaffaʿ that seems most Qur'ānic, however, with Satan prompting Adam's posterity to veer from the 'favours' of *al-raḥmān* (الرحمان ; the merciful). Derived not from the Bible's beginnings, but from the opening to a Qur'ānic chapter, Ibn al-Muqaffa' infuses his own account of Genesis with the genesis of Sūra 55 (al-Raḥmān), invoking 'the merciful' to designate the divine gifts 'rejected' by Adam. Contrasting satanic rebellion with the sublime name of *al-raḥmān*, Ibn al-Muqaffa' offers a Christian account of human deviance that itself deviates from Christian exclusivity, penning Coptic historiography and miaphysite apologetics that 'favour' monotheistic expressions unmistakably overlapping with the Qur'ān.

III

'SEVERITY AGAINST THE *NAṢĀRĀ*'

الباب الثالث
في المجامع ومن كان السبب فيها ومن اى موضع كان الافتراق
ولم تزل الناس على هذا الامانة المستقيمة التى للابا الحواريين مايتى وستة وسبعين سنة الى ان
ولى ديكلاديانوس ومكسميانوس الملوك الكفار فعبدوا الاوثان واخربوا البيع وقتلوا خلقا كثيرا
من النصارى

CHAPTER THREE
Concerning the Councils, and the reasons thereof,
and from what occasions the divisions arose
The people strayed not from this upright fidelity, which was that of the fathers, the disciples, for two hundred and seventy-six years, up until the reign of Diocletian and Maximian, the infidel emperors. And they worshiped idols, destroyed churches, and killed a great number from amongst al-Naṣārā (the Christians)[28]

Appealing to Islamic names in his account of 'the Fall', Ibn al-Muqaffa' inflected the paradisal past with an interreligious flavour; the names used throughout his *Kitāb al-Majāmi'* also help, however, advance Ibn al-Muqaffa''s intra-religious polemic, supporting his struggle against Chalcedonian contemporaries. As Jeanne Saint-Laurent has recently remarked, Ibn al-Muqaffa' advocates for his Coptic heritage by 'playing with the etymologies of the labels of the competing Christian Churches', accenting, for instance, that his adversaries are labelled 'Melkites' due to their compromised commitments to an 'earthly *malik*' (i.e., 'king').[29] The schisms that shaped Ibn al-Muqaffa''s writings at the end of the first millennium, however, were themselves rooted in controversies that surfaced during the Church's first centuries – controversies that Ibn al-Muqaffa' himself charts in the third chapter to his *Kitāb al-Majāmi'*'s first book, the opening of which is quoted above. Introducing this chapter on the Christian 'Councils' and their 'partitions', it is the persecution of the faithful that Ibn al-Muqaffaʿ initially emphasises, electing to begin his 'Chapter Three' even before the first Ecumenical Council in 325 AD, recounting the Roman violence suffered by ante-Nicene Christians.[30] Ironically, however, Ibn al-Muqaffaʿ again recalls Islam even as he outlines this third-century Christian persecution, celebrating his own faithful 'fathers' with interfaith diction. Describing Diocletian and Maximian not only as 'kings', but as '*al-kuffār*' (الكفار ; infidels), these emperors cruelly kill believers who ascribe to a 'fidelity' that is 'straight' or 'upright' (المستقيمة ; *al-mustaqīma*) – a term typical of the orthodox 'way' proclaimed by the Qurʾān, here applied to the Christian creed.[31] More striking, and simple, are the labels Ibn al-Muqaffaʿ offers for the patriarchs themselves; calling the early Christians 'al-Naṣārā' (النصارى), Ibn al-Muqaffaʿ invokes a name for Christians which is 'peculiar[ly]' Qurʾānic, as Gabriel Said Reynolds has recently emphasised.[32] Perhaps even more idiomatic is the 'apostolic' appellation that intersects Ibn al-Muqaffaʿ's account; designating the fathers of the Christian faith, Ibn al-Muqaffaʿ utilises the term '*al-ḥawāriyyīn*' (الحواريين ; nominative *ḥawāriyyūn*; 'disciples', or 'apostles'). A term of unclear etymology, perhaps deriving from a Semitic root signifying 'whiteness', '*ḥawāriyyīn*' reflects a clear textual source, claiming precedent in several Qurʾānic *āyāt* (cf. 3:52, 5:11).[33] A term colourless in significance, '*ḥawāriyyīn*' nevertheless allows Ibn al-Muqaffaʿ to colour anew the patriarchs, whitewashing clear divides between Christian 'fathers' and Qurʾānic phraseology, with Islam aiding Ibn al-Muqaffaʿ as he celebrates 'apostolic' resistance to the kingly '*kuffār*'.

Opening his third chapter with two emperors of Rome who begin their oppressive reign at the end of the third century, it is the beginning to the present study's own Chapter 3 that also seems echoed in Ibn al-Muqaffaʿ's account, recalling the initial quotation from Ibn Baṭrīq's historiography cited above.[34] Introduced with a selection on the deposed bishop 'Ammonius' sourced from *String of Gems*, the present chapter opens with a quotation also centred in Christianity's third century, citing Ibn Baṭrīq's account of 'transgression' during the papacy of Heracles, who headed the Egyptian church from 232 to 246. Immediately after this same *String of Gems* passage, however, Ibn Baṭrīq himself also recounts Christian oppression suffered in imperial Rome, retreating two centuries to address not the famed 'Diocletian' persecution depicted by Ibn al-Muqaffaʿ at the opening to his Chapter 3, but rather the much earlier martyrdoms of the first century. Just a few sentences after the selection that opens the present chapter, Ibn Baṭrīq offers further context for Christian persecution, returning to the very time of 'the evangelist[s]':

> وخرج مرقص البشير الى برقة يدعوا الناس الى الايمان بالمسيح ابن الله ومات قلوديوس قيصر الملك وملك بعده ابنه نارون قيصر برومية ثلث عشرة وهو اول من اهاج علي النصارى

> الشر والبلا وكان رجلا شريرا جدا ردى السيرة وفي عصر نارون قيصر كتب بطرس ريس الحواريين انجيل مرقص عن مرقص بالرومية في مدينة رومية ونسبه الى مرقص
>
> Mark the Evangelist went out to Barqa, calling the people there to belief in the Messiah, the son of God. The Emperor, Claudius Caesar, died, and his son, Nero, reigned as caesar in Rome after him for thirteen years. And he was the foremost of those inciting evil and tribulation on the Christian (*naṣārā*), being a man most evil in mores. And in the era of Caesar Nero, Peter, the head of the disciples (*ḥawāriyyīn*), recorded the Gospel of Mark from Mark in Latin, in the city of Rome, and ascribed it to Mark.[35]

Straddling the divide between the death of Emperor Claudius (c. 54 CE), and reign of his adopted 'son' Nero (c. 54–68 CE), Ibn Baṭrīq offers a brief account that anticipates Ibn al-Muqaffaʿ, retreating not only to tell of severe persecutions suffered by the earliest Christians, but also infusing this episode of violence with Qur᾽ānic vocabulary.[36] Gesturing to the genesis of the anti-Christian campaign conducted by Nero, the new Emperor is seen as oppressing the '*naṣārā*' in Ibn Baṭrīq's account, sharing with Ibn al-Muqaffaʿ this Qur᾽ānic idiom for the Christian faithful. Also shared, however, is '*al-ḥawāriyyīn*' (الحواريين), with Ibn Baṭrīq anticipating his Coptic successor in utilising this same Qur᾽ānic term to designate the Christian 'disciples', labelling Christ's own 'rock', Peter, as the 'head' of the '*ḥawāriyyīn*'.[37]

Transmitting Qur᾽ānic terms even while tracing acts of biblical transmission, Ibn Baṭrīq fittingly appeals to Islamic diction in the very passage that depicts not only the 'travels' of the 'evangelists', but also the conveying of a scripture across cultures and continents – a concern with apostolic transmission that seems especially apt, however, considering the wide reception of Ibn Baṭrīq's own writings.[38] Read by Egyptian antagonists such as Ibn al-Muqaffaʿ, *String of Gems* will be more sympathetically received much further afield, stretching northward and westward across Europe during the following centuries, attracting especial attention in early modern England. Appearing in an edition that intersected the pivotal seventeenth century, portions of Ibn Baṭrīq's *String of Gems* would ultimately be published in Arabic and Latin under the title of *Eutychii Aegyptii, Patriarchae Orthodoxorum Alexandrini, Ecclesiae suae origins* – an edition produced in London, and which has been claimed as 'the first Arabic text […] printed in England'.[39] Edited by pioneering orientalist and jurist, John Selden – himself acclaimed as the 'Great Light of the English Nation' – Ibn Baṭrīq's unprecedented edition was published in 1642, the very year that ignited England's own Civil War.[40] Arising from Christian schisms in North Africa, Ibn Baṭrīq's *String of Gems* surfaces in the West at the opening to another Christian schism in the north of Europe; pitting Puritan dissenters against Anglican conservatives, the first year of England's Civil War in 1642 ironically witnessed the printing not only of the nation's 'first Arabic text', but also a text that itself reflects internecine struggles for ecclesiastic ascendency.

Valued for its information on 'early episcopacy' – with Ibn Baṭrīq's chronicle signalling the lack of bishops in the early Egyptian church – Selden's decision to edit *String of Gems* as his own country slid towards civil war was inevitably perceived as a political act, appearing to support English Puritan aims to 'bear down Episcopacy', as G. J. Toomer has recently outlined.[41] However, if Ibn Baṭrīq's medieval Egyptian chronicle oddly anticipated debates in early modern England, it also conveyed westward another precedent even more unexpected, with this 'first Arabic text' introducing English readers to Qur'ānic idioms. A historical treasure for opponents to the episcopacy, *String of Gems* mirrored Christian schisms across cultures and continents; yet, it would also implicitly embody ecumenical exchanges across scriptures, with the selections from Ibn Baṭrīq's historiography of most interest to English Puritans featuring splinters of Islamic diction – diction which Selden himself ensures his readers recognise in his 1642 edition. For instance, the same Ibn Baṭrīq passage quoted above concerning the 'tribulations' suffered by the first Christians would not only appear in Selden's 1642 edition, but would also come equipped with explanatory annotations, with Selden accenting especially this selection's use of *ḥawāriyyīn*. In an endnote explaining Peter's portrait as the 'head of the *ḥawāriyyīn*', Selden's edition of *String of Gems* traces the origins of Ibn Baṭrīq's two-term phrase, noting its currency among 'Mohammedans' ('Mahumedanis'), while also offering a more precise citation, tracing the term '*ḥawāriyyīn*' specifically to:

> *...Mahumedi in Alcorano; ut videre est in Azoaris 3, 5 & 61 Arabicè. Loca autem in Latina seu Retinensis versione respondentia, sunt Azoaris 5, 13 & 71.*
>
> Muhammed in the Qur'ān; as is seen in the Arabic *sūra*s 3, 5, and 61, passages which correspond also, in the Latin version of Robert of Ketton, to *sūra*s 5, 13, and 71[42]

Offering this precise annotation in the pages to his 1642 edition, Selden clarifies the Qur'ānic precedents that underlie Peter's portrait as 'head of the *ḥawāriyyīn*', defining the Islamic diction that informs Ibn Baṭrīq's depiction of early Christian leadership, even as Selden's own nation starts an armed struggle seeking to define its Christian leadership. Tracing Peter's title back to '*Muhemdi in Alcorano*' (Muhammad in the Qur'ān), Selden ensures that English readers searching for proofs against Anglican episcopacy also encounter Islamic revelation. Not merely referencing the Qur'ān's Arabic original, Selden also highlights a more domestic version, specifically, the 'Latin version' of twelfth-century English translator, Robert of Ketton. Although aware that *String of Gems* would hold particular interest to his Puritan countrymen, Selden makes certain to exhibit the richly eclectic character of Ibn Baṭrīq's idioms, excavating the Qur'ānic substrate from below its Christian surface. Complicating its partisan relevance to England's stark religious struggle, Ibn Baṭrīq's 'orthodox' text instead emerges in Selden's edition as inter-religiously implied, its diction reflecting origins in Muslim Egypt with cross-references to a medieval Englishman's edition of the Qur'ān.[43]

Emphasising Qur'ānic foregrounds in his marginal footnotes, Selden's edition of Ibn Baṭrīq helped to convey westward slices of the Muslim scripture, with England's 'first Arabic text' offering a subtle vehicle for Islamic vocabulary. However, due to the precedence of his Civil War edition, and to Selden's own prominence, his 1642 *String of Gems* would stretch well beyond England, reaching readers in New England even as America itself approached its own first 'civil war': the Revolution.[44] Impacting another British internecine struggle, it is not only Selden's *String of Gems*, but precisely this annotated passage on Peter, which would emerge in Revolutionary America, recorded in the private writings of New England's own leading intellectual, Ezra Stiles, American pastor and future President of Yale, whose interest in Arabic was sparked by his reading of Selden's Ibn Baṭrīq edition, as I have recently discussed.[45] Committed to congregationalism, belonging to an American church opposed to Anglican bishops, Ezra Stiles engaged with Ibn Baṭrīq in the eighteenth century for the same reasons attackers of episcopacy in Britain were attracted to *String of Gems* in the seventeenth century.[46] However, Stiles not only reviewed, but rendered, selections of *String of Gems*, privately transcribing and translating Ibn Baṭrīq's Arabic from Selden's edition in the years leading up to the Revolution. More intriguingly, Stiles also pays particular attention to a selection from *String of Gems* now very familiar to us, as witnessed in Figure 1 – Ezra Stiles's manuscript translation of an Ibn Baṭrīq passage, which the American penned on 28 August 1769.

Punctuating his English, Stiles's rendered passage on Peter preserves Arabic fragments from Ibn Baṭrīq's original, with Stiles isolating in his translation the very same terms that Selden himself had highlighted as Qur'ānic in his annotations. Inscribed just a few short years before the outbreak of America's Revolution, Stiles records this ancient instance of imperial tyranny, recounting an Emperor's own 'severity' against his oppressed subjects; and yet, although endowed with domestic resonance, Stiles's appeal to Ibn Baṭrīq equally accents foreign idioms, allowing Islamic nomenclature to surface in this Christian chronicle. Instead of merely rendering Ibn Baṭrīq's '*al-naṣārā*', for instance, Stiles supplies both translation and transcription, recording Nero's persecution of 'the Nazarenes النصارى'. And rather than portray 'Peter' merely as 'the head of the Apostles', Stiles instead records the Arabic source of this phrase, writing its original 'ريس الحواريون' ('head of the *ḥawāriyyūn*' [*sic*]).[48] Rendered into English, yet retaining pivotal pieces of Arabic, this early American reception of Ibn Baṭrīq finds Qur'ānic phrases forwarded again across centuries and continents, even as the text itself recounts the dissemination of 'the انجيل' (*injīl*), that is, 'the Gospel'. Originally authored amid Christian schisms in Egypt, *String of Gems* stretches to the threshold of American republicanism; however, even as Ibn Baṭrīq's chronicle crosses the Atlantic, its Qur'ānic substrate refuses to stay submerged, the Islamic echoes interwoven into this antique Christian history floating up to its surface as the New World starts its own pivotal struggle for the future.

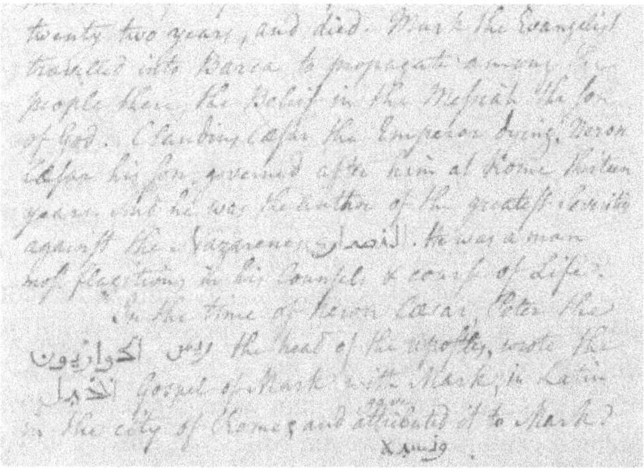
twenty two years, and died. Mark the Evangelist travelled into Barca to propagate among the people there, the Belief in the Messiah the son of God. Claudius Caesar the Emperor dying, Neron Caesar his son, governed after him at Rome thirteen years. And he was the author of the greatest Severity against the Nazarenes النصارى. He was a man most flagitious in his Counsels & course of Life.
In the time of Neron Caesar, Peter the ريس الحواريون the head of the Apostles, wrote the انجيل Gospel of Mark with Mark, in Latin in the city of Rome, and attributed it to Mark.
ونسبه

Figure 1. Ezra Stiles, 'The Antiquities of the Church of Alexandria' (1769), page 4, comprising Stiles's rendition from Ibn Baṭrīq's *String of Gems* made available to Stiles via John Selden's edition. Image courtesy of Beinecke Rare Book and Manuscript Library, Yale University.[47]

TRANSCRIPTION:

[…] Mark the Evangelist travelled into Barca to propagate among the people there, the Belief in the Messiah the son of God. Claudius Caesar the Emperor dying, Neron Caesar his son, governed after him at Rome thirteen years. And he was the author of the greatest Severity against the Nazarenes النصارى. He was a man most flagitious in his Counsels & course of Life.

In the time of Neron Caesar, Peter the ريس الحواريون the head of the Apostles, wrote the انجيل Gospel of Mark with Mark, in Latin in the city of Rome, and gave attributed it to Mark.
ونسبه

IV

FROM *AL-NAṢĀRĀ* TO SŪRAT AL-NAṢR

انه علي كل شيء قدير
for He is over all things powerful[49]

Final words to the Introduction of Ibn Baṭrīq's
String of Gems from its 1658–59 British edition.

A dozen years after his *String of Gems* edition appeared in 1642, John Selden died at home in London; Selden's decline and death in 1654 did not mark the end, however, but a new beginning, for *String of Gems*, with this project passing to his friend and collaborator, Edward Pococke (1604–1691). England's next great Arabist, Pococke was persuaded and supported by Selden to produce a full Arabic edition and Latin rendition of *String of Gems*, receiving funds from Selden's own estate, with money set aside in his will specifically for the project.[50] And it would be in the same year that Selden died that Pococke's subsidised edition of *String of Gems* began to appear, printed partially in 1654, with a first full edition published in 1656, and then again in 1658 – the very year that marked the beginning of the end to the English Civil War, coinciding with Oliver Cromwell's death and the imminent collapse of the 'puritan cause'.[51] It is this *String of Gems* edition published by Pococke in 1658 – entitled in Latin as *Contextio Gemmarum* – that also features the above 'powerful' appeal to Allah, with the preface to Ibn Baṭrīq's history closing by praising God's comprehensive control over 'all things'. Forming not only an end to this Christian chronicle's introduction, this phrase also qualifies as the most common of Qur'ānic endings, matching precisely the last words of *āyāt* such as Qur'ān 22:6, which also concludes with:

وَأَنَّهُ عَلَىٰ كُلِّ شَيْءٍ قَدِيرٌ
for He is over all things powerful[52]

Published in royalist Oxford in 1658 – the year that presages England's Restoration and the nation's imminent return to monarchy – Pococke's edition opens by offering his readers an entirely alternate source of sovereignty, ascribing to Allah all control via phraseology that concretely recalls the Qur'ān.

Selden's own edition of Ibn Baṭrīq had appeared at the opening to England's sectarian struggle; Pococke's posthumous edition, funded by a bequest from Selden, was published and republished as the Civil War came to a close. However, even as English republicanism began to shift back to royalism, Pococke's own attentions also shifted, transitioning away from Ibn Baṭrīq and towards yet another Eastern Christian writer and his Arabic chronicle. Instead of an anti-Miaphysite history authored by a Chalcedonian, Pococke dedicated the last months of the war to producing an edition of a pro-Miaphysite history by a non-Chalcedonian: Gregory Bar Hebraeus (1226–1286). Celebrated Syrian polymath, Bar Hebraeus led a career both astonishingly prolific and surprisingly diverse, writing on multiple topics and in multiple tongues, producing works of philosophy, exegesis, and history, composed in both Syriac and Arabic.[53] It is the latter language that was selected for his *Mukhtaṣar Ta'rīkh al-Duwal*, Bar Hebraeus's 'Short History of the Nations', which seems relatively 'concise' in comparison with his more capacious Syriac chronicle, commonly known under its Latin title *Chronicon Ecclesiasticum*.[54] Serving early in his career as Anglican chaplain in Aleppo, Pococke first encountered texts by Bar Hebraeus in the 1630s, and eventually produced a partial edition of Bar Hebraeus's *Mukhtaṣar*, published in 1650 – an edition that 'ends with a dedication' to none other than Selden himself. Returning to complete a full edition of Bar Hebraeus as the Civil War came to its own end, Pococke's comprehensive *Mukhtaṣar* appeared in 1663 with an accompanying Latin translation, published under the title *Historia Compendiosa Dynastiarum*.[55] Acquired before the Civil War began, but not printed until the war's conclusion, Bar Hebraeus's *Historia* is framed for Pococke by the struggle for England's sovereignty; however, English sovereignty also emerges as the literal frame to Pococke's Arabic edition, with the Restoration of the monarchy vividly reflected at its very opening. Introduced with a Latin dedication to the recently-crowned King Charles II, Pococke launches his publication in 1663 with lavish praise, devoting his work to:

> The Most Serene Majesty
> Charles the Second,
> By the Grace of God, most powerful King
> of England, Scotland, France, Ireland,
> Defender of the Faith, &c.
>
> Most August King,
>
> Whereas, not without good reason is the saying from the Arabs –
> السلطان ظل الله في الأرض 'The King is God's shade upon the earth'[56]

Son of a deposed and decapitated king, and survivor of the tumult of the Revolution, Charles II yet first emerges in Pococke's edition as 'most serene' (*sereniſsimæ*), this 'majestic' figure of English history elevated to appear at the head of a classic Arabic *Historia*. Named as not only the 'most august' monarch, but as Anglican 'Defender of the Faith', England's king is also, however, endowed with an 'Arabian' quotation, Pococke contextualising his own sovereign in this early modern edition with an ancient citation:

السلطان ظل الله في الأرض

The sultan is Allah's shadow upon the earth

Celebrated as an English '*sulṭān*', Charles II's imperial power is associated with Allah's 'shadow upon the earth', drawing a direct line between divine authority and England's '*fidei defenſori*'. If apt in significance, however, this Arabic aphorism seems curiously unattributed, Pococke confessing no source for this '*dictum*'. Instead of a Christian Arabic epigram to describe the 'defender' of the Christian 'faith', the epigram that Pococke invokes derives instead from an alternate source, with these words framing the head of Anglicanism original to Islam's founder. Although unacknowledged, it is none other than Muḥammad to whom this monarchal adage has been historically ascribed, Pococke covertly appealing to words attributed to the Prophet of Islam even while celebrating Charles II.[57]

Adapting a *ḥadīth* for English history, invoking Allah while addressing an Anglican patron, this majestic quotation ascribed to the Qur'ān's own messenger anticipates the ecumenical texture of Bar Hebraeus's entire Arabic chronicle as edited by Pococke. Himself celebrated as 'king of the scholars' (ملك العلماء), Bar Hebraeus's own history begins with a Muslim quotation that Pococke applies to Christian kingship, merging discrete traditions of politics and prophecy that reflect Bar Hebraeus's own composite background.[58] Serving as a miaphysite primate in Muslim lands, the interreligious span of Bar Hebraeus's own biography is reflected in the actual biography that prefaces Pococke's edition, which launches with a hagiographic portrait of Bar Hebraeus himself before his own *Historia* begins:

بسم الله الرحمن الرحيم
قال مولانا وسيدنا الاب القديس الطاهر النفيس العالم العلامة ملك العلماء افضل الفضلاء
قدوة الزمان فريد الوقت والاوان افتخار اهل الفضل والحكمة المفريان المؤيد مار كريغوريوس
ابو الفرج بن الحكيم الفاضل اهرون المتطبب الملطي تغمدة الله برحمته
الحمد لله الاول بلا بداية والاخر بلا نهاية...

In the name of Allah, the Merciful, the Compassionate
(Thus) said our Master and Liege-lord, the father, holy, pure and precious, the *ʿālim*, most learned, king of the scholars, superlative in merits, the era's exemplar, peerless in the period and the times, the pride of the folk of favour and wisdom, the Maphran, the Advocate, Mar Gregory Abū al-Faraj son of the superior doctor, Aaron, the healer, the Melitine, may Allah encompass him in His mercy:

Praise be to Allah, the Primary, without beginning, the Final, without end…[59]

A rhyming foreword that reflects Bar Hebraeus's own religious foregrounds, his Arabic chronicle begins with stylised biography, celebrating Bar Hebraeus himself with assonant epithets such as '*al-qadīs…al-nafīs*' (holy…precious). It is not these poetic credentials, however, but the Qur'ān's own lyric opening, that comprises the very first words to Bar Hebraeus's *Historia*, beginning with the *basmala* itself: (*bismillāh al-raḥmān al-raḥīm*; In the name of Allah, the merciful, the compassionate'). Prefacing Christian history with Qur'ānic introduction, Pococke's edition transitions from this Islamic doxology into a description of the author, before finally beginning with Bar Hebraeus's own first words – first words which also subtly extend the assonance, as well as Islamic ethos, witnessed in this opening page. Praising Allah with poetic phrases in parallel – '*bi-lā bidāya…bi-lā nihāya*' (without beginning…without end) – Bar Hebraeus's own very first phrase echoes the *Fātiḥa*, comprising the opening words to the Qur'ān's first chapter after the *basmala*, that is, '*al-ḥamdu lillāh*' (Praise be to Allah; cf. Qur'ān 1:2).

Inserting Bar Hebraeus's credentials within a Qur'ānic envelope, the introduction to Pococke's edition aptly reflects the Islamic terminology that regularly surfaces throughout this Arabic *Historia*, as well as throughout Bar Hebraeus's substantive corpus of writings – terminology previously treated in-depth by Hidemi Takahashi and Sidney H. Griffith.[60] Recalling his Christian predecessors, Arabic chroniclers such as Ibn Baṭrīq and Ibn al-Muqaffaʿ, Bar Hebraeus's own *Historia* too opens with creation, before soon transitioning to treat Christian persecutions, addressing the oppression suffered under Roman emperors. Rather than Nero or Diocletian – as described above by Ibn Baṭrīq and Ibn al-Muqaffaʿ – Bar Hebraeus's *Historia* offers a vivid portrait of the anti-Christian campaign of Domitian (reigned 81–96 CE). Despite suffering the Emperor's violence, Bar Hebraeus suggests that Christians not only remained committed to their faith, but ironically the Christian community increased in numbers, asserting in his *Historia* that:

> و في السنة التاسعة لملكه اضطهد النصاري اضطهادا شديدا ومع هذا كان الناس يدخلون في دين المسيح افواجا
>
> In the ninth year of his (Domitian's) reign, he oppressed *al-naṣārā* with a severe oppression, but, despite this, the people were entering the religion of the Messiah in multitudes[61]

Published in 1663 Oxford, soon after the end to England's own sectarian war, this passage from Pococke's *Historia* edition concerns Christian suffering under a hostile regime, testifying to spiritual victory despite political persecution. Invoking issues of religious violence and imperial force that would have been all too familiar to English readers in the 1660s, Bar Hebraeus's passage also ironically implies a more intimate exchange between discrete traditions, testifying to Christian endurance even while employing Qur'ānic terms. Recalling both Ibn Baṭrīq and Ibn al-Muqaffaʿ before him, Bar Hebraeus identifies the Christians themselves with a Qur'ānic idiom, naming the faithful as '*al-naṣārā*'. However, a more creative and extensive appeal to the Qur'ān emerges in the very same sentence in which Bar Hebraeus signals the success of the Christians. Although persecuted for their belief, Bar Hebraeus suggests that 'the people' continued converting to Christianity, with Domitian unable to prevent:

...الناس يدخلون في دين المسيح افواجا
...the people entering the religion of the Messiah in multitudes

Rather than a vague Qur'ānic echo, this passage from Bar Hebraeus precisely parallels, with only a single substitution, the second verse of Sūrat al-Naṣr, which promises that 'you will see' (رأيت):

النَّاسَ يَدْخُلُونَ فِي دِينِ اللَّهِ أَفْوَاجًا
the people entering the religion of Allah in multitudes[62]

Forecasting the 'victory' (*al-naṣr*) of God's religion, this second verse from Sūrat al-Naṣr ironically provides Bar Hebraeus with an Islamic precedent for the primacy and triumph of Christianity. However, rather than verbatim quotation, Bar Hebraeus refashions Sūrat al-Naṣr to chronicle the *naṣārā*, removing Allah from these words borrowed from Qur'ān 110:2, with 'Messiah' inserted instead ('المسيح'). Proclaiming Christian 'victory' in this adapted *āya*, Bar Hebraeus heralds his own sect's ascendency even as he undertakes an act of scriptural schism, literally breaking apart a verse from Sūrat al-Naṣr to insert silently the founder of his own faith. Embodying the broader ironies implicit in the Qur'ān's westward endurance via Christian Arabic chronicles, Bar Hebraeus's passage on religious persecution and political repression is printed by Pococke at the very conclusion to his own nation's fractious civil war – a passage which itself celebrates the rise of the Messiah's 'multitudes', but only by fracturing and reformulating an Islamic phrase, reporting to English readers in 1663 the successful conversion of early Christians, even as this same Christian text covertly converts an alternate scriptural tradition.

NOTES

1. Saʿīd ibn Baṭrīq, *Eutychii Patriarchae Alexandrini Annales*, ed. L. Cheikho, B. Carra de Vaux, and H. Zayyat (Paris: C. Poussielgue, 1906), p. 96 (subsequently

cited as 'Ibn Baṭrīq, *Annales*'). For this same passage as found in an early modern edition of Ibn Baṭrīq, see note 8, below.

2. For a summary of Ibn Baṭrīq's life and literary achievements, see the entry on 'Sa'īd Ibn Baṭrīq' by Uriel Simonsohn in *Christian–Muslim Relations: A Bibliographical History. Volume 2, 900–1050*, ed. David Thomas, Alexander Mallett, and Barbara Roggema (Leiden: Brill, 2011), pp. 224–233, which charts the sections of *Naẓm al-Jawhar*, beginning with 'the creation of Adam' (p. 227).
3. For Heracles as 'the head of the church of Alexandria', and the first to be 'accorded the title pope', see Otto F. A. Meinardus, *Christians in Egypt: Orthodox, Catholic, and Protestant Communities Past and Present* (Cairo: The American University in Cairo Press, 2007), p. 36.
4. Although not concerned with the specific Qur'ānic echoes throughout *Naẓm al-Jawhar* addressed in the present chapter, Simonsohn has previously recognised the Muslim contexts for Ibn Baṭrīq's historiography, noting that '[i]n addition to his explicit reliance on Muslim sources for relating the period following the Muslim conquest, Ibn Batrīq's work suggests an awareness of the Muslim environment. Two examples are particularly striking. The first is his presentation of Judaeo-Christian apocryphal narratives in a manner that had been adapted by Muslim authors, particularly narrators of *qiṣaṣ al-anbiyā'* ("Tales of the prophets"). […] The second example pertains to his description of the encounter between the second caliph, 'Umar ibn al-Khaṭṭāb (d. 644) and the patriarcḥ of Jerusalem, Sophronius (d. 638)' ('Sa'īd Ibn Baṭrīq', *Christian–Muslim Relations*, p. 229).
5. For more modern mention of the 'depos[ing]' of 'Ammonius, bishop of Thmuis' due to 'disobedience', see Thomas W. Allies, *The Throne of the Fisherman: The Root, the Bond, and the Crown of Christendom* (London: Burns & Oates, 1887), p. 75.
6. Griffith's 'heresiographical milieu' is a phrase formed in response to John Wansbrough, whose seminal and controversial 1978 study – *The Sectarian Milieu* – suggested 'Islam [to be] the response to inter-confessional (Judaeo-Christian) polemic' (see *The Sectarian Milieu: Content and Composition of Islamic Salvation History* (New York: Prometheus, 2006), p. 161). For this phrase, see Sidney H. Griffith, '"Melkites", "Jacobites" and the Christological Controversies in Arabic in Third/Ninth-Century Syria' in *Syrian Christians under Islam: The First Thousand Years*, ed. David Thomas (Leiden: Brill, 2001), pp. 9–55 (p. 9). For 'Christian self-definition' in 'the World of Islam', see Griffith, *The Church in the Shadow of the Mosque*, p. 129ff. In tracking Islamic contexts for texts reflecting later splits in the Christian communion, the present chapter is naturally indebted to Griffith; however, I am unaware of foregoing studies which address the Qur'ānic diction of the particular passages addressed in this chapter, and more broadly, the Qur'ān's transmission westward via Christian texts composed within the 'heresiographical milieu'. For recent recognition of 'intra-Christian religious controversy' as contouring 'early-modern' Western Qur'ānic receptions, however, see Ziad Elmarsafy, *The Enlightenment Qur'an: The Politics of Translation and the Construction of Islam* (New York: Oneworld Publications, 2014), p. 211, and addressed further below). For Ibn Batrīq's own zealous championing of his Chalcedonianism contra non-Chalcedonianism in Egypt, see Mark N. Swanson, *The Coptic Papacy in Islamic Egypt (641–1517)* (Cairo: American University in Cairo Press, 2010) who notes that Ibn Batrīq 'claimed that, during the first century of

Islamic rule, 'the Jacobites had seized all the churches in Misr and Alexandria' [...] While this claim is exaggerated, it no doubt reflects the vigour with which the anti-Chalcedonian patriarchs pressed their claims on existing churches' (p. 161).

7. See Chapter 2, note 4, above, for critical neglect of al-Ghazzī as accented by Griffith.
8. For the English Civil War linked with 'revolution', see Keith Lindley, *The English Civil War and Revolution: A Sourcebook* (London: Routledge, 1998), p. 1. The 1642 edition of Ibn Baṭrīq's *String of Gems* is *Eutychii Ægyptii, Patriarchæ Orthodoxorum Alexandrini*, ed. John Selden (London: Excudebat Richardus Bishopus, 1642). The Ibn Baṭrīq passage quoted at the opening to the present chapter concerning 'Ammonius' is found on page xxxiii of this 1642 edition.
9. Ibn Batrīq's own Qur'ānic engagements have, however, been previously recognised once again by Griffith, who addresses Ibn Batrīq's efforts to 'replace the narrative [i.e., of the "Youths of Ephesus"/"Companions of the Cave", cf. Sūrat al-Kahf] into its Christian context'. See Sidney H. Griffith, 'Christian Lore and the Arabic Qur'ān: The "Companions of the Cave" in Sūrat al-Kahf and in Syriac Christian Tradition' in *The Qur'ān in its Historical Context*, ed. Gabriel S. Reynolds (London: Routledge, 2008), pp. 124–137 (pp. 130–131).
10. Ibn Baṭrīq's account of creation and 'the Fall', although following Genesis, has also received notice due its added details, especially his stipulating 'a Mountain in India' as the place inhabited by Adam and Eve after 'being cast out' of paradise; see, for instance, and for these quotes, Simon Patrick, *A Commentary upon the First Book of Moses called Genesis* (London: R. Chiswell, 1704), p. 82.
11. For this passage in the critical edition of Ibn Baṭrīq, i.e., *Annales*, see p. 6. For this passage in an early-modern English edition of Ibn Baṭrīq's *String of Gems*, treated later in this chapter, see Ibn Baṭrīq, *Contextio Gemmarum, sive, Eutychii Patriarchæ Alexandrini Annales*, ed. and trans. Edward Pococke, 2 vols. (Oxford: Humphrey Robinson, 1658–59), vol. 1, p. 14, subsequently cited as '*Contextio Gemmarum*'.
12. For '*'azza wa-jalla*' in the *ḥadīth* see, for instance, Muslim ibn al-Ḥajjāj al-Qushayrī, *Mukhtaṣar Saḥīḥ Muslim*, ed. 'Abd al-'Aẓīm ibn 'Abd al-Qawī al-Mundhirī (Beirut: Dār wa-Maktabat Hilāl, 1987), p. 300.
13. This rendition of Qur'ān 2:36 reflects Arberry's English, but with my parenthetical additions.
14. Ibn Baṭrīq, *Annales*, p. 6.
15. This rendition of Qur'ān 20:120 reflects Arberry's English, but with my parenthetical additions.
16. For these quotes on Ibn Baṭrīq's *Annales*, see *Encyclopedia of Arabic Literature: Volume 1*, ed. Julie S. Meisami and Paul Starkey (London: Routledge, 1998), p. 211.
17. For Ibn al-Muqaffa''s death date as 'after 987', see Simonsohn's entry on Ibn Baṭrīq in *Christian–Muslim Relations*, p. 230. Kees Versteegh, *The Arabic Language* (Edinburgh: Edinburgh University Press, 2014), p. 128, characterises Ibn al-Muqaffa' as 'one of the first Coptic authors to write exclusively in Arabic'.
18. This quoted phrase derives from Simonsohn's entry on Ibn Baṭrīq in *Christian–Muslim Relations*, p. 230. Simonsohn is also responsible for a more sustained consideration of Ibn al-Muqaffa''s polemical engagements with Ibn Baṭrīq; see 'Motifs of a South-Melkite Affiliation in the *Annales* of Sa'īd ibn Baṭrīq' in *Cultures in Contact: Transfer of Knowledge in the Mediterranean Context: Selected*

Papers, ed. Tovar S. Torallas and J. P. Monferrer-Sala (Córdoba: CNERU, 2013), pp. 243–254 (esp. pp. 243–245).

19. See Sidney H. Griffith, 'The *Kitab Misbah al-Aql* of Severus Ibn al-Muqaffa': A Profile of the Christian Creed in Arabic in Tenth Century Egypt', *Medieval Encounters* 2 (1996): 15–42 (p. 28). Griffith's assessment of *Kitāb Miṣbāḥ al-'Aql* is also cited by Stephen J. Davis in his recognition of the 'Islamic terminology' of *Kitāb al-Majāmi'*; see Stephen J. Davis, *Coptic Christology in Practice: Incarnation and Divine Participation in Late Antique and Medieval Egypt* (Oxford: Oxford University Press, 2008), p. 213.
20. See Davis, *Coptic Christology in Practice*, esp. pp. 211–214; it is on page 213 that Davis recognises that 'in reading the *History of the Councils* in Arabic, one is struck not only by Sāwīrus' extensive use of Islamic terminology, but also by the nature of his rhetoric and argumentation'. In these pages, Davis catalogues several of Ibn al-Muqaffa''s 'Islamic' echoes, including his usage of '*rabb al-'ālamīn*' (p. 213) and '*al-Naṣārā*' (p. 212), which I also highlight below. I am unaware, however, of previous treatments of Ibn al-Muqaffa''s specific passages on 'the Fall' which I discuss in the present chapter.
21. '*Réfutation de Sa'īd ibn Batriq*' is the French title offered in the critical edition of the first published instalment of Ibn al-Muqaffa''s *Kitāb al-Majāmi'*; see *Réfutation de Sa'īd ibn Batriq (d'Eutychius) (Le Livre des Conciles)*, ed. and trans. P. Chebli in *Patrologia Orientalis* vol. 3 (Paris: Librairie de Paris, 1909; first printed in 1905), pp. 121–242. When Ibn al-Muqaffa''s second book was published, however, this polemical title was dropped; see *Histoire des Conciles (Second Livre)*, ed. and trans. L. Leroy in *Patrologia Orientalis* vol. 6 (Paris: Librairie de Paris, 1911), pp. 465–600. It is these two editions from which I quote and translate Ibn al-Muqaffa''s Arabic below, benefitting too from the foregoing French translations offered by both Chebli and Leroy. In the opening to his *Kitāb al-Majāmi'* as edited by Chebli, Ibn al-Muqaffa' explicitly situates his work as responding to Ibn Baṭrīq and his 'history' (see Ibn al-Muqaffa', *Réfutation de Sa'īd ibn Batriq*, pp. 128–29); however, see Simonsohn, 'Motifs of a South-Melkite Affiliation in the *Annales* of Sa'īd ibn Baṭrīq', who emphasises variations in the *Kitāb al-Majāmi'* manuscript witnesses, with some 'lack[ing] these introductory remarks' (p. 243). Also see Alois Grillmeier and Theresia Hainthaler, *Christ in Christian Tradition: Vol. 2, Part 4*, trans. O. C. Dean (London: Mowbray, 1996), p. 273, which describes Ibn Baṭrīq as writing 'in such a polemical form that he challenges an anti-Chalcedonian counter-presentation by Severus ibn al-Muqaffa''.
22. Ibn al-Muqaffa', *Réfutation de Sa'īd ibn Batriq*, pp. 132–133.
23. See Chapter 1, note 48, above, for 'Iblīs'; for the plural of '*shayṭān*' – i.e., '*shayāṭīn*' ('devils') – in the Qur'ān, see, for instance, 2:102.
24. In the Qur'ānic account of Satan's disobedience in Sūrat al-Baqara, it is precisely the action cited by Ibn al-Muqaffa' – i.e., '*sujūd*' – that is invoked. See Qur'ān 2:34, which reads '*wa-idh qulnā lil-malā'ikati sjudū li-ādama fa-sajadū illā iblīs 'abā*' (And when We said to the angels, 'Bow (*isjudū*) yourselves to Adam'; so they bowed themselves (*fa-sajadū*), save Iblis; he refused; Arberry's translation, with transliterations added). The biblical precedent Ibn al-Muqaffa' invokes in opposition to the Qur'ānic account derives from Isaiah 14:13–14 (in the KJV: 'For thou hast said in thine heart, I will ascend into heaven, I will exalt my throne above the stars of God: I will sit also upon the mount of the congregation, in the

sides of the north: I will ascend above the heights of the clouds; I will be like the Most High').

25. Ibn al-Muqaffa', *Histoire des Conciles* (*Second Livre)*, pp. 543–544.
26. The Qur'ān 55:78 opens with the same two terms, although without the final personal pronoun marker ('His') on 'name', i.e., '*tabāraka smu rabbika dhī l-jalāli wa'l-ikrām*' ('Blessed be the Name of thy Lord, majestic, splendid'; Arberry's translation).
27. For the phrase '*iblīs al-la'īn*', for instance, see Samer Akkach, *Intimate Invocations*: *Al-Ghazzi's Biography of Abd al-Ghani al-Nabulusi* (*1641–1731*) (Leiden: Brill, 2012), p. 479.
28. Ibn al-Muqaffa', *Réfutation de Sa'īd ibn Batriq*, p. 161.
29. See Jeanne-Nicole M. Saint-Laurent, *Missionary Stories and the Formation of the Syriac Churches* (Oakland: University of California Press, 2015), p. 136. For this passage from Ibn al-Muqaffa', with his etymologic critique of the Melkites, see *Réfutation de Sa'īd ibn Batriq*, pp. 204–205.
30. Ibn al-Muqaffa''s survey of the early Church advances speedily from this opening to his Chapter 3, however, reaching 'Nicaea' by the next page (see *Réfutation de Sa'īd ibn Batriq*, p. 162).
31. The feminine adjective '*al-mustaqīma*' recalls, for instance, the very first adjective applied to Muslim belief in the Qur'ān, appearing in the masculine in the scripture's sixth *āya* '*ihdinā al-ṣirāṭ* <u>*al-mustaqīm*</u>'.
32. See Gabriel S. Reynolds, 'The Quran and the Apostles of Jesus', *Bulletin of the School of Oriental and African Studies* 76:2 (2013): 209–227, in which Reynolds recognises that '[i]t has long been noted that the appearance of this term in the Quran is peculiar, in as much as the word for 'Christians' in the languages (Semitic or otherwise) of late antiquity is generally (as in English) some sort of calque of the Greek term Χριστιανοί' (p. 212). The most in-depth exploration of 'al-Naṣārā' is Sidney H. Griffith's 'Al-Naṣārā in the Qur'ān: A Hermeneutical Reflection', in *New Perspectives on the Qur'ān: The Qur'ān in its Historical Context 2* (London: Routledge, 2011), pp. 301–332, which also notes that although 'al-Naṣārā' is 'almost always translated "Christians"', this 'translation is not exact', hiding distinctions between these two terms (p. 301). Although Qur'ānic in source, 'al-Naṣārā' is, of course, also used by other early Arabic-speaking Christians, beyond Ibn al-Muqaffa'; see, for instance, a similar usage in Griffith, *The Church in the Shadow of the Mosque*, p. 58, as well as below. Davis, in his *Coptic Christology in Practice*, also emphasises Ibn al-Muqaffa''s use of 'al-Naṣāra' in his *Kitāb al-Majāmi'* (*Coptic Christology in Practice*, p. 212).
33. For a recent study of '*ḥawāriyyūn*', and its traditional association with 'whiteness', and this term's possible Ethiopic origins, see Reynolds, 'The Quran and the Apostles of Jesus', esp. p. 211.
34. See above, as well as Ibn Baṭrīq, *Annales*, p. 96.
35. Ibn Baṭrīq, *Annales*, p. 96.
36. For Nero as the 'adopted son' of Claudius, see David Shotter, *Nero Caesar Augustus: Emperor of Rome* (London: Routledge, 2014), p. 56.
37. For another Arabic Christian text applying the very same phrase (i.e., '*ra'īs al-ḥawāriyyīn*') to Paul, see *Acta Mythologica Apostolorum: Transcribed from an Arabic Ms. in the Convent of Deyr-Es-Suriani, Egypt, and from Mss in the Convent of St. Catherine, on Mount Sinai*, ed. Agnes Lewis (London: Clay, 1904), p. 58.

38. Simonsohn, 'Motifs of a South-Melkite Affiliation in the *Annales* of Saʿīd ibn Baṭrīq', suggests Ibn Baṭrīq's impact on later writers beyond Ibn al-Muqaffaʿ, noting that 'the polemical works of the East Syrian Elias of Nisibis (d. c. 1049), and of the Muslim Ḥanbalī scholar Ibn Taymiyya (d. 1328), can be seen as additional examples of apologetic responses to the *Annales*' (p. 244).
39. For this claim for Selden's edition, see G. J. Toomer, *Eastern Wisedome and Learning: The Study of Arabic in Seventeenth-Century England* (Oxford: Clarendon Press, 2007), p. 66.
40. Selden's acclaim as the 'Great Light of the English Nation', pronounced at his 1654 death, is reported in Ofir Haivry, *John Selden and the Western Political Tradition* (Cambridge: Cambridge University Press, 2017), p. 1.
41. For this phrase, see Toomer, *Eastern Wisedome and Learning*, p. 164. This assessment was initially offered in the early biography of Edward Pococke – i.e., Leonard Twells, Zachary Pearce, Thomas Newton and Samuel Burdy, *The Lives of Dr. Edward Pocock, the Celebrated Orientalist by Dr. Twells; of Dr. Zachary Pearce, Bishop of Rochester, and of Dr. Thomas Newton, Bishop of Bristol, by Themselves; and of the Rev. Philip Skelton, by Mr. Burdy*, 2 vols. (London: Rivington, 1816), vol. 1, p. 226 – which asserts that '[f]or in the year 1642, to bear down Episcopacy, which was then sinking in this nation, he [Selden] published, what he could have to be thought a mighty argument against it; namely, the account which this Eutychius gives of the Church of Alexandria, during the three first centuries' (p. 226). However, also see George W. Johnson's *Memoirs of John Selden and Notices of the Political Context During His Time* (London: Orr and Smith, 1835), p. 289, which asserts that '[i]t would be erroneous to conclude that by publishing this work [i.e., his Eutychius edition], Selden intended to declare his enmity to the episcopal form of church government'. Johnson also notes that 'Selden had imbibed a great opinion of Eutychius as an author, from Erpenius [i.e., Thomas van Erpe], who, as he says, gave him a copy of this work when in London' (p. 289).
42. Ibn Baṭrīq, *Eutychii Ægyptii*, p. 151 (cited first in note 9, above).
43. For Selden's familiarity with, and critique of, Robert of Ketton's Qur'ān translation, see Toomer, *Eastern Wisedome and Learning*, p. 65.
44. For the American Revolution as the nation's 'first Civil War', see Ray Raphael, *A People's History of the American Revolution: How Common People Shaped the Fight for Independence* (New York: The New Press, 2016), p. 5.
45. The first chapter of my 2016 *The Islamic Lineage of American Literary Culture: Muslim Sources from the Revolution to Reconstruction* (New York: Oxford University Press) is dedicated to Ezra Stiles's Arabic studies (pp. 1–32), including his engagements with Ibn Baṭrīq made available to Stiles via Selden's works (see pp. 14–17, 20, 22, 29). For the edition of Ibn Baṭrīq consulted by Stiles – entitled *Eutychii Origines Ecclesiæ Alexandrinæ* – see John Selden, *Opera Omnia*, ed. David Wilkins, 3 vols. in 6 vols. (London, 1726), vol. 3, pp. 219–226.
46. For a critical and contemporary appraisal of the role played by Ibn Baṭrīq in early American debates regarding the episcopacy, as initiated by Stiles himself, see John H. Hobart, *A Charge to the Clergy of the Protestant Episcopal Church in the State of New-York* (New York: T. and J. Swords, 1815), pp. 48–52.
47. My 2016 *The Islamic Lineage of American Literary Culture*, p. 15, publishes an image from the first page of Ezra Stiles, 'The Antiquities of the Church of Alex-

andria' (1769). The above inclusion of the fourth page of Stiles's six-page manuscript, however, represents the first time this page has appeared in print.

48. Stiles mistakenly transcribes the nominative '*al-ḥawāriyyūn*' (الحواريون) rather than the correct oblique form for the genitive '*al-ḥawāriyyīn*' (الحواريين).
49. This quote is sourced from Ibn Baṭrīq, *Contextio Gemmarum*, p. 13; this phrase immediately anticipates Ibn Baṭrīq's account of creation, that begins on page 14 of this edition (i.e., the passage cited above from the critical edition; see this chapter's note 11, above). The biographical Introduction to *String of Gems*, which ends with these Arabic words, itself begins on page 2 of Ibn Baṭrīq, *Contextio Gemmarum*.
50. For Selden 'provid[ing] funds in his will for Pococke's edition of Eutychius', see Jason Peacey '"Printers to the University" 1584–1658' in *History of Oxford University Press, Volume I, Beginnings to 1780*, ed. Ian Gadd (Oxford: Oxford University Press, 2014), pp. 51–78 (p. 75).
51. For Cromwell's 1658 death and this specific phrase, see Nancy L. Matthews, *William Sheppard, Cromwell's Law Reformer* (Cambridge: Cambridge University Press, 1984), p. 64.
52. For parallel *āya* endings, see, for instance, Qur'ān 3:26 ('*innaka ʿalā kulli shayin qadīr*'; Thou art powerful over everything), and Qur'ān 5:40 ('*wa-Allāhu ʿalā kulli shayin qadīr*'; and God is powerful over everything; Arberry's translations).
53. It is Hidemi Takahashi who has most comprehensively catalogued Bar Hebraeus's diverse literary labours, and his composite life; see Takahashi's impressive *Barhebraeus: A Bio-Bibliography* (Piscataway, NJ: Gorgias Press, 2013).
54. For the relationship between Bar Hebraeus's two histories – i.e., his Arabic *Mukhtaṣar Taʾrīkh al-Duwal* and his Syriac *Chronicon* – see Herman Teule, 'The Crusaders in Barhebraeus' Syriac and Arabic Secular Chronicles. A different approach', in *East and West in the Crusader States. Context-Contacts-Confrontations*, ed. Krijnie Ciggaar, Adelbert Davids, and Herman Teule (Leuven: Peeters, 1996), pp. 39–49. Teule highlights in particular the Muslim audience for Bar Hebraeus's *Mukhtaṣar*, noting 'there is no reason to doubt that Barhebraeus composed this work at the request of his Arab (Muslim) friends' (p. 49).
55. Pococke's first partial edition of Bar Hebraeus appeared in 1650 as *Specimen Historiae Arabum, Sive, Gregorii Abul Farajii Malatiensis*, ed. Edward Pococke (Oxford: Humphrey Robinson); for its dedication to Selden, see P. M. Holt, *Studies in the History of the Near East* (London: Frank Cass, 1973), p. 34. The two volumes of Pococke's edition of Bar Hebraeus's Arabic chronicle – *Historia Compendiosa Dynastiarum* – were published in Oxford in 1663.
56. The dedication page to *Historia Compendiosa Dynastiarum* is unpaginated, forming the first page of the preliminaries in its volume 1, before the text proper begins on its page 1.
57. For this *ḥadīth*, and parallel quotations attributed to the Prophet identifying the 'sultan' as 'Allah's shadow', see Christian Mauder, 'Al-Suyūṭī's Stance Toward Worldly Power: A Reexamination based on Unpublished and Understudied Sources' in *Al-Suyūṭī, a Polymath of the Mamlūk Period: Proceedings of the Themed Day of the First Conference of the School of Mamlūk Studies*, ed. Antonella Ghersetti (Leiden: Brill, 2017), pp. 81–97 (p. 89).
58. For Bar Hebraeus as '*malik al-ʿulamā*', see *Historia Compendiosa Dynastiarum*, vol. 2, p. 1 and below.

59. Bar Hebraeus, *Historia Compendiosa Dynastiarum*, vol. 2, p. 1. Although lacking from this early-modern edition, I supply several instances of *hamza* in this Arabic quotation for clarity (e.g., offering '*al-fuḍalā'*' (الفضلاء), rather than merely '*al-fuḍalā*' (الفضلا), as this word reads in Pococke's printing).
60. For previous and wide-ranging treatments of Bar Hebraeus's engagements with Islamic sources, see Hidemi Takahashi, 'Reception of Islamic Theology among Syriac Christians in the Thirteenth Century: The Use of Fakhr al-Dīn al-Rāzī in Barhebraeus' Candelabrum of the Sanctuary', *Intellectual History of the Islamicate World*, 2:1–2 (2014): 170–192, as well as his 'Barhebraeus und seine islamischen Quellen. Têgrat têgrātā (Tractatus tractatuum) und Ġazālīs Maqāṣid al-falāsifa', in *Syriaca. Zur Geschichte, Theologie, Liturgie und Gegenwartslage der Syrischen Kirchen. 2.* (Münster: LIT Verlag, 2002), pp. 147–175. While Takahashi's concern does not centre primarily on Bar Hebraeus's own usage of Qur'ānic idioms, this topic is treated by Sidney H. Griffith in his 'Disputes with Muslims in Syriac Christian Texts: From Patriarch John (d. 648) to Bar Hebraeus (d. 1286)', in *Religionsgespräche im Mittelalter*, ed. Bernard Lewis and Friedrich Niewöhner (Wiesbaden: Harrassowitz, 1992), pp. 251–273. Especially relevant is page 269 and following of this 1992 chapter, where Griffith explores Bar Hebraeus's explicit engagement with the Qur'ān in his *Candelabra of the Sanctuary* – a work that contends with the Muslim scripture, offering actual quotations from the Qur'ān in Syriac (see Bar Hebraeus, *Le Candélabre du Sanctuaire de Grégoire Abou'lfaradj dit Barhebraeus. Quatrième base, De l'Incarnation*, ed. and trans. Joseph Khoury, in *Patrologia Orientalis*, vol. 31 (Paris: Firmin-Didot, 1966), esp. pp. 111–113 for Qur'ānic selections in Bar Hebraeus's Syriac).
61. Bar Hebraeus, *Historia Compendiosa Dynastiarum*, vol. 2, p. 118.
62. I select and render this portion of the Qur'ān 110:2 to highlight the overlap with Bar Hebraeus's usage; cf. Arberry's translation of the full verse, i.e., 'and thou seest men entering God's religion in throngs'.

4

'ADHERES TO THE ARABIC IDIOM': LUDOVICO MARRACCI'S QUR'ĀNIC VULGATES

I

'NULLAM REM ESSE SIMILEM'

> Dicunt enim (teste Sciaher Settanio, quem citat Pocokius in suis notis ad Abulpharegum): عرفنا بمقتضي العقل ان الله ليس كمثله شيء فلا يشبه شيا من المخلوقات *Nos scimus ex dictamine judicioque intellectus, nullam rem esse similem Deo, nec Deum ulli rei creatae esse similem.*
>
> Thus they say (according to Shahrastānī, who Pococke cites in his notes to Bar Hebraeus) that 'we know from the dictates of the intellect that there is nothing like unto God, and that He is unlike anything amongst created things'.
>
> Ludovico Marracci's *Alcorani Textus Universus* (1698)[1]

Dizzyingly allusive, this dense bilingual passage was printed in 1698, featured in the labyrinthine introduction to *Alcorani Textus Universus*, 'the first scholarly edition of the Quran in Arabic and Latin'.[2] Published in Padua by Pope Innocent XI's own confessor – Father Ludovico Marracci (1612–1700) – *Alcorani Textus Universus* reflects not only Marracci's key ecclesiastic position, but also his role as religious apologist. Rather than merely a rendition, Marracci's *Alcorani* also supplies extensive paratextual 'refutations'. Spanning hundreds of pages, Marracci introductory materials – including a *Praefatio* and a four-part *Prodromi* – critique Islam while championing Catholicism.[3] It is his *Prodromi*'s third part in which Marracci includes the above Latin and Arabic lines, which surface in a section that discusses a doctrine that divides Christianity and Islam: the Trinity. Offering 'proof' for this central 'mystery' of his own faith, Marracci's section oddly discovers 'the Most Holy Trinity' not in the Bible, but instead borne out 'by Mohammedan principles' ('*Mahumetanorum principiis*').[4] Seeking Catholic confirmation in Qur'ānic traditions, the third part of Marracci's massive *Prodromi* leads up to the short interreligious selection cited above, which merges what Muslims 'say' with Christian sources, packing into parentheses a citation that pairs together two non-Muslim scholars whose names should sound familiar. At the centre of this brief extract, Marracci twins Christian authorities that reach across centuries and continents, opening his Qur'ān translation by quoting an English orientalist – Edward Pococke – as well as Pococke's 'notes' to 'Abulpharagius', the author better known as Bar Hebraeus.[5]

Invoking a British Protestant and a Syrian polymath to explain Muslim 'dictates' in Latin, Marracci defends the Trinity with references both inter- and intra-religious, advocating Catholic doctrines in the opening to his *Alcorani Textus Universus* even as he spans Christian communions in his secondary sources. Marracci's appeal to Edward Pococke is, in particular, characteristic of his Qur'ān translation; as P. M. Holt notes, following C. A. Nallino, 'the Arabic authors quoted by Marracci [in the preface to his *Alcoran*] at second-hand are mainly from Pococke'.[6] The irony of Marracci's composite quotation is heightened, however, by its intensely singular content. Credited to 'Mohammedans', yet arising from Christian references, the mixed background to Marracci's citation is at odds with the unity of its focus, announcing that 'there nothing is like unto God' ('*nullam rem esse simile Deo*') – a proclamation of Allah's oneness whose ultimate source is Qur'ān 42:11:

لَيْسَ كَمِثْلِهِ شَيْءٌ

There is nothing like Him[7]

At the heart of Marracci's layered quotation on God's singularity is a kernel from the Qur'ān, this *āya* on divine uniqueness carried by diverse sources across dispensations, Marracci seeking to 'prove' the 'Most Holy Trinity' in the first pages of his *Alcoran* with a verse of *tawḥīd* itself transmitted to him via two Christian figures: Pococke and Bar Hebraeus.

This 'mysterious' marriage of holy singularity and textual multiplicity also embodies the extended background and complex environs that envelope Marracci's Catholic and 'universal' translation of the Muslim scripture. Printed on the cusp of the eighteenth century, traditionally seen as inaugurating 'a new period of western scholarship' concerning the Qur'ān, Marracci's translation yet also signals the end of a long tradition of Qur'ān translation into classical languages, recalling foregoing versions of the Muslim scripture into Latin, for example, as Thomas Burman has explored.[8] Reaching back a half a millennium to Europe's first Qur'ānic receptions, while poised on the brink of a new century that will witness the advent of an 'Enlightenment Qur'ān' (in the words of Ziad Elmarsafy), Marracci's *Alcoran* would also mark, however, a more personal culmination, appearing only two years before Marracci's own death, capping a long life filled with multiple 'orientalist' efforts.[9] Although now known for his final achievement, Marracci's Latin *Alcoran* recalls yet another complex act of translation that occupied Marracci earlier in his career. Published in Rome, and arising from decades of prior rendition and revision, Marracci helped oversee the 1671 publication of a three-volume work that bore the title *Biblia Sacra Arabica* – a complete Arabic translation of the Latin Bible, correlated and corrected to be 'more conformable to the Vulgate'.[10]

Aiming to 'propagate' the Catholic 'faith' in the Middle East – published under the auspices of the Vatican's *Sacra Congregatio de Propaganda Fide* – Marracci's own work on *Biblia Sacra Arabica* spanned a quarter century, from 1646 to 1671, preparing to dispatch this Arabic Vulgate to Muslim lands during the very same decades that led up to his rendition of the Muslim scripture into Latin.[11] And although remembered for this latter work – for his 1698 *Alcorani Textus Universus* – the largely-forgotten *Biblia Sacra Arabica* in 1671 comprised an instructive foreground to Marracci's Qur'ān translation, these two works of scriptural rendition reflecting inverse processes, yet an identical perspective. In 1698, Marracci's *Alcoran* offered European Christians a Qur'ān rendered into Latin; in 1671, however, Marracci had helped publish for Middle Eastern Christians a Latin Bible rendered into Qur'ānic idioms, with expressions from Islam's scripture recurrently enriching this Arabic Vulgate. As quoted above, Marracci prioritises his own Christian convictions in his Latin introduction to the Qur'ān; however, years before, he had encouraged the Christian scriptures themselves to speak in Qur'ānic terms. Largely overlooked by existing scholarship on Marracci, the *Biblia Sacra Arabica* forms a primary focus of the following chapter, which finds this Arabic Vulgate exemplifying in 1671 a tension between textual multiplicity and creedal singularity that previews Marracci's subsequent and more celebrated Qur'ān translation.[12] Published in a triad of volumes which are themselves 'unlike anything else', Marracci's *Biblia Sacra Arabica* offers both an opposing, yet anticipatory, text to his *Alcorani Textus Universus*, circulating a sacred corpus beyond its original expressions, even while seeking to 'propagate' the Christian creed by relying on the very 'principles' of 'Mohammedan' language.

II

'*IDEST* LIBRUM DEI'

> Vocant etiam Alcoranum simpliciter per Antonomasiam الكتاب, idest *Librum*, sicut Graeci Sacra Volumina, τὰ βιβλία: & كتاب الله, idest *Librum Dei*: aliisque nominibus, ac titulis honorificis illum insigniunt.
>
> They also call the Qur'ān simply, via antonomasia, '*al-kitāb*', that is 'the book', like the Greek sacred books, *ta Biblia*: & *kitāb Allāh*, that is, 'the Book of God', as well as other names and honorific titles to distinguish it
>
> from Marracci's *Praefatio* to his *Alcorani Textus Universus* (1698)[13]

Marracci's *Prodromi* to his *Alcoran*, quoted at the outset of this chapter, voiced Catholic apologetics via Qur'ānic exegesis; however, even earlier, in his *Praefatio*, Marracci had defined the term 'Qur'ān' itself. Aptly entitled '*De Alcorano*', the second section of Marracci's *Praefatio* includes the selection quoted above, categorising the Qur'ān nominally, accenting especially its title as '*al-kitāb*' – 'the book'. Although less polemical, these prefatory sentences concerning what the Qur'ān is 'call[ed]' do, however, anticipate Marracci's *Prodromi*; rather than reading Trinitarian 'mystery' via 'Mohammedan principles', Marracci offers an inverse interreligious appeal, contextualising the Qur'ān with biblical labels. Genetically linked to the Bible by its very genre, Islam's Arabic scripture, like the Greek '*Sacra Volumina*', is 'honorifically' known as '*al-kitāb*', or '*kitāb* Allāh' ('The Book of God') – precisely the phrase included in the introduction to Ḥafṣ al-Qūṭī's initial psalm ('but his passion is in the *kitāb Allāh*'; see Chapter 1). Invoking this shared scriptural title in his critical prose, rather than the psalmody of al-Qūṭī, Marracci's appeal to '*Librum Dei*' identifies this common label for the Bible and the Qur'ān as a type of semantic substitution – an '*antonomasia*' (an 'instead naming').[14] Theologically, the Qur'ān praises the God to Whom 'nothing is similar' (*nullam rem esse similem*). Bibliographically, however, the Qur'ān is 'called' by the very name as the Bible – '*al-kitāb*' – the Muslim scripture transported '*per Antonomasiam*' to emerge under the identical title shared also by the same *Sacra Volumina* cherished by Marracci and his fellow Catholics.

If introduced theoretically in his *Praefatio*, this process of 'antonomasia' is practically performed in Marracci's own Qur'ān translation. Indeed, even as his rendition reaches Qur'ānic passages that invoke images of 'the book', Marracci subtly appeals to the Christian *kitāb*, inserting biblical idioms into the Muslim scripture. Consider, for instance, Sūrat al-Takwīr, the Qur'ān's eighty-first chapter, whose apocalyptic opening features the following *āyāt* (10–11):

وَإِذَا ٱلصُّحُفُ نُشِرَتْ
وَإِذَا ٱلسَّمَآءُ كُشِطَتْ

when the scrolls shall be unrolled,
when heaven shall be stripped off[15]

Picturing the cosmos in terms of pagination, the universe's destruction is portrayed as bookish disclosure, with the 'stripping off' of the skies paralleled with the 'unroll[ing]' of 'the scrolls'. This apocalyptic publishing of 'pages' (ٱلصُّحُف ; *al-ṣuḥuf*) leads Marracci himself to turn to other pages, with the Qur'ān's bookish analogy for the *eschaton* rendered via a biblical analogy, Marracci offering the following Latin rendition for these verses:

Et, cùm libri expansi fuerint
Et, cùm Cœlum pelle spoliatum fuerit

and, when the books are spread open
and, when Heaven (as) a skin is stripped[16]

Slightly extending the Qur'ān's more economical Arabic, it is the 'skin' of the second verse above that seems most striking. In Marracci's version, unlike in the Muslim scripture, the sky's peeling away is supplemented with '*pelle*', likening 'Heaven' in Latin to a 'hide' or a 'skin'. Seemingly an innovation, this image of the sky as a 'skin' is not, however, new. As Marracci acknowledges in his footnotes, a clear precedent for '*pelle*' is found not in Qur'ānic *āyāt*, but in a verse from the Vulgate; explaining his own translation, Marracci traces a biblical precedent for Sūrat al-Takwīr, suggesting that this Qur'ānic verse (81:11):

> Vedetur alludere ad verba illa Psalmi 103. *Extendens Cœlum, sicut pellem.*
>
> Appears to allude to the words of Psalm 103, 'Stretching the Heavens, like a skin'.[17]

To justify his grafting 'skin' on to Sūra 81, Marracci notes that its eleventh *āya* itself 'appears to allude' to Psalm 103 – an 'allusion' that prompts Marracci to borrow '*pelle*' from this biblical account of creation, infusing *al-Takwīr* with the description of God in Psalm 103 as 'stretching the heavens, like a skin'. Taking '*verba*' from the Vulgate, the Islamic *eschaton* is merged in Marracci's rendition with a cosmic act of creation, the celestial origins of Psalm 103 echoing into the world's end in Sūra 81, the '*pelle*' of the sky stretched out in the former, and stripped off in the latter. Confessing his psalmic intervention into Sūrat al-Takwīr, Marracci himself discloses his own bibliographic debts even as the Qur'ān pictures a universal disclosure, Marracci unfolding a term from another 'Book' – the Bible – to enrich the Qur'ān's portrait of the eschatological 'unrolling' of 'scrolls' and the 'stripping' off of the sky.[18]

Although problematic, this process of substitution – re-covering the Qur'ān with biblical 'skin' – is yet consistent with the kerygmatic overlap suggested in Marracci's *Praefatio* to his *Alcoran*, which itself acknowledges the shared 'calling' of both the Bible and the Qur'ān as '*al-kitāb*'. A concrete instance of 'antonomasia' – an 'instead naming' – the sky assumes a new surface in the Qur'ān, the 'heaven' of the Muslim scripture covered over by Marracci's own '*Sacra Volumina*', these two scriptural canons now sharing a single term in translation, even as they bear in tandem the title '*Librum Dei*'. Reminiscent of his *Alcoran*'s introduction, the psalmic 'skin' of Marracci's Sūra 81 also recalls his earlier career, both echoing and inverting the three-volume Arabic Bible that appeared seventeen years earlier, in 1671 – an Arabic Bible that imports not vocabulary from the Latin

Vulgate to render the Qur'ān, but imports Qur'ānic vocabulary to render the Vulgate. Featuring reciprocal instances of '*antonomasia*', the *Biblia Sacra Arabica*, unlike Marracci's *Alcoran*, will 'instead' derive 'names' from Islam's scripture. Moreover, considering Marracci's psalmic revisions to Sūra 81 in 1698, the 1671 *Biblia* aptly features a single book that seems especially amenable to Qur'ānic expressions: the Book of Psalms.

III

'*AL-SĀLIKĪN FĪ ṬARĪQIHI*'

Stretching over two thousand pages, the three weighty volumes of the *Biblia Sacra Arabica* that appeared in 1671 offers the entire biblical corpus in two languages, aligning in parallel columns Latin 'original' with its Arabic rendition. Multiple in both volume and vernacular, this Arabic Vulgate from the Vatican also reflected and targeted multiple perspectives; crafted over a half century by the *Congregatio de Propaganda Fide*, the published *Biblia Sacra Arabica* represented the work of numerous translators in Rome, while also reaching out to diverse readers in the Middle East. However, despite its 'congregational' origins and its global aspirations, Marracci's own individual mark on the 1671 *Biblia Sacra Arabica* emerges from its very opening pages. Contributing a small segment of composition to this massive translation, Marracci not only oversaw this Arabic Bible's correlation with the Vulgate, but is also credited with producing the sole portion in the *Biblia Sacra Arabica* that qualifies not as rendition, but as original writing: 'The Introduction' (المقدمة ; *al-muqaddama*).[19] Aptly, considering the *Biblia*'s bilingualism, Marracci's own preface also straddles expressions, East and West, offered first in Latin, and followed by an Arabic equivalent. And, anticipating the stylistic complexities that contour this entire translation, Marracci's foreword to the 1671 *Biblia* emerges with Islamic touches. Tracing the genesis of biblical revelation in the pages just before 'Genesis' itself begins, the Arabic iteration of Marracci's 'Introduction', for instance, opens with the following words:

المقدمة
تبارك الله فاطر الارض والسمآء بجزيل الشكر والاعظام وبجميل الحمد والاكرام فانه بسبوغ
احسانه وبفضل انعامه على الناس انزل كلامه الكريم الى رسله الطاهرين وانبيآئه المختارين
قانونا تميما لحقيقة الدين ورشادا امينا للايمان المستقيم * واما بعد *

Introduction
Blessed be Allah, the creator (*fāṭir*) of the earth and heaven, with abundance of gratitude and glorifications, and with beauty of praises and graces, for He is ample of His beneficences, and gracious of His blessings upon mankind, sending down His noble Word upon His pure mes-

> sengers and chosen prophets as a complete canon for the verification of religion, and as trustworthy guidance for the straightforward faith * and regarding that which follows *[20]

Although Christian in content, Islamic conventions surface from the very start of this inventive 'Introduction', beginning with phrases that echo specific Qur'ānic *sūra*s; Marracci's own first words, for instance, seem to be inspired by the opening of the first *āya* of Sūrat al-Fāṭir – that is, 'Praise be to Allah, the creator of the heavens and earth', i.e. *al-ḥamdu lillāhi fāṭir al-samāwāti wa'l-arḍ* (Qur'ān 35:1). Shifting from its opening to its open ending, this first passage of Marracci's *Biblia* culminates also with '*wa-ammā ba'd*' (and regarding that which follows), a transition from introduction to main text which is standard to Muslim sermons, sourced ultimately from the Prophet's own practice.[21] Intersecting this envelope of Islamic rhetoric, Marracci outlines an economy of revelation that befits his own faith. However, even Marracci's description of the Bible's reception by man is again Islamically consistent, with Qur'ānic actions and epithets surrounding the Christian scripture; for instance, God's 'gracious Word', borne by 'pure apostles and prophets', is not merely revealed, but specifically 'sent down' – that is, '*anzala*' (انزل), a verb recalling numerous Qur'ānic verses, beginning with Sūrat al-Baqara's fourth *āya*. This process of revelatory reception leads finally to the above selection's last phrase, qualifying 'faith' as '*al-mustaqīm*' (المستقيم ; straightforward) – an adjective which possesses especial Qur'ānic relevance, as previously noted, comprising the very first qualifier in the Fātiḥa, invoked as the initial descriptor for the 'path' of the Muslim faithful (i.e., Qur'ān 1:6: *al-ṣirāṭ al-mustaqīm*).

Stylised in diction yet 'straightforward' in doctrine, this Arabic opening to Marracci's introduction anticipates the biblical translation it prefaces. Beginning with poetic touches – including an initial row of rhyming epithets that describe the divine ('*bi-jazīm al-shukr wa'l-ā'ẓām wa-bi-jamīl al-ḥamd wa'l-ākrām*') – it will be biblical poetry that especially attracts Qur'ānic idioms in the edition that follows Marracci's introduction. Published seven hundred years after al-Qūṭī's own psalter, and yet tracing itself to the very same source – Jerome's Latin translation – the 1671 *Sacra Biblia Arabica* features psalms that follow its Vulgate sources faithfully, even while pursuing Qur'ānic directions whenever possible. In the *Biblia*'s first Arabic psalm, for example, it is the 'orthodox path' that is again addressed – an introductory topic that broadly overlaps with the Qur'ān's own first chapter, while also endowed with expressions that are Qur'ānically consistent:

المزمور الاول
طوبا للرجل الذى لم يسلك في مشورة المنافقين
وفي طريق الخطاة لم يقف
وعلى مجلس المستهزيين لم يجلس

Psalm 1
Blessed be the man who journeys not
in the counsel of the dissemblers (*al-munāfiqīn*)
and in the way of sinners does not stand
and sits not in the *majlis* of the mockers (*al-mustahzi'īn*)[22]

In Arabic, the status of being 'blessed' (طوبا ; *ṭūbā*), is dependent on '*ṭarīq*' (طريق ; the 'path') pursued by 'the man' of piety. Framing the spiritual life in terms of '*salaka*' (سلك ; wayfaring) Psalm 1 defines orthodoxy against errancy, identifying the avenues and areas to be *avoided* by the righteous. And it is such counterexamples in this Arabic translation that reflect most clearly Qur'ānic terminology. For instance, the final term included in the above recalls Qur'ān 15:95, where precisely these 'mockers' (الْمُسْتَهْزِئِينَ ; *al-mustahzi'īn*) are rejected.[23] Perhaps more characteristic of the Qur'ān is the first clause above, which abjures not the '*mustahzi'īn*' but the '*munāfiqīn*' – the same active participate that occurs more than two dozen times in the Qur'ān.[24] Signifying 'the dissemblers' – suggesting 'hypocrites' who feign fidelity – '*munāfiqīn*' is striking in the above biblical translation not only due to its Qur'ānic background, but also due to its absence from the original of Psalm 1, which nowhere speaks of such 'hypocrites' precisely. In Jerome's Latin, it is the '*consilio impiorum*' – the 'counsel of the impious' – that should not be pursued, a phrase replaced in the 1671 *Biblia* by '*mashūrat al-munāfiqīn*' (the counsel of the dissemblers).[25] Seeming more intentional than accidental, Psalm 1 is altered to fit a very recognisable Qur'ānic term, with the insertion of 'dissemblers' itself comprising a slight dissimulation in translation. Feigning parallelism between scriptural expressions, the 'paths' of Psalm 1 and the Qur'ān are brought into 'blessed' alignment, despite their respective originals – 'impious' vs. 'hypocrites' – subtly 'deviating' one from another.

The celebration of the '*sālik*' – the 'wayfarer' – in Psalm 1 frequently recurs throughout the psalter, inviting quiet adoption of similar Islamic idioms which equally endorse 'the straight path'. Consider, for example, another psalmic opening, these verses forming the introduction to Psalm 127:

طوبي لجميع الذين يتّقون الرب السالكين في طريقه
Blessed be all of those who piously fear the Lord, the wayfarers in His way[26]

As Psalm 1, Psalm 127 begins again with a benediction, voicing a plural 'blessing' here rather than the singular. It is other echoes of Psalm 1, however, that seem more significant, Psalm 127 invoking not only the 'wayfarer' but also his 'way', synthesised in the following evocative phrase '*al-sālikīn* fī *ṭarīqihi*' (the wayfarers in His way). A fair version of its biblical source, such a sequence is also consistent with a variety of Muslim precedents, recalling diverse texts, spanning *tafsīr* literature to Sūfī manuals.[27] Ascribing 'the path' to those 'piously fearing the Lord' – a phrase recalling *āyāt* such as Qur'ān 6:32, 6:51, and 6:69[28] – this introduction to Psalm 127 also parallels the 'path' pursued in Psalm 85, whose verses 10–12 read as follows:

لانك عظيما انت وصانع العجايب انت يا الله وحدك
اهديني يا رب الى طريقك فاسلك في حقك وليفرح قلبي عند خوفه من اسمك
اعترف لك يا ربي والاهي من كل قلبى وامجد اسمك الى الدهر

For Thou art great, and the Doer of wonders, Thou, O Allah, art (God) alone

Guide me, O Lord, to Thy path, and I shall journey in Thy truth,
so that my heart may rejoice in its fear of Thy name

I confess Thee with my whole heart, O my Lord and my God,
and I glorify Thy name forever[29]

Intersecting this triad of Arabic lines is an imperative of orientation, not only invoking again God's 'path', but also imploring His direction – 'Guide me (*ihdīnī*), O Lord, to Thy path' – a command that faintly echoes the Qur'ān's own first chapter, which employs the very same plea for God's 'guidance' ('*ihdinā*', 'guide us'; see also Chapter 1 above). This light overlap seems more concrete, however, considering the creedal statements that anticipate it. Seeking to become a '*sālik*', the psalmist in Arabic also voices a familiar theological formula, invoking 'Allah' as God 'alone' (*Allāh waḥdak*) – a phrase with Islamic precedents, appearing in prayers attributed to the Prophet himself.[30] Such an assertion of God's lone oneness, so essential to Islam, is, of course, also entirely consistent with the Hebrew Psalms; and yet, considering its Christian context, rendered in Rome from the Latin Vulgate, this expression of *tawḥīd* intersecting a triad of verses from Psalm 85 seems somewhat more intriguing. Rather than religious nomenclature in general, however, it is the specific 'name' of God that forms the focus of these three verses, voicing reverence for His '*ism*' (اسم ; name) – a highlighting of nomenclature that hints at the pivotal importance which Allah's sublime *asmā'* will assume throughout the 1671 *Biblia*'s entire psalter.

IV

CHRISTIAN *DHIKR*

ذكرت في الليل اسمك يا رب وحفظت شريعتك
I make remembrance (*dhakartu*) in the night
of Thy name, O Lord, and I keep Thy *sharī'a*[31]

A single line from the longest psalm, this first-person appeal to 'the Lord' from Psalm 118 as offered by the 1671 *Biblia* again offers worship through His holy 'name'. However, it is not only divine label, but divine law, that is lauded in this line, ending with a term previously seen several times in *The Qur'ān and Kerygma*: the '*sharīʿa*'. In light of this noun's Islamic overlap, the verbs of this verse from Psalm 118 also seem apt. Portraying himself as a '*ḥāfiẓ*' – committed to 'keeping' (حفظ) the '*sharīʿa*' – the psalmist also dedicates his 'night' to the pious practice of '*dhikr*' (ذكر), undertaking nocturnal 'remembrance' of Allah's 'name', an act essential also to Muslim spirituality.[32] Intimately engaged with the '*ism*' of God, while also overlapping Islamic praxis, this line from Psalm 118 recalls earlier verses in the 1671 *Biblia* involving similar actions, such as Psalm 9:11:

ويتوكلون عليك الذين يعرفون اسمك لانك لم ترفض طالبيك يا رب
And they who rely (*yatawakkalūn*) upon Thee are those who know
Thy name, for Thou never rejects those seeking Thee, O Lord[33]

Again celebrating knowledge of the Lord's 'name', this verse features verbal forms distinct from Psalm 118, starting not with a first-person singular, but instead with a third-person plural. Continuities do emerge, however, in the Qur'ānic overtones of the activities of Psalm 9, opening with the verb 'يتوكلون' (*yatawakkalūn*) – a description of those who 'rely' upon God that itself relies upon the Muslim scripture, this verb of 'trust' entirely typical of the Qur'ān, recalling a range of *āyāt* that apply precisely this verb to the pious.[34]

It is not only actions surrounding Allah's 'name', however, but the precise names of 'the Lord' invoked by the 1671 *Biblia* that enable its Arabic psalms to overlap specific *sūra*s. Reaching back seven centuries, the *Biblia Sacra Arabica* echoes al-Qūṭī's own rendition by interweaving a range of *asmāʾ* into its psalter, leading to stunning sequences in single lines such as the following from Psalm 23:

من هو هذا ملك المجد الرب العزيز القوى الجبار القاهر فى الحروب
Who is it that is King (*malik*) of Glory?
The Lord, the Mighty (*al-ʿazīz*), the Strong (*al-qawī*),
the Compeller (*al-jabbār*), the Victorious (*al-qāhir*) in wars[35]

Stringing together divine names essential to Islam, this verse from a Catholic psalm is nominally consistent with the Qur'ān; especially striking is this line's series of epithets each prefaced by the definite article, making *dhikr* of 'the Lord' with the following four terms: *al-ʿazīz* (the mighty), *al-qawī* (the Strong), *al-jabbār* (the Compeller), and *al-qāhir* (the Victorious). All Qur'ānic epithets for Allah, perhaps most familiar is the immediate proximity of '*al-ʿazīz al-qawī*' – two terms which also appear together in *āyāt* such as 42:19, a Qur'ānic verse that ends with precisely these *asmā'*, although inverted in order (*wa-huwa al-qawī al-'azīz* ; and He is the strong, the mighty).[36]

Opening with 'king' (ملك ; *malik*), this verse from the *Biblia*'s Psalm 23 accents God's might and majesty, qualities which especially encourage overlaps with the Qur'ān throughout the 1671 Arabic Psalms. Returning to Psalm 9, for example, it is not one of the majestic *asmā'*, but a monarchal action, that recalls Islamic precedents, with the second half of this psalm's fifth verse reading:

استويت على العرش يا ديان الحق
Thou hast sat (*istawayta*) upon the throne, O Judge of Truth[37]

Echoing a Qur'ānic phrase that has itself historically sparked 'controversies', Psalm 9 integrates an intriguing idiom to depict Allah's 'sitting upon the throne', recalling *āyāt* such as Qur'ān 10:3, which similarly asserts:

إِنَّ رَبَّكُمُ اللَّهُ الَّذِي خَلَقَ السَّمَاوَاتِ وَالْأَرْضَ فِي سِتَّةِ أَيَّامٍ
ثُمَّ اسْتَوَىٰ عَلَى الْعَرْشِ
Surely your Lord is God, who created the
heavens and the earth in six days,
then sat Himself (*istawā*) upon the Throne[38]

Suggesting 'to turn' or 'to be equal', but implying in this context 'to establish', 'to settle upon', or more simply, 'to sit', the verb '*istawā*' is flexible in its precise significance, but is also highly distinctive of Qur'ānic descriptions of the divine 'Throne'. Appealing to this Islamic idiom to designate Allah's sovereignty, Psalm 9 in Arabic covertly 'establishes' itself on Qur'ānic grounds; however, this reliance seems especially ironic, with the 1671 *Biblia* not only 'settling' on an external basis, but one that is semantically unsettled, this Christian translation ironically borrowing a majestic metaphor from the Qur'ān whose own meaning is multivalent.[39]

The sovereignty of Allah as celebrated by the *Biblia*'s psalter is reciprocally complemented in the humble servanthood of humankind, with divine majesty prompting acts of obeisance. Consider, for instance, the imperative reverence voiced in verse 6 of Psalm 94:

هلموا نسجد ونركع له ونبكى امام الرب الذى خلقنا
Come, let us make *sajda* and bow (lit., perform *ruk'ū*) to Him,
and let us weep in the presence of the Lord Who created us.[40]

Recognising the devotion due to 'the Lord', the psalmist recommends 'our' supplication 'to Him'. However, rather than genuflection in general, the motions endorsed in this biblical line parallel Muslim praxis, with

Psalm 94 suggesting not only '*sajda*', but also '*rukʿū*', be performed in the presence of Allah. Consistent with Christian reverence that is due to the divine king, and yet expressed in terms that are Qurʾānic in texture, the *Biblia* traces instances of *ṣalāt* in its Arabic psalter, outlining acts central to Islamic prayer within this single line of Hebrew poetry.[41]

It is not only the august majesty of 'the Lord', but His intimate mercy, that invites Islamic overlaps throughout the 1671 *Biblia*, with psalms such as 114 echoing the Qurʾān in its portrait of God's compassion:

وباسم الرب دعوت
يا رب نجى نفسى الرب رحوم وصديق والاهنا رحيم
الرب يحفظ الاطفال اتضعت فخلصنى
ارجعى يا نفسى الى راحتك لان الرب قد احسن اليك

and in the name of the Lord, do I call
O Lord, save my soul, the Lord is merciful and truthful
and our God is compassionate (*raḥīm*)
The Lord maintains the children, I was abased, and He saved me
Return (*irjiʿī*), O my soul to thy rest, for the Lord has been beneficent
to thee[42]

Beginning with an abbreviated *basmala*, the psalmist opens his 'prayer' by pronouncing 'in the name of the Lord', while also invoking Allah via a divine epithet essential to the Qurʾān's own doxology – '*raḥīm*' (compassionate; cf. '*bismi Allāh al-Raḥmān al-Raḥīm*'). Shifting from God's *raḥma* (compassion) to human 'return', even more idiomatic is the imperative that ends this selection, inviting the individual self to come home with words similar to a Qurʾānic command – indeed, offering the *self-same* invitation inserted into Psalm 114 by al-Qūṭī. Table 4.1 shows the first words of the final psalmic line quoted above, together with the relevant selection from the Qurʾān's eighty-ninth chapter, Sūrat al-Fajr, seen previously in Chapter 1:

from the *Biblia*'s Psalm 114:7	**from Qurʾān 89:27–28**
ارجعى يا نفسى الى راحتك	يا أيتها النفس المطمئنة ارجعي إلى ربك
Return (*irjiʿī*), O my soul to thy rest	O soul at peace, return (*irjiʿī*) unto thy Lord[43]

Table 4.1. A comparison of a line from Pslam 114:7 with Qurʾān 89:27–28.

Returning to Islamic idioms even while the 'soul' returns to its heavenly origins, the psalmist voices a self-referential command that sounds once again like a Qurʾānic reference. Echoing Sūra 89 in its Arabic imperative '*irjiʿī*' (ارجعى), the biblical speaker seeks peace in the promised 'rest' of

'*Raḥīm*', even as the *Biblia Sacra Arabica* itself traces its own way back to Qur'ānic precedents.

If the dialectical polarities of divine majesty and mercy help infuse Islamic idioms into the *Biblia Sacra Arabica*, Qur'ānic echoes also surface in the 1671 psalter as it portrays devilish opposition to the divine itself. Reaching down from the celestial to the infernal, this selection from Psalm 85 opens again with '*raḥma*' but soon plunges to the 'lowest' pit:

لان رحمتك عظيمة على ونجيت نفسى من قعر الجحيم السفلى
اللهم ان المنافقين قد قاموا على وجماعة الاشداء طلبوا نفسى ولم يجعلوك امامهم
وانت ايها الرب الاهي رووف ورحوم طويل الروح وكثير الرحمة وصادق

For Thy mercy is great upon me,
and Thou hast saved my soul from the pit of the lowest *jaḥīm*

O Allah, the dissemblers (*al-munāfiqīn*) have risen up against me
and the congregations of the fierce have sought my soul,
and have not set Thee before them

But Thou, O Lord, my God are benevolent and merciful
extensive of spirit, and abundant of mercy and truthful[44]

Enveloped in 'mercy', these verses on divine compassion are interrupted by the diabolic, including the 'dissemblers' who were first condemned in the initial lines of Psalm 1, that is, the '*munāfiqīn*'. It is not 'hypocrites' merely, but hell itself, from which the psalmist seeks rescue, appealing to Allah for refuge from:

قعر الجحيم السفلى
the bottom of the lowest *jaḥīm*[45]

A name for 'hell', '*jaḥīm*' is not only common in the Qur'ān, but is itself a Qur'ānic coinage, the Arabic psalms integrating this idiom voiced initially in Islam's scripture.[46] Appealing up from 'hell', the psalmist's rendered cry retreats to Qur'ānic foundations, reaching down not only to '*al-jaḥīm*', but '*al-jaḥīm al-suflā*' (the lowest [or lower] hell). This latter term, as much as the former, offers an intriguing overlap with Islamic usages, soon recurring once again in another form and in another psalm: Psalm 87. Rather than a mere elative, '*suflā*' emerges as a superlative in Psalm 87, strengthened to form an infernal phrase even more characteristic of the Qur'ān. Redoubling his description of the abyss, the speaker of Psalm 87 again describes the extreme locale from which liberation is sought, imploring God from 'the pit' where his persecutors have 'put' him:

جعلونى في الجب اسفل السافلين في الظلمة وظلال الموت

They have put me into the pit, the lowest of the low,
into the darkness, and shade of death[47]

Adequately expressing the original sense of Psalm 87, this Arabic rendition also shadows over another source which supplies its specific expressions. Reaching up from the 'pit', this agonised petition also reaches forward in scriptures, invoking a later *Sacra Volumina* to designate the hellish depths, with the infernal region here labelled as '*asfal al-sāfilīn*' (lowest of the low), a phrase original to *sūra*s such as Sūra 95, where Allah himself proclaims:

رددناه أسفل سافلين ثم
then We restored him the lowest of the low (*asfal sāfilīn*)[48]

Situating himself in the very depths forecasted in the Qur'ān, the psalmist appeals to this superlative phrase from Sūrat al-Tīn – '*asfal sāfilīn*' (the lowest of the low) – intensifying both the Islamic character, as well as infernal characterisation, of the Vulgate's hell. Even as the psalmist suffers under 'the shade of death', it is an Islamic afterlife that he sustains in Arabic rendition, with a Qur'ānic phrase surprisingly rising up from this submerged locus in the *Biblia Sacra Arabica*.

V

'BEING IN LATIN, IT CAN BE OF NO USE'

Responsible for two scriptural renditions reciprocal in character – both a 1671 Latin Bible translated into Arabic, as well as a 1698 Qur'ān translated from Arabic into Latin – Marracci's orientalist efforts surfaced during the final decades of the seventeenth century, but would also prove seminal for scholars as the next century dawned. Known now for his *Alcorani Textus Universus*, it was Marracci's *Biblia Sacra Arabica* that most immediately invited a successor, with yet another Arabic Bible appearing in the West during the first decades of the 1700s. Produced not by a Catholic 'congregation for the propagation of the faith', but instead by English Protestants committed to 'promoting' their own traditions, an Arabic New Testament commissioned by the 'Society for Promoting Christian Knowledge' appeared in 1727; printed in London, this Arabic Bible announced itself with the following words in stylised script on its frontispiece:

العهد الجديد لربنا يسوع المسيح،
وايضا
وصايا الله العشر كما في الاصحاح العشرين من سفر الخروج،
طتبع في سنة ١٧٢٧ مسيحية

The New Testament of our Lord, *Yasū' al-Masīḥ*
and also
Allah's Ten Commandments according to the twentieth Chapter in the
Book of Exodus
Printed in the Christian year 1727[49]

An Anglican competitor to Rome's *Biblia Sacra Arabica*, this Arabic title-page hides an intriguing continuity with Marracci's own Bible, staying silent as to the English identity associated with producing this New Testament in 1727, namely, that of George Sale. London lawyer by profession, but orientalist by avocation, Sale would also prove to be the most prominent translator of the Qur'ān in the eighteenth century, his 1734 *The Koran* quickly eclipsing Marracci's *Alcoran*, becoming the West's standard edition of the Muslim scripture 'for over two hundred years'.[50]

Surpassing Marracci as translator of the Muslim scripture, Sale yet succeeded Marracci in first editing an Arabic Bible during the very years leading up to his own Qur'ān translation – a surprising parallel between Marracci and Sale that is rarely acknowledged.[51] And yet, if overlaps between their discrete careers are often overlooked, it was Sale himself who claims Marracci as his predecessor, not only critiquing the latter's Latin Qur'ān, but also recognising its reliance on biblical expressions. Mentioning Marracci in his voluminous 'Preliminary Discourse' that prefaces his 1734 English *Koran*, Sale immediately sets himself in ambivalent opposition to the Italian's own 1698 *Alcoran*:

> In 1698, a *Latin* translation of the *Koran*, made by father *Lewis Marracci*, who had been confessor to Pope *Innocent XI.* was published at *Padua*, together with the original text, accompanied by explanatory notes and a refutation. This translation of *Marracci*'s, generally speaking, is very exact; but adheres to the Arabic idiom too literally to be easily understood, unless I am much deceived, by those who are not versed in the *Mohammedan* learning. The notes he has added are indeed of great use; but his refutations, which swell the work to a large volume, are of little or none at all, being often unsatisfactory, and sometimes impertinent. The work, however, with all its faults, is very valuable, and I should be guilty of ingratitude, did I not acknowledge myself much obliged thereto; but still, being in *Latin*, it can be of no use, to those who understand not that tongue.[52]

Accenting both the fidelity and the 'faults' of the Latin *Alcoran*, Sale offers a mixed assessment of Marracci, simultaneously expressing – yet subverting – praise for the Italian's 'translation'. While Marracci's 'notes' are 'of great use', his 'refutations' are rejected by Sale as 'unsatisfactory, and sometimes impertinent'; while Marracci's 'translation' is 'exact', it is ironically understood by Sale also as 'too literal'. It is this latter critique, centred on language, which is perhaps most telling, charting the change between Marracci in late seventeenth-century Rome and Sale in early eighteenth-century London, as Ziad Elmarsafy has recently emphasised.[53] Not only staying too close to 'the Arabic idiom', it is Marracci's 'Latin' that obviates its 'use', Sale prioritising his own English vernacular, voicing Protestant discomfort with the approved classical 'tongue' of the Vatican that marks Marracci's translation.

Implying in his Qur'ān's first pages a subtle intra-Christian struggle, it is ironic that Sale indicts Marracci for 'adher[ing] to the Arabic idiom too literally' as it will also be Sale who first identifies the biblical innovations that enliven Marracci's rendition. Shifting forward from his extensive foreword to his appended footnotes, Sale annotates his own version of the Qur'ān's Chapter 81 in order to specify the 'faults' of Marracci's *Alcoran*; translating Sūrat al-Takwīr's verses 10 and 11, Sale offers a version fairly straightforward in expression:

> [10] and when the books shall be laid open;
> [11] and when the heaven shall be removed[54]

Supplementing this stark rendition, however, Sale also supplies a paratext, appending the following footnote to *āya* 11 – a marginal commentary that quotes Marracci to contextualise this verse's passive verb form (i.e., 'shall be removed'):

> *When the heaven shall be removed,* Or plucked away from its place, as *the skin is plucked off* from a camel which is flaying; for that is the proper signification of the verb here used. *Marracci* fancies the passage alludes to that in the Psalms, where, according to the versions of the *Septuagint* and *Vulgate*, GOD is said to *have stretched out the heaven like a skin.*[55]

Recalling his *Koran* introduction as quoted above, an intriguing ambivalence emerges in Sale's approach to Marracci; not only offering an extended definition for the Arabic verb in verse 11, Sale's note also subtly denigrates his Italian predecessor, suggesting that Marracci merely 'fancies' this *āya*'s source in 'the Psalms'. Recognising confusions that arise from discrete biblical 'versions' even as he annotates the Qur'ān, Sale ends by emphasising the derivative character of Marracci's own translation, with the 'skin' that surfaces in his *Alcoran* itself traced to 'the *Septuagint* and *Vulgate*', rather than the original Psalms. A Protestant critique of Marracci's Latin '*pelle*', this note to Sūrat al-Takwīr ironically finds biblical translations and transmissions discussed and debated in Muslim scriptural margins.[56] Weighing possible Hebrew Bible influence, while speaking back to his continental predecessor, Sale's *Koran* also implies, however, yet another irony entirely unexpected in 1734, anticipating a Qur'ān which will itself be both Hebrew and continental, and which will situate Sale himself as influential predecessor. Extending an intra-Christian conversation in his *Koran* annotations, the edges of Sale's edition interrogates Marracci's psalmic exegesis; however, although here considering Qur'ānic indebtedness to ancient Jewish sources in 1734, Sale's own *Koran* will itself become a source for a modern Jewish text, informing the first ever full translation of the Muslim scripture into the Bible's original idiom, Hebrew.

NOTES

1. Ludovico Marracci (trans.), *Alcorani Textus Universus Ex Correctioribus Arabum*, 2 vols. (Padua: Ex Typographia Seminarii, 1698), vol. 1, p. 31 (of *Prodromi, Pars Tertia*). Discrete paginations are offered for the preliminary sections of Marracci's *Alcorani*, with his '*Praefatio*' occupying the first forty-seven pages of Marracci's first volume, before his *Prodromi* commence.
2. For this characterisation, see Alastair Hamilton, *Europe and the Arab World: Five Centuries of Books by European Scholars and Travellers from the Libraries of the Arcadian Group* (Dublin, Ireland: Arcadian Group, 1994), p. 20.
3. Marracci himself frames his '*Prodromi*' as '*ad Refutationem Alcorani*'; he also, however, adds '*Refutationes*' after his translated Qur'ānic chapters. Also see Thomas E. Burman, *Reading the Qur'ān* in Latin Christendom, *1140–1560* (Philadelphia: University of Pennsylvania Press, 2009), p. 164, which highlights that Marracci's *Alcoran* 'is not just an edition, translation, and explanation of the Qur'ānic text; it is also a refutation of it' (p. 164).
4. Marracci (trans.), *Alcorani Textus Universus*, vol. 1, p. 29. Elmarsafy has recently emphasised Marracci's tendency 'to attack the Muslims with their own arguments and using their own sources' (see *The Enlightenment Qur'an*, pp. 38–39).
5. Although entirely unclear from Marracci's transliteration, his 'Sciaher Settanio' denotes Muḥammad al-Shahrastānī; see Pococke's biographic sketch of al-Shahrastānī in his original 1650 Bar Hebraeus edition, i.e., *Specimen Historiae Arabum, Sive*, p. 368. Also see the much later, and expanded, 1806 edition, whose inserted notes helps make clear the identity of 'Sciaher Settanio' as al-Shahrastānī, citing the latter's seminal work *al-Malik wa'l-Naḥl*; see *Specimen Historiae Arabum*, ed. Edward Pococke (Oxford: Clarendon Press, 1806), p. 420. See also Elmarsafy, *The Enlightenment Qur'an*, p. 10, who notes both George Sale's and Marracci's reliance on not only Pococke's 1650 *Specimen*, but also on 'Pococke's two other major historical works, the *Contextio gemmarum* [...] and the *Compendiosa historia dynastiarum* (a complete translation of Bar Hebraeus's *al-Mukhtaṣar fī'l-duwal*)'.
6. See Holt, *Studies in the History of the Near East*, p. 46, which appeals to this judgement of C. A. Nallino, first expressed in his article 'Le fonti arabe manoscritte di Ludovico Marracci sul Corano', in the *Rendiconti della R. Accademia nazionale dei Lincei, Cl. di scienze morali, storiche e filologiche*, 6th series, vol. 7 (1932), pp. 303–349.

7. This celebrated phrase intersects a much longer *āya*, which reads in Arberry's translation: '[t]he Originator of the heavens and the earth; He has appointed for you, of yourselves, pairs, and pairs also of the cattle, therein multiplying you. Like Him there is naught ('*laysa ka-mithlihi shay*''); He is the All-hearing, the All-seeing' (transliterated Arabic added).
8. Burman in his *Reading the Qur'ān* in Latin Christendom, *1140–1560*, p. 53 invokes the view of Marracci's *Alcoran* as 'initiator of this new period of western scholarship' – a view which Burman not only invokes, however, but also questions. Despite acknowledging Marracci's *Alcoran* as a 'towering achievement', Burman also locates this translation within a long tradition of Latin rendition, reaching back to not only Robert of Ketton's version, but also an unpublished attempt by Dominicus Germanus. The Byzantine translation of the Qur'ān into Greek by Euthymius Zigabenus also formed a precedent for later European renditions; see, for example, Zigabenus as cited in George Sale's 1734 *Koran*, treated further below (George Sale (trans.), *The Koran: Commonly called the Alcoran of Mohammed* (London: C. Ackers, 1734), p. 505). For extant selections from Zigabenus's translation, see Karl Förstel, *Schriften Zum Islam von Arethas und Euthymios Zigabenos und Fragmente der Griechischen Koranübersetzung*: Griechisch-Deutsche Textausgabe (Wiesbaden: Harrassowitz Verlag, 2009), p. 44ff.
9. 'Enlightenment Qur'ān' comprises the primary title to Elmarsafy's 2014 study (cited above), which also critiques Marracci's *Alcoran* as 'embattled' (p. 63).
10. The full title of this Arabic Bible, published in three volumes in 1671 by Rome's Sacra Congregatio de Propaganda Fide, is *Biblia Sacra Arabica Sacrae Congregationis De Propaganda Fide Jussu Edita, Ad Usum Ecclesiarum Orientalium*, subsequently cited simply as *Biblia Sacra Arabica*. For this Bible's aim of offering an Arabic rendition 'more conformable to the Vulgate' see James Townley, *Illustrations of Biblical Literature: Exhibiting the History and Fate of the Sacred Writings, from the Earliest Period to the Present Century*, 3 vols. (London: Longman, Hurst, Rees, Orme, and Brown, 1821), vol. 3, p. 378.
11. For Marracci as being 'taken first into [the project of the *Biblia Sacra Arabica*] in the year 1646', see Osborne et al. (eds.), *A New and General Biographical Dictionary*, vol. 8, p. 249.
12. Marracci has merited increasing critical attention in recent years; however, scholarship has emphasised almost exclusively his 1698 *Alcorani Textus Universus*, largely neglecting the 1671 *Biblia Sacra Arabica*. See, for example, Roberto Tottoli, 'New light on the translation of the Qur'ān of Ludovico Marracci from his manuscripts recently discovered at the Order of the Mother of God in Rome', in *Books and Written Culture of the Islamic World: Studies Presented to Claude Gilliot on the Occasion of his 75th Birthday*, ed. Andrew Rippin and Roberto Tottoli (Leiden: Brill, 2015), pp. 91–130, which impressively surveys the background to Marracci's *Alcoran*, but makes no mention of *Biblia Sacra Arabica*. The polemical purpose, and inexact character, of Marracci's *Alcoran* has recently led to critical assessments of his 'achievement'; in addition to Elmarsafy, who judges Marracci's *Alcoran* to be an act of 'verbal warfare' (*The Enlightenment Qur'an*, p. 38), Bruce Lawrence in his recent *The Koran in English: A Biography* (Princeton, NJ: Princeton University Press, 2017), p. 217 asserts that 'Marracci's [rendition of the Fātiḥa] is at once an inept and demeaning rendition of the core Qur'ānic text for ritual and belief'.

13. Marracci (trans.), *Alcorani Textus*, vol. 1, p. 33 (of the *Praefatio* section).
14. For '*antonomasia*' (ἀντονομασία) as 'to name instead', see Douglas R. McGaughey, *Strangers and Pilgrims: On the Role of Aporiai in Theology* (Berlin: Walter De Gruyter, 1997), p. 265.
15. This is Arberry's rendition of the Qur'ān's 81:10–11.
16. Marracci (trans.), *Alcorani Textus Universus*, vol. 2, p. 783.
17. Marracci (trans.), *Alcorani Textus Universus*, vol. 2, p. 784.
18. Marracci here appeals to the second verse of the Vulgate's Psalm 103 (KJV, number 104). However, as George Sale himself will note, '*pelle*' is original to the '*Septuagint* and *Vulgate*' versions of this verse, and is somewhat at variance with the original Hebrew, which reads 'כַּיְרִיעָה' (as a curtain); see discussion below, and especially note 55. Marracci's insertion of '*pelle*' into this Qur'ānic passage, which also concerns the 'unroll[ing]' of 'scrolls' does, however, intriguingly accord with earlier Latin appeals to 'Psalm 103'; see, for instance, St. Augustine's *Confessions*, which includes a passage merging 'skins' and 'book', i.e., 'you have like a skin [*sicut pellem*] stretched out the firmament of your book' – an allusion to 'the sky as a skin (Psalm 103.2)' (this passage, and its interpretation, are quoted from Eric Jager, *The Tempter's Voice: Language and the Fall in Medieval Literature* (Ithaca: Cornell University Press, 1993), p. 70).
19. For Marracci as credited with the *Biblia Sacra Arabica*'s 'preface', see Osborne et al. (eds.), *A New and General Biographical Dictionary*, vol. 8, p. 249, which asserts that, among other tasks, 'the preface' of *Biblia Sacra Arabica* was 'executed' by Marracci. It is unclear, however, whether Marracci produced merely the Latin version of the Introduction (spanning the unpaginated first five pages of the first volume of *Biblia Sacra Arabica*) or also contributed to producing the Arabic version of this same material, treated below.
20. *Biblia Sacra Arabica*, vol. 1, p. vii (my pagination, as no pagination provided for these preliminaries).
21. For this formulation – i.e., '*amma ba'd*' – in '[d]oxological statements', see Adam Gacek, *Arabic Manuscripts: A Vademecum for Readers* (Leiden: Brill, 2012), p. 202.
22. *Biblia Sacra Arabica*, vol. 2, p. 179.
23. See Qur'ān 15:95, '*innā kafaynāka al-mustahzi'īn*' (in Arberry's translation 'We suffice thee against the mockers'); however, this same participle, but in the nominative case (مُسْتَهْزِئُونَ ; *mustahzi'ūn*), appears in Qur'ān 2:14.
24. For the participle *al-munāfiqīn* (المنافقين ; nominative المنافقون / *al-munāfiqūn*) in the Qur'ān's fourth chapter alone, see, 4:61; 4:88; 4:138; 4:140; 4:142; 4:145.
25. I cite the Latin of Psalm 1 from *Biblia Sacra Arabica*, vol. 2, p. 179. This Arabic translation of Psalm 1, with its characteristic '*mashūrat al-munāfiqīn*' (مشورة المنافقين) in verse 1, is still in liturgical use; see, for instance, the Arabic version of Psalm 1 printed in the Coptic Church's *Agpeya*.
26. *Biblia Sacra Arabica*, vol. 2, p. 313.
27. For '*al-sālikīn fī ṭarīqa*' in *tafsīr*, see 'Abd al-Raḥmān ibn Nāṣir al-Sa'dī's *Taysīr al-Karīm al-Raḥmān fī Tafsīr Kalām al-Mannān* (Riyadh: Obeikan, 2013), p. 749. A similar phrase – i.e., '*al-sālikīn* fī *ṭarīqa*' – appears within the very title of a Sūfī treatise by 'Abd al-Ṣamad al-Falimbant, i.e. his *Sayr al-Sālikīn fī Ṭarīqat al-Sādāt al-Ṣufiyya*, 2 vols. (Singapore: Pustaka Nasional, 1953).

28. For this verb, see, for example, Qur'ān 6:32, which includes the assertion that '*wa-lal-dār al-ākhiratu khayrun lil-ladhīna yattaqūn*' (in Arberry's translation: 'surely the Last Abode is better for those that are godfearing').
29. *Biblia Sacra Arabica*, vol. 2, p. 267.
30. For each of these terms, see the prayer as transliterated by Sviri in 'Words of Power and the Power of Words: Mystical Linguistics in the Works of al-Hakim al-Tirmidhi', p. 235, i.e., '*annaka anta Allāh lā ilāha illā anta waḥdaka*'.
31. *Biblia Sacra Arabica*, vol. 2, p. 303.
32. For the practice of 'all-night *dhikr*', see Pnina Werbner, '*Du'a*: Popular Culture and Powerful Blessing at the 'Urs' in *South Asian Sufis: Devotion, Deviation, and Destiny*, ed. Clinton Bennett and Charles M. Ramsey (London: Bloomsbury, 2013), pp. 83–94 (p. 87).
33. *Biblia Sacra Arabica*, vol. 2, p. 185.
34. See, for instance, Qur'ān 42:36: '*wa-mā ʿinda Allāhi khayrun wa-abqā lil-ladhīna āmanū wa-ʿalā rabbihim yatawakkalūn*' ('but what is with God is better and more enduring for those who believe and put their trust [*yatawakkalūn*] in their Lord'; Arberry's translation with transliteration added).
35. *Biblia Sacra Arabica*, vol. 2, p. 200.
36. Arberry renders this phrase from Qur'ān 42:19 as 'He is the All-strong, the All-mighty'. For other *āyāt* with these same divine names invoked in tandem, see Qur'ān 22:40 and 22:74.
37. *Biblia Sacra Arabica*, vol. 2, p. 185.
38. This excerpt from Qur'ān 10:3 is rendered by Arberry, with my transliteration inserted. For '*istawā*' implied in 'controversial issues in early Islamic theology', see Mahmoud M. Ayoub, 'Literary Exegesis of the Qur'an: The Case of al-Sharīf al-Raḍī', in *Literary Structures of Religious Meaning in the Qur'an*, ed. Issa J. Boullata (Richmond: Curzon Press, 2000), pp. 292–309 (p. 297).
39. The multivalence of '*istawā*' is suggested by the variety of renditions that it has attracted merely in the context of the *āyāt* which describe God's relation to His 'throne'; see also Christoph Luxenberg, '*Al-Najm* (Q 53), Chapter of the Star: A New Syro-Aramaic Reading of Verses 1–18' in *New Perspectives on the Qur'ān*: The *Qur'ān* in its Historical Context 2, pp. 279–297 (pp. 288–289).
40. *Biblia Sacra Arabica*, vol. 2, p. 276.
41. For '*rakʿa*' and '*sajda*' (or '*sujūd*') as acts of prayerful obeisance portrayed by the Qur'ān, see 2:43 and 50:40, respectively.
42. *Biblia Sacra Arabica*, vol. 2, p. 298.
43. This is Arberry's rendition of this excerpt from Qur'ān 89:27–28, with my transliteration inserted.
44. *Biblia Sacra Arabica*, vol. 2, p. 267.
45. I render '*qaʿr*' (قعر) as 'bottom', but this term could equally suggest 'pit' (the Vulgate's Latin reads as '*inferno inferiori*').
46. For '*jaḥīm*' as occurring twenty-six times in the Qur'ān, and for O'Shaughnessy's theory that this term represents a 'distortion of *jahannam*', see Michael Carter, 'Foreign Vocabulary' in *The Blackwell Companion to the Qur'ān*, ed. Andrew Rippin (Oxford: Blackwell, 2006), pp. 120–139 (p. 137).
47. *Biblia Sacra Arabica*, vol. 2, p. 268.
48. This is Arberry's rendition of the 95:5 with my transliteration inserted.
49. For this title, see the coverpage of George Sale and Sulaymān ibn Yaʿqūb al-Ṣāliḥānī (eds.), *al-ʿAhd al-Jadīd* (London: S.P.C.K., 1727).

50. For the enduring influence of Sale's *Koran*, see Lawrence, *The Koran in English: A Biography*, p. 38, who notes: 'For over 200 years, [Sale's] translation persisted as the longest lasting, most popular, and influential English translation having gone through at least 123 editions in both Britain and the United States up to 1975'. For Sale's involvement with the S.P.C.K.'s 1727 Arabic New Testament see George Sale (trans.), *The Koran: with Explanatory Notes from the Most Approved Commentators* (London: Warne, 1909), p. x: 'it is on the Society's records that on August 30, 1726, [Sale] offered his services as one of the correctors of the Arabic New Testament and soon became the chief worker on it'.
51. See, however, Elmarsafy, *The Enlightenment Qur'an*, pp. 22–23, who does note Sale's work on the S.P.C.K. Arabic bible; mention is not made, however, of Marracci's contribution to the 1671 *Biblia Sacra Arabica*.
52. George Sale (trans.), *The Koran* (1734), pp. vi–vii.
53. See Elmarsafy, *The Enlightenment Qur'an*, which has previously contrasted the 'differences between Sale's and Marracci's approaches to the Qur'ān' with reference to their alternate linguistic, cultural, and religious commitments (p. 63), without, however, treating this specific passage from Sale's 'Preliminary Discourse'.
54. Sale (trans.), *The Koran* (1734), p. 482. I supply the verse numbering in the above, which is absent in Sale's edition.
55. Sale (trans.), *The Koran* (1734), p. 482. Italics in the original; there is also a closing square bracket in the original following the term '*removed*' which has been here excised for the sake of clarity.
56. Elmarsafy has also tracked Sale's critical engagement with Marracci in his 1734 *Koran*'s 'paratexts' (although this specific note to Sūrat al-Takwīr is not addressed). See, for instance, *The Enlightenment Qur'an*, p. 41, where Elmarsafy notes 'Not unexpectedly, Sale's paratexts take aim at Marracci [...]'.

5

'BY ORIGIN AND LANGUAGE AN HEBREW': THE GENESIS OF A JUDAIC QUR'ĀN

I

'THE POSTERITY OF ISMAEL'

> The learned Sale, who first gave the world a genuine version of the Koran, and who had so zealously laboured in forming that 'Universal History' which was the pride of our country, pursued his studies through a life of wants – and this great Orientalist, I grieve to degrade the memoirs of a man of learning by such mortifications, when he quitted his studies, too often wanted a change of linen, and often wandered in the streets in search of some compassionate friend who would supply him with the meal of the day.[1]

Published in 1812, these sentences are submerged in a small-print footnote in *Calamities of Authors* – two volumes of literary wit and worldly wisdom by one of Britain's most celebrated authors of Jewish descent: Isaac D'Israeli (1766–1848). Father of Benjamin Disraeli, who was to become British Prime Minister, Isaac discretely inserted these 'memoirs of a man of learning' in a section ironically entitled 'The Rewards of Oriental Students', memorialising George Sale as an exilic mendicant forced to 'search' through London 'streets' for a 'friend who would supply him with the meal of the day'. Publishing works that would prove to be 'the pride of our country', Sale emerges as a British national treasure, but also a wandering beggar – an indigent Englishman in need of charity, who also graciously 'gave the world a genuine version of the Koran'. Perhaps most intriguing in this portrait of Sale is that it is preserved by Isaac D'Israeli himself – a Jewish author who in 1812 is grappling with his own national and religious identity, eventually electing to break with his synagogue, baptising his children as Christians in the years following his *Calamities of Authors*.[2]

Leading 'a life of wants' – merging vagrant displacement and patriotic neglect – this portrait of the eighteenth century's foremost Qur'ān translator, reported by the nineteenth century's leading Anglo-Jewish author, is intriguing too as it aptly recalls an identity that is essential to Sale's historiography of Islam, namely, that of Ishmael. The archetypal exile, expelled from family and forced to wander, Ishmael occupies a key place in the 'Preliminary Discourse' to Sale's 1734 *Koran*, helping to bridge between Sale's Christian audience and Islamic origins. Not only son of Abraham, but also 'father of the Arabs', the itinerant Ishmael is a peripatetic Hebrew and yet the patriarch 'from whom Muhammad was descended', both belonging within, yet straying beyond, the biblical story. A familiar figure linking biblical beginnings with Islamic origins, Ishmael is aligned by Sale not only with sacred lineages, but also with sacred language; in the middle of his 'Preliminary Discourse' to his 1734 *Koran*, for example, Sale characterises the Ishmaelite background to 'the *Arabs*', declaring that:

> The posterity of *Ismael* have no claim to be admitted as pure *Arabs*; their ancestor being by origin and language an *Hebrew*, but having made an alliance with the *Jorhamites*, by marrying a daughter of *Modad*, and accustomed himself to their manner of living and language, his descendants became blended with them into one nation.[3]

Although the 'ancestor' of the '*Arabs*', Ishmael's marriage to 'a daughter of *Modad*', and his 'alliance with the *Jorhamites*', does not negate his Hebrew 'origin'. Indeed, according to Sale, 'the posterity of *Ismael*' remains Hebraic, having 'no claim' to be called 'pure *Arabs*'. However, it is not merely family, but philology, Sale accents, with Hebraic Ishmael joined genetically, but also verbally, to his Arab descendants. Reflecting Sale's own role as Arabic translator, Ishmael is here portrayed as a biblical outsider who linguistically 'blends' with the Arabs, becoming 'accustomed' not only to 'their manner of living', but also their 'language'. As Sale's 'Preliminary Discourse' develops, it is the Qur'ān's own 'dialect' that becomes increasingly tied to Ishmael's Hebrew 'ancestor[y]', with problems of 'purity' emerging again as Sale addresses the very language of the Prophet and his tribe, 'the *Koreish*':

> The dialect of the *Koreish* is usually termed the *pure Arabic*, or, as the *Korân*, which is written in this dialect, calls it, *the perspicuous* and *clear Arabic*; perhaps, says Dr. *Pocock*, because *Ismael*, their father, brought the *Arabic* he had learned of the *Jorhamites* nearer to the original *Hebrew*.[4]

Recalling the introduction to Marracci's own *Alcoran*, it is '[Edward] *Pocock*' that again surfaces in another *Koran* preface, with Sale reaching back to his own British forbearer, even as he once more addresses the 'father' of the Arabs, 'Ismael'. Perhaps more importantly, however, 'Dr. *Pocock*' is ascribed a startling claim by Sale concerning the Qur'ān's 'dialect', the scripture deriving its linguistic 'purity' from kinship with biblical idioms. For Pococke, the '*perspicuous* and *clear*' quality of the Qur'ān's Arabic arises from its being 'brought nearer to the original *Hebrew*'. Consistent with his Hebraic 'origin and language', Ishmael again forms a linguistic and lineal bridge between biblical patriarchy and Muslim posterity, infusing his native Hebrew into 'the *Arabic* he had learned', which eventually culminates in the '*Korân*' itself.

Sourced from 'Dr. *Pocock*', this biblical genealogy for both Arab descendants and Arabic 'dialect' is subsequently questioned by Sale himself, who prefers instead to trace the linguistic 'pur[ity]' of the Qur'ān back to the Koreish's custody of the '*Caaba*', as well as his tribe's residence 'in *Mecca*'.[5] However, Hebraic precedents continue to shape Sale's 'Preliminary Discourse' even as he turns attention from Ishmael's impact on Islamic language to consider the language that defines Islam's scripture itself. Parsing the very title of the Qur'ān, it is again Judaic 'origins' that seem uppermost in Sale's mind:

> The word *Korân*, derived from the verb *karaa, to read*, signifies properly in *Arabic*, *the reading*, or rather, *that which ought to be read*; by which name the *Mohammedans* denote not only the entire book or volume of the *Korân*, but also any particular chapter or section of it; just as the *Jews* call either the whole scripture, or any part of it by the name of *Karâh*, or *Mikra*, words of the same origin and import.[6]

In light of Sale's prior link between 'original *Hebrew*' and 'pure *Arabic*', it is perhaps unsurprising to find Hebraic precedents invoked as Sale explains the very name of the Muslim scripture. First expounding its Arabic etymology, 'the word *Korân*' is immediately contextualised Hebraically, Sale likening the title 'Qur'ān' to '*Karâh*, or *Mikra*' – terms applied by 'Jews' to their own 'scripture'. Identified as 'words of the same origin and import', Sale's appeal to these Semitic analogues is entirely consistent with the 'Ishmaelite' contexts he outlines for the Qur'ān throughout his 'Preliminary Discourse'. However, in highlighting these Hebrew equivalents for 'the word *Korân*' – that is, '*Karâh*, or *Mikra*' – Sale could not possibly have anticipated that he was also setting a precedent for the Qur'ān's actual appearance in Hebrew, laying foundations in his 1734 'Preliminary Discourse' for the very first Jewish translation of the Muslim scripture, which would appear over a century later. A pioneering act of Islamic reception, surprisingly often overlooked by contemporary critics, it was in 1857 that a four-hundred page volume appeared in Leipzig under the title *al-Qōrān ō ha-Miqrā* – a comprehensive Hebrew rendition of the Qur'ān whose very title echoes the cognate term suggested by Sale: '*Mikra*' (*miqrā*).[7] Memorialised by Isaac D'Israeli as 'giv[ing] the world a genuine version of the Koran', it is Sale who also helps inspire yet another nineteenth-century Jewish author to 'give the world' a 'version of the Koran' in Hebrew. Treated in detail for the first time in the following chapter, the 1857 *al-Qōrān ō ha-Miqrā* not only implicitly echoes Sale in its title, however, but explicitly invokes Sale in its very text, with his 1734 *Koran*'s 'Preliminary Discourse' and its interests in 'the original Hebrew' resurfacing to appear in the initial pages of the first Hebrew Qur'ān.[8]

II

JEWISH 'FATHERS' AND A HEBREW *FĀTIḤA*

הקוראן*
אלקראן (התקרא) הוא הספר אמר לדעת הישמעאלים נגלה מהמלאך גבריאל אל מחמד...

The Qur'ān*
Al-Qorān ('the reading'), this is the book which, it is said according to the Ishmaelites, was revealed by the angel Gabriel to Muḥammad (...)[9]

The above passage appears in the Preface to the 1857 *al-Qōrān ō ha-Miqrā*, inaugurating a section dedicated to defining the very term 'Qur'ān' itself.[10] Opening with a Hebrew transliteration, 'הקוראן' (*ha-Qōran*), this introductory section offers Jewish readers not only a familiar, but a familial, genealogy for Islam's scripture, recording its 'revela[tion]' via 'Gabriel', but also its interpretation by 'the Ishmaelites' (הישמעאלים): a term for 'Muslims' that again accents not creedal boundaries, but biblical kinship.[11] Recalling Sale, it is Ishmael and his legacy that is once more linked to Islamic origins, with the Qur'ān heralding a discrete faith, yet tied to the same Abrahamic family shared by Jewish readers. Invoking 'the posterity of Ishmael' within another Qur'ānic preface, the above section not only overlaps Sale's own 'Preliminary Discourse', however, but also situates Sale himself as an explicit precedent. Appended to 'the Qur'ān' at the top of this brief passage is an asterisk directing readers down to the bottom of the Hebrew page, where a simple English footnote is found that reads 'Sale, Prel. Disc. 56–122'.[12]

In the first pages of the first Hebrew Qur'ān, the Hebrew term for 'Qur'ān' itself points back to '[George] Sale' and his 'Prel[iminary] Disc[ourse]'. Framing the Muslim scripture in biblical terms in his 1734 translation, Sale himself is invoked to frame the Muslim scripture even as it first appears in the Bible's own original language.[13] Aptly invoking Sale's *Koran* at its Hebrew opening, *al-Qōrān ō ha-Miqrā*'s appeal to England's 'great Orientalist' also seems somewhat ironic, however, considering their contrasting fame; unlike Sale's 1734 translation, celebrated by D'Israeli as the 'first [...] genuine version' given to 'the world', the 1857 *al-Qōrān ō ha-Miqrā* has been altogether forgotten, despite itself qualifying as genuinely unprecedented. Linked in their forewords, the afterlives of these two

Qur'ānic translations, and their translators, are entirely inverse; while Sale has been remembered and referenced for centuries, *al-Qōrān ō ha-Miqrā* has largely been lost to history, as has the name of the 'pioneer[ing]' figure behind its production: Tzvi Chaim 'Hermann' Reckendorf (1825–1875).[14]

Jewish author and German orientalist, Hermann Reckendorf's present-day obscurity seems especially surprising in light of the influence he enjoyed during his own age, not only well-connected to scholarly coteries from Halle to Heidelberg, but also well read by Jewish contemporaries across Europe.[15] Rising through university ranks, first in Leipzig, and then in Heidelberg, Reckendorf's career led him to lecture on 'oriental languages' alongside Gustav Weil, fellow Jewish Orientalist and author of the prominent prophetic biography, *Mohammed der Prophet, sein Leben und seine Lehre* (1843).[16] Appearing in 1857, while still in Leipzig, Reckendorf's own Hebrew *al-Qōrān* also shared its year of publication with the work for which he was primarily known, the five-volume *Die Geheimnisse der Juden* (1856–7) – a 'historical novel' that not only 'tells the tale of the descendants of King David', but also reflects Reckendorf's Islamic interests, featuring fictional vignettes of 'Jewish history' that integrate quotations from the Qur'ān.[17] Although overshadowed by his own concurrent and colossal *Geheimnisse der Juden*, Reckendorf's 1857 *al-Qōrān ō ha-Miqrā* yet merited immediate attention from Jewish peers such as Moritz Steinschneide. Born nearly a decade before Reckendorf, Steinschneide was another German orientalist who had long contemplated publishing a Hebrew Qur'ān, but elected to 'abando[n]' his own 'project upon the appearance of Hermann Reckendorf's Hebrew translation'.[18] Discouraging elder competitors, Reckendorf also offered encouragement to younger successors, and especially his own son and namesake, Hermann Reckendorf Jr. (1863–1923), who also pursued a prominent career in Middle Eastern studies. Born in Heidelberg, Reckendorf Jr. not only followed in his father's footsteps, but surpassed him in fame, producing a seminal study of Arabic syntax in 1921, as well as a work centred on the Prophet's own family, published in 1907 as *Mohammed und die Seinen*.[19]

Surrounded by domestic legacies, Judaic and Islamic, Hermann Reckendorf's 1857 *al-Qōrān* itself opens with paternal concerns and familial contexts, featuring a preface that reaches not forward to his future son, but back to his revered father. While Jewish antiquity played a prominent role in Sale's preface to his *Koran*, Reckendorf introduces his own *al-Qōrān* by invoking a more immediate and personal Jewish past; rather than Hebrew ancestry in general, Reckendorf's rendition instead opens with his actual ancestor and Hebrew instructor, his father, Shlomo Reckendorf. In the leading pages to *al-Qōrān*, Reckendorf's readers find first not the Fātiḥa, but instead a prose epigraph and three-page poem dedicated to Shlomo

Reckendorf, who is honoured as Reckendorf's 'dear father' (*'Avī Hayyaqar*).[20] Celebrating his father's preservation of Judaic traditions, Reckendorf memorialises Shlomo first and foremost, however, for his 'teaching' the 'Torah', passing on this sacred text to the 'children of Judah' (*bənei Yəhūdāh*).[21] At the outset to his Muslim translation, it is biblical transmission that forms the intimate focus of Reckendorf's *al-Qōrān*; commencing in Hebrew for the first time in 1857, the Qur'ān surprisingly opens by commemorating Jewish family and faith, with Hebrew pedagogy and paternity highlighted at the opening to Islamic prophecy.

Prefacing his Hebrew Qur'ān with a poem to his own Jewish father, the actual body text of Reckendorf's *al-Qōrān* also opens with a poetic chapter that engages Jewish fathers. In the very first verses that he renders into Hebrew, it is Hebraic history that Reckendorf emphasises, translating the Qur'ān's introductory chapter – the Fātiḥa – in full as follows:

בשם אלה הרחמן והרחום

(א) השבח לאלה רב העולמים. (ב) הרחמן והרחום. (ג) מלך ביום הדין. (ד) אותך נעבד ואליך נשוע. (ה) הורנו דרך המישרים ארחותיהם. (ו) דרך האנשים אשר חנות אותם. (ז) ולא דרך מכעיסיך ולא דרך התועים.

In the name of God, the Merciful, and the Compassionate

i) Praise be to God, the Lord of the worlds. ii) the merciful, and the compassionate. iii) the king upon the Day of Judgement. iv) Thee do we worship, and unto Thee do we supplicate. v) Show us the path of those straight of ways. vi) the path of people who have been favoured. vii) And not the path of those provoking Thee to anger, and not the path of those who are astray[22]

In the 'Preliminary Discourse' to his 1734 *Koran*, George Sale had posited a kinship between biblical and Qur'ānic traditions, invoking Ishmael as a common link between Hebrew and Arab ancestries. In this preliminary chapter to Reckendorf's *al-Qōrān*, a linguistic kinship between Hebrew and Arabic is not merely theorised, but actually exhibited, with original Qur'ānic terms surviving almost unaltered in Judaic rendition. Practically performing bonds between sister Semitic languages, Arabic roots are repeated in Reckendorf's Hebrew, beginning with his *basmala*, which seems almost a transliteration, rather than a translation, of its Qur'ānic original, the two appearing together in Table 5.1, with Arabic in the lefthand column, and Hebrew in the righthand column.

Although shifted in script, the sounds of Arabic stay largely stable in Hebrew, the *basmala* altering very little as it enters a biblical idiom. Rather than an '*antonomasia*' – an 'instead naming', à la Marracci – the Qur'ān's translation into Hebrew allows for a literal retaining of 'the name', with the scripture's very first Arabic word *bismi* (بِسْمِ ; in the name) paralleled by the same letters of Hebrew's own 'in the name' (בשם ; *bəshem*).[23] Additional original phrases from the Fātiḥa also easily fit Hebrew form; rendering 'Lord of the worlds', for instance, Reckendorf is able simply to replace the Arabic's *rabb al-ʿālamīn* with the very similar sounding Hebrew *rabb ha-ʿōlamīm*.

بِسْمِ اللَّهِ الرَّحْمَٰنِ الرَّحِيمِ	בשם אלה הרחמן והרחום
bismi Allāh al-Raḥmān al-Raḥīm	*bəshem Eloah ha-Raḥmān va-ha-Raḥōm*

Table 5.1. The *basmala* in original Arabic and as translated into Hebrew in Hermann Reckendorf's 1857 *al-Qōrān*.

It is not only kinship with the Hebrew language, but a critique of his own Hebraic lineage, however, that Reckendorf finds as he renders the Fātiḥa. Typically understood as the 'Mother of the Book', the Qur'ān's first chapter also implies Jewish fathers according to Reckendorf, who translates and annotates the Fātiḥa's final verse with diction that is distinctly biblical. Below is Reckendorf's Hebrew version of the first words to the Fātiḥa's seventh *āya*, as well as the footnote which he adds, contextualising the 'paths' of the people who have deviated from divine favour:

(ז) ולא דרך מכעיסיך*

*אלו היהודים אשר הכעיסו אל במעלליהם.

vii) And not the path of those provoking Thee to anger,*

*These are the Jews who provoked God with their deeds[24]

In this opening to the Fātiḥa's final verse as rendered by Reckendorf, a single word stands out as intriguing. While the Qur'ān's original Arabic had condemned those with whom Allah is 'angered' (ٱلْمَغْضُوب), Reckendorf's Hebrew reprimands those 'provoking Thee to anger' (מכעיסיך), preferring an active and causative form, rather than passive participle.[25] As evidenced in the quotation above, however, this replacement itself 'provokes' a paratext, Reckendorf offering his readers a footnote that parses his own Hebrew expression, explaining that it gestures specifically to 'the Jews who provoked God with their deeds'. Integrating into the Qur'ān a biblical idiom to reference the recalcitrant Israelites, Reckendorf's own Hebrew rendition, that is, 'מכעיסיך' (provoking Thee to anger) recalls verses such as 1 Kings 14:15, where this same participle is used, surfacing in close proximity to the Jewish 'fathers', whose progeny have angered 'the LORD':

וְהִכָּה יְהוָה אֶת־יִשְׂרָאֵל כַּאֲשֶׁר יָנוּד הַקָּנֶה בַּמַּיִם וְנָתַשׁ אֶת־יִשְׂרָאֵל מֵעַל הָאֲדָמָה הַטּוֹבָה הַזֹּאת
אֲשֶׁר נָתַן לַאֲבוֹתֵיהֶם וְזֵרָם מֵעֵבֶר לַנָּהָר יַעַן אֲשֶׁר עָשׂוּ אֶת־אֲשֵׁרֵיהֶם מַכְעִיסִים אֶת־יְהוָה׃

For the LORD shall smite Israel, as a reed is shaken in the water, and he shall root up Israel out of this good land, which he gave to their fathers, and shall scatter them beyond the river, because they have made their groves, provoking the LORD to anger.[26]

Building from such biblical precedents, Reckendorf infuses a 'provocative' Hebrew participle into the Muslim scripture, recalling in his Qurʾān rendition this earlier usage from 1 Kings, where the very same verbal idiom appears, i.e. 'מַכְעִיסִים' (*makh'īsīm* ; 'provoking'). Fashioning a Qurʾānic critique of the Israelites that ironically echoes their own scriptures, Reckendorf finds in Jewish revelation a reprimand of the Jewish people that also fits his rendered Hebrew Fātiḥa. First dedicating the Qurʾān to his own 'dear father' – his own beloved 'teacher' of 'Torah' – Reckendorf soon inserts into the Qurʾān's very opening a Hebrew Bible censure of the ancient Hebrew 'fathers', with this self-reflective Judaic usage surprisingly mirrored in the Muslim scripture even as it is offered for the first time to a Jewish readership.

III

ALLĀH HA-'ELYŌN

Opening with Hebrew verses dedicated to his father, Reckendorf sets a poetic precedent for his *al-Qōrān* that echoes throughout this 'pioneering' translation. Reflecting the Muslim scripture's own innate 'poeticity', Reckendorf regularly endows his rendition with assonance, relying again on the kinship between Hebrew and Arabic, with these two Semitic languages sharing not only roots, but able to sustain similar rhymes. Consider, for example, verses 8 to 10 from Sūrat al-Balad, whose Arabic original is compared with Reckendorf's Hebrew version, which follow below:

أَلَمْ نَجْعَلْ لَهُ عَيْنَيْنِ وَلِسَانًا وَشَفَتَيْنِ وَهَدَيْنَاهُ النَّجْدَيْنِ
Have We not appointed to him two eyes (*ʿaynayn*),
and a tongue, and two lips (*shafatayn*),
and guided him on the two highways (*al-najdayn*)?

הלא נתנו לו עינים, לשון ושפתים, ונורהו את שתי הדרכים?
Have we not given to him two eyes (*ʿeynāyim*)
and a tongue, and two lips (*səfāṭayim*),
and guided him to two paths (*ha-dərākayim*)?[27]

Capitalising on corresponding morphologies, Arabic rhymes are mirrored in Reckendorf's version, the Qur'ān's own line endings in '*ayn*' are echoed in the recurring final syllable of '*ayim*' in Hebrew. Derived from a dual form shared by Semitic languages, Reckendorf offers his readers a sonorous repetition that itself repeats the Qur'ān's own euphony, allowing Sūrat al-Balad in both languages to speak with a similar 'tongue', its 'two lips' resonating with rhyme equally in Hebrew as in Arabic.[28]

It is not solely simple rhyme that suggests Reckendorf's poetic priorities in his Hebrew *al-Qōrān*, however, but also his appeal to psalmic conventions. Recalling translators already treated in this study – Ḥafṣ al-Qūṭī and Ludovici Marracci – Reckendorf establishes links between the Hebrew psalter and the Qur'ān; however, unlike al-Qūṭī and Marracci, Reckendorf is unmediated by an intervening language, working not through Latin psalmody, but rendering instead the Qur'ān directly into psalmic Hebrew. In the first verse of yet another short *sūra*, for instance, Reckendorf implicitly echoes terms typical of the psalter, offering the following for the opening *āya* of Sūra 87, that is, Sūrat al-A'lā:

חזון העליון
(א) הלל את שם אדונך העליון!
Chapter of the Most High (*ha-'Elyōn*)
i) Praise (*hallel*) the name of thy Lord, the Most High (*ha-'Elyōn*)[29]

Recalling several psalms, this *sūra* starts with its own *hallelujah*, voicing an imperative that begins multiple biblical chapters, that is, *hallel* (הלל ; praise!). Opening with the same command in the singular that commences Psalms such as 113 and 150 in the plural, Reckendorf's first verse to Sūra 87 also ends with an epithet typical of the Bible, designating '*Allāh*' as '*ha-'Elyōn*' (העליון ; Most High).[30] Cognate to the Qur'ān's own original term and title – that is, '*al-A'lā*' (الْأَعْلَى) – the Hebrew ''*Elyōn*' offers a suitable fit for Sūra 87; however, it is also a divine name that recalls psalmic passages such as the very first verse of Psalm 92:

טוֹב, לְהֹדוֹת לַיהוָה; וּלְזַמֵּר לְשִׁמְךָ עֶלְיוֹן.
It is a good thing to give thanks unto the Lord,
and to sing praises unto thy name, O Most High (*'Elyōn*)[31]

Psalm 92 opens by invoking directly the 'Most High' (*'Elyōn*), pledging to 'give praise' to 'thy name' ('*shimkha*'); in Reckendorf's rendition, Sūra 87 similarly launches with a second-person appeal, encouraging the reader to 'praise the name of thy Lord, the Most High' (*shem 'Adōnkha ha-'Elyōn*). Fashioning a first verse to Sūrat al-A'lā that follows psalmic conventions, from its directive to 'praise' to its divine 'name', Reckendorf rewrites Qur'ānic poeticity with biblical psalmody, opening *sūra*s such as 87 with lines that sound as much like a Hebrew *hallelujah* as an Islamic *āya*.

Infusing his translation with psalmic accents, the psalter itself frequently surfaces as an explicit subject of Reckendorf's rendition. As noted in Chapter 1 above, the 'psalms' (*zabūr*) are named in several *sūra*s, challenging Reckendorf to translate into Hebrew the Qur'ān's references to this Hebrew book.[32] Nearing the finale of the Qur'ān's fourth chapter, for instance, the verses 'given' by God to 'David' are listed among the foregoing revelations, with the following passage stretching from the end of this chapter's *āya* 163 to its *āya* 164:

وَآتَيْنَا دَاوُودَ زَبُوراً
وَرُسُلا قَدْ قَصَصْنَاهُمْ عَلَيْكَ مِنْ قَبْلُ وَرُسُلا لَمْ نَقْصُصْهُمْ عَلَيْكَ وَكَلَّمَ اللَّهُ مُوسَى تَكْلِيمًا
and We gave to David Psalms (*zabūr*);
and Messengers We have already told thee of before,
and Messengers We have not told thee of; and unto Moses God spoke directly[33]

From the later 'Messengers' to the earlier ones, this passage retreats back from 'David' to 'Moses', with other prophets – both known and unknown – anonymously cited in-between. Rather than a literal rendition of this source, however, Reckendorf instead offers a truncated translation, while also elaborating in Hebrew on the most Hebraic elements offered in these Qur'ānic verses:

גם נתנו לדוד את זמירות ישראל. במשה דבר אלהים פה אל פה.
We also gave to David the Songs of Israel (*Zəmīrōt Yisrael*).
With Moses, God spoke mouth to mouth[34]

Although the Qur'ān's original *āyāt* had mentioned other 'Messengers' – including those 'We have not told thee of' – Reckendorf himself suppresses this revelatory silence, cutting the scripture's own references to additional prophets.[35] Transitioning in his translation directly from 'David' to 'Moses', Reckendorf not only refuses to relay the Qur'ān's mentioning of untold 'Messengers', but also further specifies the Qur'ān's references to Hebrew revelations. Rather than the single Arabic word '*zabūr*' (psalms), Reckendorf instead offers the full Hebrew phrase 'זמירות ישראל' (*Zəmīrōt Yisrael* ; Songs of Israel), a phrase entirely absent from the Qur'ān, but which claims a biblical background, surfacing in the final chapter to David's story in 2 Samuel, with his 'last words' introduced in 2 Samuel 23:1:

וְאֵלֶּה דִּבְרֵי דָוִד, הָאַחֲרֹנִים: נְאֻם דָּוִד בֶּן-יִשַׁי, וּנְאֻם הַגֶּבֶר הֻקַם עָל--מְשִׁיחַ אֱלֹהֵי יַעֲקֹב,
וּנְעִים זְמִרוֹת יִשְׂרָאֵל.

Now these *be* the last words of David. David the son of Jesse said, and the man *who was* raised up on high, the anointed of the God of Jacob, and the Darling of the Songs of Israel (*Zəmirōt Yisrael*)[36]

Precisely the same phrase recruited by Reckendorf for his Qur'ānic rendition, '*Zəmirōt Yisrael*' originally appears here in the very first verse to 2 Samuel 23, defining David as 'the Darling of the Songs of Israel' even as he nears his death. Rewriting Qur'ān 4:163 with a phrase from 2 Samuel, Reckendorf's *al-Qōrān* perhaps most importantly adds a domestic adjective to David's psalmic revelation; qualifying his 'songs' with 'Israel' (יִשְׂרָאֵל), Reckendorf repatriates David's poems, reaffirming their Judaic origins within Islam's own scripture. It is not this description of David alone, however, but the 'direct' exchange between God and Moses that receives a biblical rendition in Reckendorf's translation above. Replacing the concise Qur'ānic phrase '*wa-kallama Allāhu Mūsā taklīman*' (and unto Moses God spoke directly), Reckendorf instead offers:

במשה דבר אלהים פה אל פה
With Moses, God (*Elohīm*) spoke mouth to mouth (*peh 'el peh*)[37]

Replacing the Qur'ān's '*Allāh*' with Hebrew '*Elohīm*', it is Reckendorf's gloss that he adds to God's speech that seems most intriguing, inserting an 'anthropomorphic' phrase that is absent from his Arabic original. According to Reckendorf's rendition, Moses and God spoke '*peh 'el peh*' (lit., 'mouth to mouth') – a Hebrew synecdoche often understood to suggest 'face to face'.[38] Accenting their intimacy, this phrase implies not only Moses's familiarity with God, however, but Reckendorf's own familiarity with the Hebrew Bible, this three-word sequence claiming origins in passages such as Numbers 12:8, where God and Moses are again aligned 'mouth to mouth', with 'the Lord' Himself asserting:

פֶּה אֶל־פֶּה אֲדַבֶּר־בּוֹ וּמַרְאֶה וְלֹא בְחִידֹת וּתְמֻנַת יְהוָה יַבִּיט
Mouth to mouth (*peh 'el peh*) with him (Moses) will I (God) speak, even apparently, and not in dark speeches; and the similitude of the LORD shall he behold[39]

Expressing their 'apparent' relationship, this Torah passage prioritises the openness of divine-human exchange, starting with precisely the same phrase Reckendorf recruits to characterise Moses in the Qur'ān, that is, 'mouth to mouth' (*peh 'el peh*). Appealing to precedents such as Numbers 12:8, in which God communicates with man 'mouth to mouth', rather than via 'dark speeches', Reckendorf himself secretly borrows a biblical depiction for intimate Qur'ānic dialogue, indirectly exchanging Judaic idiom for Islamic original, even as he renders a passage that accents exchange that is open and direct. A label for sacred speech that passes from God to his prophet, the idiom '*peh 'el peh*' itself passes between discrete traditions of the sacred, Reckendorf placing two canons of scripture in confrontation in order to portray Moses's own coming face to face with his Lord.

IV

YESHŪ BEN MIRYAM

Although often able to domesticate Qur'ānic characters with biblical qualifications, Reckendorf is also challenged by terms in his Arabic source that have no easy Hebrew substitutes. In the very title of Sūra 72, for instance, Reckendorf is required to derive a Judaic rendition for 'the *jinn*' (الجن) prompting him to offer the following Hebrew heading and first verses for his own Sūrat al-Jinn, which appears below after the original Arabic of Qur'ān 72:1–4:

سورة الجن
بِسْمِ اللهِ الرَّحْمٰنِ الرَّحِيْمِ
قُلْ أُوحِيَ إِلَيَّ أَنَّهُ اسْتَمَعَ نَفَرٌ مِّنَ الْجِنِّ فَقَالُوا إِنَّا سَمِعْنَا قُرْآنًا عَجَبًا (1) يَهْدِي إِلَى الرُّشْدِ فَآمَنَّا بِهِ
وَلَن نُّشْرِكَ بِرَبِّنَا أَحَدًا (2) وَأَنَّهُ تَعَالَىٰ جَدُّ رَبِّنَا مَا اتَّخَذَ صَاحِبَةً وَلَا وَلَدًا (3)
Sūrat al-Jinn
In the Name of God, the Merciful, the Compassionate
1) Say: 'It has been revealed to me that a company of the *jinn* gave ear, then they said, "We have indeed heard a Koran wonderful, 2) guiding to rectitude. We believe in it, and we will not associate with our Lord anyone. 3) He – exalted be our Lord's majesty! – has not taken to Himself either consort or a son

חזון השדים
בשם אלה הרחמן והרחום.
(א) אמור: הוגד לי, כי צבא שדים הקשיב לקולי ויאמרו: הן שמענו את הקוראן הנשגב!
(ב) הוא ידריכנו אל מעגל יושר; מאמינים אנחנו בו, ולא נדמה לאלהינו אלהי נכר! (ג)
אדונינו, ברוך שם כבודו, לא נשא אשה ולא הוליד בנים;
The Chapter of the *Shedīm*
In the Name of God, the Merciful, and the Compassionate
1) Say: 'It has been revealed to me that a company of the *shedīm* listened to my word, then they said, "Behold, We have heard a sublime Qur'ān! 2) It guides us to a straight path. We are believers in it, and we will not bring into comparison with our God foreign gods! 3) Our Lord, blessed be His glorious name, He married not a wife, nor beget sons.[40]

Reckendorf's Hebrew revisions to Sūra 72 start in its very title, replacing the Qur'ān's eponymous '*Jinn*' with 'The Chapter of *Shedīm*', that is, 'שדים' (devils). Accurately implying the otherworldly origins of the *jinn*, this Hebrew substitute yet adjusts their genealogy, offering a biblical background for these Qur'ānic creatures, while also making more concrete their moral character. A term typically understood as implying the demonic, '*shedīm*' appears in biblical books that span the entire Tanakh, used as a designation for 'devils', surfacing in verses such as Deuteronomy 32:17 and Psalm 106:37, which read below respectively:

יִזְבְּחוּ לַשֵּׁדִים לֹא אֱלֹהַ

They sacrificed unto devils (*shedīm*), not to God

וַיִּזְבְּחוּ אֶת בְּנֵיהֶם וְאֶת בְּנוֹתֵיהֶם לַשֵּׁדִים

they sacrificed their sons and their daughters unto devils (*shedīm*)[41]

Instead of the '*jinn*' – characters in the Qur'ān who are considered 'morally ambiguous' – the Bible's '*shedīm*' are decidedly diabolic, not only challenging divine sovereignty, but even demanding human 'sacrifices'.[42] Appealing to a term that is fantastic, yet also biblically familiar, Reckendorf's '*shedīm*' not only domesticates, but demonises, the Qur'ān's invisible creatures, making visible only their evil, while erasing any 'benevolent' potential in the *jinn*.[43] And yet, in close proximity to this devilish term, a pious doxology is also voiced in Reckendorf's rendition of Sūra 72, the first words of the last verse quoted above comprises a classic Hebrew blessing. Instead of the Arabic 'exalted be our Lord's majesty!', Reckendorf offers 'ברוך שם כבודו' (*bārūkh shem cəvōdō*; blessed be His glorious name), another phrase that builds from biblical precedents, based in pivotal passages such as this final verse to Psalm 72:

וּבָרוּךְ שֵׁם כְּבוֹדוֹ לְעוֹלָם וְיִמָּלֵא כְבוֹדוֹ אֶת כֹּל הָאָרֶץ אָמֵן וְאָמֵן

And blessed be his glorious name (ū-*vārūkh shem cəvōdō*) for ever and let the whole earth be filled with his glory; Amen, and Amen.[44]

Echoing this conclusion to Psalm 72 in his introduction to Sūra 72, Reckendorf balances out the devilish implications of the '*shedīm*' by blessing the divine '*shem*' (שם ; name), colouring biblically both the dark and light shades of this Qur'ānic chapter concerning the 'unseen' *jinn*.

Although sourced from an alternate scripture, this second biblical import into Sūra 72 seems theologically apt, lending a Judaic benediction to the 'Chapter of the *Jinn*' even as this same *sūra* affirms God's oneness and denies Him a 'wife' or 'sons' – Muslim beliefs which are, of course, entirely shared by Reckendorf and his Jewish readers. Indeed, the monotheism of Chapter 72 is magnified by Reckendorf via another biblical borrowing; rather than the *jinn*'s original pledge not to 'associate with our Lord anyone', the *shedīm* in Reckendorf's rendition instead abjure all 'foreign gods' ('*Ēlōhei nēkhār*') – an idiom which is itself 'foreign' to the Qur'ān, but entirely original to the Torah, where this very same phrase is also used to critique polytheism.[45] Accenting in translation Judaic ties with the Qur'ān, Reckendorf's rendition also implicitly resists the dominant religion of its own land of publication, his Hebrew *al-Qōrān* appearing in Christian Leipzig even as it also refuses that God has a 'son'. Agreeing with his Arabian source in denying the dominant creed of his European homeland, Reckendorf discovers in the Qur'ān a surrogate resistance to Christian tenets – a complex continuity between Islamic text and Jewish translator that seems especially urgent as Reckendorf comes to render *sūra*s that address Jesus specifically. Transitioning forward in testaments, it is the Gospels, not the Hebrew Bible, that are evoked in Qur'ānic chapters such as Sūrat Maryam (Sūra 19) which recounts not only Jesus's nativity, but also narrates Mary's return to her family. Facing questions concerning her newborn baby, Mary gestures to her son, leading the Qur'ān to report Jesus's first miraculous words – a passage rendered into Hebrew by Reckendorf as follows, starting with the accusatory words of Mary's family who address her with a curious epithet:

> (ל) אחות אהרון! אביך לא היה בליעל, ואמך לא היתה זונה! (לא) ותבט אל הילד; ויאמרו: איך נדבר אל ילד רך וקטון? (לב) ויאמר הילד: אני עבד ד'; הוא נתן לי כתב וישימני לנביא. (לג) ויצו אתי את ברכתו בכל אשר אהיה, ויצוני להתפלל אליו ולחון דלים כל ימי חיי. (לד) שלום על יום הולדי ושלום על יום מותי ושלום על יום הקיצי מעפר. (לה) זה ישו בן מרים; דברי אמת, גם אם הם מריבים בו. (לו) לא לאלהים להוליד בן; חלילה לו! אם יגזר אומר ויאמר: יהי! ויהי.

> (30) Sister of Aaron! Thy father was not a wicked man, nor was thy mother a fornicator! (31) And she (Mary) looked to the child; but they said, 'How should we speak with a child, tender and little?' (32) And the child said, 'I am the slave of G-D; He gave me writings, and made me a prophet (33) And He has appointed to me His blessing wherever I am; and He has enjoined me to pray to Him, and to charity all the days of my life. (34) Peace be upon the day of my birth and peace be upon the day of my death and peace be upon the day of resurrection from the earth.' (35) That is *Yeshū ben Miryam*; words of truth, even if they dispute him. (36) It is not for *Elohīm* to beget a son. Far be He from it! When He decrees a matter, thus he says: Let there be! and it was[46]

Opening with a direct address to Mary herself, Reckendorf's first rendered verse above invokes Jesus's mother not by her specific name, but by a familial phrase. Rather than her own name, Mary's community calls her 'sister of Aaron' (i.e., *āḥōt Aharōn*), a Hebrew substitute that closely follows the Qur'ān's original Arabic (*ukht Hārūn*; sister of Aaron).[47] Oft-debated, this phrase is frequently seen as a marker of Mary's tribe, rather than suggesting a literal sibling relationship, identifying Mary as Aaron's distant descendant, as a 'sister' in his Levite lineage. For readers of Reckendorf's translation, however, Mary's label as 'sister of Aaron' is especially confusing, as her Hebrew name is indeed exactly the same as the name of Aaron's actual sister, that is, Miriam.[48] While English distinguishes between New Testament 'Mary' and Old Testament 'Miriam' – between the mother of Jesus in the Gospels, and the sister of Aaron first named in Exodus – no such distinction is available in Hebrew, both female figures from the two testaments named identically as 'מרים' (*Miryam*). Reckendorf himself recognises this confusion, prompting the translator to append a footnote to his Hebrew phrase, explaining the Qur'ān's surprising usage – that is, 'sister of Aaron' – as non-literal, asserting:

> וקצת מפרשי הישמעלים עלו בסכלותם כל כך לאמר, כי מרים אחות משה ואהרן ומרים אם ישו גוף אחר היו!!!
>
> And some of the Ishmaelite exegetes were so foolish to say that *Miryam*, sister of Moses and Aaron, and *Miryam*, mother of Jesus, were (actually) one and the same!!![49]

Although annotations are common in his *al-Qōrān*, this Hebrew annotation by Reckendorf is uniquely exclamatory, punctuating his paratext with three exclamation marks in order to accent the supposed 'foolishness' of equating 'Mary' with 'Miriam'. Mocking the error of 'some' Muslim 'exegetes', Reckendorf signals his scorn. However, even as he derides Muslims who identify two Hebrew figures as 'one and the same', Reckendorf himself identifies Muslims again with a Hebraic label – 'Ishmaelite' – situating Qur'ānic 'exegetes' as sibling members within the 'same' family of Abraham shared by Reckendorf and his readers.

Querying the confusion caused by the Qur'ān's epithet for Mary, it is her Messianic son whose identity is most at stake in Reckendorf's version of Sūrat Maryam. In both the body text and footnote annotation quoted above, Jesus's own name is intriguingly altered by Reckendorf. Rather than offer the full Hebrew name for 'Jesus', that is, '*Yeshūa'*' (יֵשׁוּעַ) or '*Yəhōshua'*' (יְהוֹשֻׁעַ), etymologically implying 'God saves' – Reckendorf instead identifies Mary's son as '*Yeshū*' (ישו), an abbreviation lacking such divine significance. Sounding somewhat similar to the Qur'ān's own two-syllable name for Jesus, that is, '*'Īsā*' (عيسى), Reckendorf's shortened '*Yeshū*' also enables him to stay faithful to his own religious tradition, subtly resisting Christian views of Jesus as being the one who 'saves' (יֵשׁוּעַ).[50] Avoiding etymologic equation of Christ with divine 'salvation', Reckendorf's shortened '*Yeshū*' also has rabbinic precedents, with this same moniker appearing in early Judaic literatures to contend against Christian claims for Jesus.[51] '*Yeshū*' is not, however, the only abbreviation in Reckendorf's above rendition that serves to merge Judaic monotheism with the Muslim scripture. The very first words of Jesus quoted in the Qur'ān's Chapter 19, that is, 'I am the slave of Allah' (*innī ʿabdu Allāh*), are translated into Hebrew by Reckendorf as:

אני עבד ד'
I am the slave of G-D[52]

Consistent with the Qurʾān, Reckendorf's rendition expresses Jesus's subservience to God; however, this Hebrew version amplifies Jesus's subordination, reverentially refusing even to voice God's name: 'Jehovah'. Reflecting Judaic conventions, the sacred tetragrammaton is euphemistically suppressed in Hebrew, Reckendorf supplying not 'Jehovah' but substituting instead ''ד' – an abbreviation that signals, but does not spell out, this most holy identity.[53] Distinguished from the divine, *Yeshū* also refrains from even speaking the divine name, with Reckendorf's 'Jesus' not only shortened in Hebrew, but also appealing to God with a pious Hebrew ellipsis.

Withholding sacred letters to stay within his own tradition, Reckendorf's translation also echoes his own sacred text in order to Judaically contextualise the Qurʾānic Jesus. Emphasising Allah's sovereignty, this selection from Sūrat Maryam quoted above ends with an *āya* that declares: 'When He decrees an affair, He only says to it, 'Be', and it is (*kun fa-yakun*)' – a declaration that Reckendorf renders as:

אם יגזר אומר ויאמר: יהי! ויהי.
When He decrees a matter, thus he says:
Let there be! and it was (i.e., *yehī va yehī*)

Although sensible, Reckendorf's rendition is also stylised, embellished by features such as assonance and repetition. Replacing the Qurʾān's decree – '"Be", and it is' – Reckendorf expresses this creative command with a reduplication, replacing the Arabic's '*kun fa-yakun*' with the Hebrew '*yehī va yehī*' (יהי! ויהי). Twice voicing the same verbal form in a single statement – '*yehī*' – Reckendorf's repetition is not original to him, however, but itself comprises a repetition of a sacred source, recalling the very first words spoken by God in the Hebrew Bible, the third verse of Genesis reading as follows:

וַיֹּאמֶר אֱלֹהִים יְהִי אוֹר וַיְהִי אוֹר
And *Elohīm* said, Let there be (*yehī*) light: and there was (*va yehī*) light.[54]

Immediately after rendering Jesus's initial words as reported in the Qurʾān, Reckendorf's Hebrew echoes God's own initial words from the Book of Genesis: '*yehī va yehī*' (Let there be and there was) – an echo of biblical creation that helps to contextualise Jesus as a contingent creature, dependent on *Elohīm*'s sovereign 'decree'. Translating the Qurʾān, even while addressing events most associated with the Gospels, Reckendorf retreats even further back in the biblical corpus, returning to the very opening of the sacred canon, inserting words from 'in the beginning' into this account of Jesus's own beginnings. Mocking 'Ishmaelite' exegetes who equate identities from the Old Testament and the New Testament, it is Reckendorf himself who renders the Qur'ān's nativity story via idioms from the Tanakh, triangulating Abrahamic traditions by appealing to the Jewish scriptures within Islam's account of Christian origins. In this episode dedicated to the maternity of Mary, and to the denial of God's paternity, Reckendorf inscribes yet another genealogy which is textually Judaic, ensuring that the Qur'ān's own modern genesis in Hebrew is yet accompanied by the original divine words from Genesis itself.

NOTES

1. Isaac D'Israeli, *Calamities of Authors; Including Some Inquiries Respecting Their Moral and Literary Characters*, 2 vols. (John Murray: London, 1812), vol. 2, p. 191. For the title of the chapter in which this passage appears – i.e., 'The Rewards of Oriental Students' – see D'Israeli, *Calamities of Authors*, vol. 2, p. 184.
2. Although 'Isaac did not covert' to Christianity, 'on July 11, 1817' he had 'his two youngest sons [...] baptized'; see Bernard Glassman, *Benjamin Disraeli: The Fabricated Jew in Myth and Memory* (Lanham, MD: University Press of America, 2003), p. 39.
3. Sale (trans.), *The Koran* (1734), p. 9 (italics in the original). For the 'Ismaílites' as the peoples 'from whom Muhammad was descended' – a note inserted into a later edition to Sale's 'Preliminary Discourse' by E. M. Wherry – see George Sale (trans.), *A Comprehensive Commentary on the Qurán: Comprising Sale's Translation and Preliminary Discourse*, ed. E. M. Wherry, 4 vols. (Boston: Houghton, 1882–1886), vol. 1, p. 126.
4. Sale (trans.), *The Koran* (1734), p. 25 (italics in the original).
5. See Sale (trans.), *The Koran* (1734), pp. 25–26, which continues on to assert that: 'But the politeness and elegance of the dialect of the *Koreish*, is rather to be attributed to their having the custody of the *Caaba*, and dwelling in *Mecca*, the centre of *Arabia*, as well more remote from intercourse with foreigners, who might corrupt their language [...]' (italics in the original).
6. Sale (trans.), *The Koran* (1734), p. 56 (italics in the original). Sale's comparative approach in his *Koran* commentary has been recently emphasised by Elmarsafy who notes at the beginning to his Chapter 3 that 'Sale uses his translation of the Qur'ān to conduct an exercise in comparative religion' (*The Enlightenment Qur'an*, p. 64).
7. The complete reference for this Qur'ān rendition is Hermann Reckendorf (trans.), *al-Qōrān ō ha-Miqrā* (Leipzig: Wolfgang Gerhard, 1857); cited subsequently as 'Reckendorf (trans.), *al-Qōrān*'.
8. Beyond an original and anonymous review of Reckendorf's *al-Qōrān* published in the 1857 *Monatsschrift für Geschichte und Wissenschaft des Judentums* (cited

in note 13 below), this earliest Hebrew edition of the Qur'ān has received very little critical attention. For a helpful overview of the few foregoing sources that address Reckendorf's rendition as well as its Hebrew successors, however, see Robert Singerman, *Jewish Translation History: A Bibliography of Bibliographies and Studies* (Amsterdam: John Benjamins Publishing Company, 2002), p. 199. Most recently, Reckendorf's *al-Qōrān* has been critiqued by Subhi Ali Adawi, who has produced the latest Hebrew rendition of the Qur'ān, published in 2015 under the title *ha-Qōrān*: *bəLashōn Aḥer* (Haifa: Gasṭliṭ, 2015). In an article entitled 'Reading the Quran in Hebrew', Jacky Hugi notes that 'Adawi considers this pioneer work [Reckendorf's *al-Qōrān*] to be an affront. Reckendorf claimed that the stories in the Quran were stolen from Jewish scriptures, and that the Arabic is of inferior quality'; see Jacky Hugi, 'Reading the Quran in Hebrew', *Al-Monitor*, 29 December 2015.

9. Reckendorf (trans.), *al-Qōrān*, p. xxii.
10. This section on '*ha-Qōran*' (הקוראן) – which comprises the third section in Reckendorf's preface – spans pages xxii to xxx of his *al-Qōrān*.
11. See Carol Bakhos, *Ishmael on the Border: Rabbinic Portrayals of the First Arab* (Albany, NY: State University of New York Press, 2006), p. 104, for Judaic usage of 'the Ishmaelites' as 'represent[ing] Islam'.
12. Reckendorf (trans.), *al-Qōrān*, p. xxii.
13. This appeal to Sale's 1734 *Koran* at the opening to his 1857 Hebrew Qur'ān reflects Reckendorf's broad agreement with Sale, including their shared accenting of Judaic foregrounds for Islam's revelation. In the preliminaries to *al-Qōrān ō ha-Miqrā*, the section following the one quoted above is itself entitled 'What Muḥammad took from the Jewish Faith and Books' (p. xxx). This section also takes its title from, and explicitly cites, Abraham Geiger's *Was Hat Mohammed Aus Dem Judenthume Aufgenommen*? (Bonn: F. Baaden, 1833). The supposed Judaic influence upon the Qur'ān is also highlighted in the review of *al-Qōrān ō ha-Miqrā* published in *Monatsschrift für Geschichte und Wissenschaft des Judentums* which asserts that 'the Qur'ān has itself appropriated (lit. smuggled in) many things from Judaic/Midrashic literature' (i.e., 'Der Koran selbst hat Manches aus der judish-midrashischen literature eingeschmuggelt'); see π, 'Review of Hermann Reckendorf (trans.), *al-Qōrān ō ha-Miqrā*', *Monatsschrift für Geschichte und Wissenschaft des Judentums*, vol. 6 (1857): 357–359 (p. 358).
14. For recognition of Reckendorf's work as 'pioneer[ing]', invoked in tandem with Subhi Ali Adawi's critique of *al-Qōrān ō ha-Miqrā*, see note 8 above.
15. Published before his move to Heidelberg, the frontispiece of *al-Qōrān ō ha-Miqrā* characterises Reckendorf in 1857 as a 'standing member of the German Orientalist Society in Halle and Leipzig, as well as the Schiller Society there' ('ordenlichem Mitgliede der deutschen morgenlaendishen Gessellschaft in Halle und Leipzig, und des Schillervereins daselbst').
16. An in-depth biographical study of Reckendorf has not yet been published; however, Reckendorf's life is briefly outlined in an entry in the tenth volume of *The Jewish Encyclopedia* (1909), which observes that 'Having acquired a thorough acquaintance with the Hebrew language and literature, Reckendorf devoted himself to the study of the other Semitic languages. In 1856 he went to Leipsic, where he occupied himself with the study of history; later he became lecturer in the University of Heidelberg' (see *The Jewish Encyclopedia: A Descriptive Record of the History, Religion, Literature, and Customs of the Jewish People from the*

Earliest Times to the Present Day, Volume X (New York: Funk and Wagnalls, 1909), p. 343). For Gustav Weil teaching 'Oriental languages at the University of Heidelberg, alongside Hermann Reckendorf', see Michael L. Miller, 'European Judaism and Islam: The Contribution of Jewish Orientalists', in *A History of Jewish–Muslim Relations: From the Origins to the Present Day*, ed. Abdelwahab Meddeb and Benjamin Stora (Princeton, NJ: Princeton University Press, 2013), pp. 828–836 (p. 829).

17. See Hermann Reckendorf, *Die Geheimnisse der Juden*, 5 vols. (Leipzig: Wolfgang Gerhard, 1856–57). This description of *Die Geheimnisse der Juden* is from David Assaf, *Untold Tales of the Hasidim: Crisis & Discontent in the History of Hasidism* (Waltham, MA: Brandeis University Press, 2011), p. 295. See also John M. Efron's *German Jewry and the Allure of the Sephardic*, which describes Reckendorf's 'novel' as seeking 'among other things, to show that the line of King David never disappeared but persisted all the way through to the Abravanels in Spain and beyond, with their descendants in post-1492 exile' (John M. Efron, *German Jewry and the Allure of the Sephardic* (Princeton, NJ: Princeton University Press, 2016), p. 214). For citations and quotations from the Qur'ān in *Die Geheimnisse der Juden*, see, for instance, its third volume, pp. 25, 64, 66, 80, 90.
18. For Moritz Steinschneider (b. 1816), see Paul B. Fenton, 'Moritz Steinschneider's Contribution to Judaeo-Arabic Studies', in *Studies on Steinschneider: Moritz Steinschneider and the Emergence of the Science of Judaism in Nineteenth-Century Germany*, ed. Reimund Leicht and Gad Freudenthal (Leiden: Brill, 2012), pp. 363–382 (pp. 364–365), which notes that 'using Delitzsch's German translation of the Koran, Steinschneider began what was to be one of his first important translations from the Arabic: an Arabised Hebrew rendition of the Koran, which would, in Mendelssohnian spirit, facilitate the study of the Koran for Jews. He subsequently abandoned this project upon the appearance of Hermann Reckendorf's Hebrew translation in 1857 in Leipzig'. Steinschneider himself mentions this decision to abandon his own 'Hebrew translation' of the 'Koran' due to 'Reckendorf's translation', although adding that Reckendorf's 1857 *al-Qōrān ō ha-Miqrā* did not enjoy 'success' (see Moritz Steinschneider, *Die Arabische Literatur der Juden: ein Beitrag zur Literaturgeschichte der Araber grossenteils aus handschriftlichen Quellen* (Frankfurt am Main: Kauffmann, 1902), pp. xlvi–xlvii).
19. See Hermann Reckendorf [Jr.], *Arabische Syntax* (Heidelberg: Carl Winter Universitätsverlag, 1921) and *Mohammed und die Seinen* (Leipzig: Quelle & Meyer, 1907). For continued references to Reckendorf's 1921 *Arabische Syntax* in recent works, see Arik Sadan, 'The Mood of the Verb following Ḥattā, according to Medieval Arab Grammarians', in *The Foundations of Arabic Linguistics: Sībawayhi and early Arabic Grammatical Theory*, ed. Amal E. Marogy and M. G. Carter (Leiden: Brill, 2012), pp. 173–185 (p. 182).
20. See Reckendorf (trans.), *al-Qōrān*, p. v, for his Hebrew epigraph to his father, named here as '*Shlomoh Ra'qa'ndārf*'. Reckendorf's dedicatory poem to his father spans pages vii to ix of his *al-Qōrān*.
21. For Reckendorf's memorialising his father as 'teaching [...] Torah' to the 'children of Judah' see Reckendorf (trans.), *al-Qōrān*, page v, where he also ties his father to 'Trebitsch' in 'Moravia'.
22. Reckendorf (trans.), *al-Qōrān*, p. 1. Above Reckendorf's *basmala*, he includes the title of the Fātiḥa in Hebrew (i.e., פותח); as all other *sūra*s in his translation,

however, Reckendorf also here records contextual details, including where the chapter was revealed ('Mecca'), as well as its verse count ('seven').

23. For Marracci and '*antonomasia*', see Chapter 4, note 14, above.
24. Reckendorf himself notes that the Fātiḥa is known as 'Mother of the Book'; see Reckendorf (trans.), *al-Qōrān*, p. 1.
25. For '*al-maghḍūb*' (الْمَغْضُوب), see Qurʾān 1:7. I represent the footnote marker in Reckendorf's rendition of the final verse of the Fātiḥa with an asterisk; however, in the original, the footnote marking is a superscript '2', i.e., '[2]מכעיסיך'. Reckendorf's version above differs from the Fātiḥa's standard verse numbering, breaking apart its seventh *āya* to comprise his Hebrew verses six and seven, while also not counting the *basmala* as the Fātiḥa's first *āya*.
26. This comprises the KJV of 1 Kings 14:15 with underlining added. See also a similar usage in 2 Kings 21:15, which not only includes the term 'מַכְעִסִים' (*makhʿisīm*) – cognate with Reckendorf's 'מכעיסיך' (*makhʿīsēkhā*) – but also makes mention of 'their fathers' ('אֲבוֹתָם'; *ʾAvōtām*).
27. Reckendorf (trans.), *al-Qōrān*, p. 355.
28. As Reckendorf regularly does not supply vowels in his rendition, these transliterated Hebrew nouns could possibly (though less plausibly) be read as plurals rather than duals. However, while 'eyes' (עינים) and 'lips' (שפתים) are most likely to be read in the dual, due to their significance, there is also biblical precedent for 'paths' (הדרכים) also being read in the dual. See Proverbs 28:18, whose dual 'paths' are discussed by Michael V. Fox, *Proverbs 10–31: A New Translation with Introduction and Commentary* (New Haven: Yale University Press, 2010), p. 822.
29. Reckendorf (trans.), *al-Qōrān*, p. 352.
30. Psalms 113 and 150 both begin with the same imperative utilised by Reckendorf, not in the singular, however, but in the plural, i.e., '*haləlū*' (הַלְלוּ ; Praise (ye all)).
31. This translation of Psalm 92:1 is from the KJV (with my transliteration of 'עֶלְיוֹן' – i.e., '*ʿElyōn*' – added).
32. For Qurʾānic occurrences of '*zabūr*'/ '*al-zabūr*', see Chapter 1, note 14, above.
33. This selection from Qurʾān 4:163–64 is rendered by Arberry, with my added transliteration of '*zabūr*' (زَبُور).
34. Reckendorf (trans.), *al-Qōrān*, p. 56.
35. The 1857 anonymous review of Reckendorf's *al-Qōrān*, published in *Monatsschrift für Geschichte und Wissenschaft des Judentums*, itself recognised Reckendorf's translation's tendency 'to cut full sentences' ('ganze Satztheile ausgelassen'); π, 'Review of Herman Reckendorf (trans.), *al-Qōrān ō ha-Miqrā*', p. 359.
36. This rendition mostly represents the KJV's translation of 2 Samuel 23:1, except for the final words 'and the Darling of the Songs of Israel', which is the literal significance of the Hebrew original *ūnʿīm zəmirōt Yisrael* according to the *Lexicon in Veteris Testamenti Libros* of Ludwig Hugo Kohler and Walter Baumgartner (cited in Gnana Robinson, *Let Us be Like the Nations: A Commentary on the Books of 1 and 2 Samuel* (Grand Rapids: Eerdmans, 1993), p. 278). For this same Hebrew phrase, the KJV instead offers 'and the sweet psalmist of Israel', which contextually interprets the plural noun '*zəmirōt*' (זְמִרוֹת) as signifying 'songster/ psalmist', rather than its more patent meaning simply as 'songs' (which concurs with this term's significance in other biblical *loci*, e.g., Psalm 95:2, Psalm 119:54, and Isaiah 24:16). Although the same in meaning, Reckendorf's usage – 'זמירות'

(*zəmīrōt*) – differs very slightly in orthography from this term's appearance in 2 Samuel 23:1, which does not include the long *i*, i.e. 'זְמִרוֹת' (*zəmirōt*').

37. Reckendorf (trans.), *al-Qōrān*, p. 56.
38. For the 'anthropomorphic' character of this Hebrew phrase, see Esther J. Hamori, *When Gods were Men: The Embodied God in Biblical and Near Eastern Literature* (Berlin: Walter De Gruyter, 2008), p. 31. Ceslaus Spicq conjectures that 'St. Paul' himself 'probably substituted 'face to face' for 'mouth to mouth' of Numbers 12:8' (see Ceslaus Spicq, *Agape in the New Testament. Vol. II, Agape in the Epistle of St. Paul, the Acts of the Apostles and the Epistles of St. James, St. Peter and St. Jude* (St. Louis: Herder, 1965), p. 165).
39. This translated selection from Numbers 12:8 is from the KJV, with my parenthetical transliteration and clarifications inserted.
40. The rendition provided of the Qur'ān's original verses (i.e., 72:1–4) follows Arberry. For Reckendorf's Hebrew translation quoted here, see Reckendorf (trans.), *al-Qōrān*, p. 337.
41. This is the KJV's translations from Deuteronomy 32:17 and Psalm 106:37 with my added transliterations, i.e., '*shedīm*'.
42. For the *jinn* as 'morally ambiguous', see Mark R. Woodward, *Java, Indonesia and Islam* (Dordrecht: Springer, 2011), p. 87.
43. For some *jinn* as 'benevolent', see again Woodward, *Java, Indonesia and Islam*, p. 87. Reckendorf's 'devil[ish]' rendition of the *jinn* is especially ironic at the opening to Chapter 72, as the *jinn* not only here testify to *tawḥīd*, but also explicitly describe in *āya* 11 their 'differing' moral characters, i.e., 'And some of us are the righteous, and some of us are otherwise; we are sects differing' (Arberry's translation).
44. This translated selection from Psalm 72:19 derives from the KJV, with my parenthetical transliteration inserted; Psalm 72 marks the close to the second book of the Psalms, and Psalm 72:19 is thus followed by a verse that comprises the conclusion to the book as a whole, i.e., '*kallū təfillōt Dāvid ben-yishāy*' ('The prayers of David the son of Jesse are ended'; KJV 72:20). For a similar benediction of God's name in the Hebrew Bible, see, for instance, Nehemiah 9:5, i.e., '*vīvārəkhū shēm kəvōdēkha*' ('and blessed be thy glorious name'; KJV).
45. See, for instance, Joshua 24:20, i.e., 'If ye forsake the LORD, and serve strange gods (*Ēlōhei nēkhār*), then he will turn and do you hurt, and consume you, after that he hath done you good' (KJV, with original Hebrew phrase added).
46. Reckendorf (trans.), *al-Qōrān*, p. 175.
47. For '*ukht Hārūn*' (sister of Aaron), see Qur'ān 19:28.
48. For this coincidence of names, see Deirdre J. Good, 'The Miriamic Secret', in *Mariam, the Magdalen, and the Mother*, ed. Deirdre Good (Bloomington: Indiana University Press, 2005), pp. 3–26 (p. 12), who notes in reference to another Semitic language – Syriac – that '[r]eadings of the Syriac Bible would thus view Mary the mother of Jesus as having the same name as Miriam in Exodus and Mary Magdalene. Where there are three names in English there is one in Syriac'.
49. Reckendorf (trans.), *al-Qōrān*, p. 175. In the sentence that precedes the one here quoted, Reckendorf's footnote suggests that the epithet of Qur'ān 19:28 – 'sister of Aaron' – was said 'sardonically' to Mary.
50. For '*Yeshū'a*' as signifying 'God saves', see Gerald O'Collins, *Jesus Our Redeemer: A Christian Approach to Salvation* (Oxford: Oxford University Press, 2010), p. 7.

51. For usage of 'Jēshū' as a means of avoiding 'pronounc[ing] the real name' of 'Jēshūaʿ', see Gustaf Dalman, *Jesus-Jeshua: Studies in the Gospels* (trans.), Paul P. Levertoff (London: S.P.C.K.; New York: Macmillan, 1929), p. 6. See also the polemical *Toledot Yeshu*, including its report of 'the rabbis call[ing] him Yeshu' within a pejorative context; see *Toledot Yeshu: the Life Story of Jesus: Two Volumes and Database*, ed. and trans. Ya'aḳov Doiṭsh and Michael Meerson (Tübingen: Mohr Siebeck, 2014), p. 57. It should be noted that other expressions with evocative Judaic precedents also impact this passage as rendered by Reckendorf, for example, '*ḥalīlāh lō*' (far be He from it!) – a phrase also employed by Maimonides when critiquing the attribution of human actions to God; see Moses Maimonides, *Moreh Nevukhim*, ed. Profiat Duran, vol. 1 (Ṿarsha: Bi-defus Y. Goldman, 1872), p. 30.
52. As its Arabic original, *ʿabd* (عَبْد), Reckendorf's Hebrew rendition '*ʿeved*' (עבד) could also be understood as 'servant', rather than the more intensive 'slave'.
53. Reckendorf utilises 'ד'' from the outset of his translation, frequently substituting this pious euphemism for 'Allah'; see, for instance, Reckendorf's rendition of Qurʾān 2:15 (Reckendorf (trans.), *al-Qōrān*, p. 3).
54. Compare the KJV's translation of Genesis 1:3, i.e., 'And God said, Let there be light: and there was light'. For this verse, and the beginning of Genesis overall, as 'rhythmic', and featuring instances of 'chiasmus', see Val Vinokur, *The Trace of Judaism: Dostoevsky, Babel, Mandelstam, Levinas* (Evanston, IL: Northwestern University Press, 2008), p. 129.

6

A 'TOTALLY TYPOLOGICAL' CHRISTIAN QUR'ĀN: NORTHROP FRYE'S TRIPLE MIRROR

I

'IDENTIFYING MIRIAM AND MARY'

> [...] you remember that in the Gospel account, Jesus is taken to Egypt by Joseph and Mary. In the earlier account [the Book of Exodus], Moses grows up in Egypt. And the names 'Joseph' and 'Mary' recall the 'Joseph' who led the Israelites into Egypt in the first place, and the 'Miriam' who was Moses' older sister. In fact there is a sura of the Koran that identifies the Miriam of the Exodus story with Mary of the Gospels. And naturally, Christian commentators on the Koran say that this is ridiculous, but we must remember that the Koran is speaking from a totally typological and ahistorical point of view, and from that point of view the identification makes sense.[1]

Recalling Reckendorf's shocked commentary to Sūrat Maryam – infusing his footnote with triple exclamations ('!!!') – it is the very same link across biblical testaments that is highlighted here, these sentences also finding 'the Koran' equating 'the Miriam of the Exodus story with Mary of the Gospels'.[2] Centred again on Qur'ānic 'identification', the above quotation repeats, yet also reverses, Reckendorf's surprise; unlike his Hebrew annotations, this English explanation *endorses* the same Islamic 'identity' between biblical 'Miriam' and 'Mary'. Asserting that this equation 'makes sense', the above selection not only forms a general apology, but also specifically defends the Muslim scripture against 'Christian commentators on the Koran'. These remarks seem especially surprising, however, due to their speaker, Northrop Frye, himself the most prominent 'Christian commentator' on the literary Bible, and the 'most cited literary critic' of the last century.[3]

Offering his apology for Qur'ānic 'identification', Frye spoke the above words in a lecture entitled 'The Double Mirror: Exodus and the Gospel' – the twelfth instalment within a cycle of thirty lectures delivered and recorded over a single academic year as part of his 'famous course' on 'The Bible and Literature'.[4] Expositing the closed structure of reflection between the two bibles, Hebrew and Greek, Frye's lecture title gestures to the mutual 'mirroring' of the testaments, with 'Old' and 'New' paralleled in perfect confrontation. Twinning the literary characters of Exodus and the Gospels, Frye literally charts for his students the duplicate careers of Moses and Christ, sketching on his blackboard a series of Mosaic 'types' and Christian 'antitypes'.[5] In Moses' Egyptian youth, for instance, Frye finds the precedent for Jesus' own early exile in Egypt – a correspondence ultimately leading Frye to voice the above selection, invoking the Miriam–Mary identity as a context for the Moses–Jesus correspondence. Aligning these predictable parallels between 'Old Testament' and 'New Testament', it is, however, a third testament that abruptly emerges in Frye's lecture – 'the Koran'. Bolstering his biblical correspondence, Frye's typological teaching receives surprising support from the Muslim scripture, its alignment between 'the Miriam of the Exodus story' and 'Mary of the Gospels'. And yet, if helping to synthesize the textual subjects of his lecture – 'Exodus and the Gospel' – the Qur'ān also curiously presents an implicit challenge to the first part of his lecture's title – 'The Double Mirror' – resisting the Bible's hermetic self-reflection, belying Frye's argument that the biblical corpus comprises 'a double mirror reflecting only itself to itself'.[6] Positing a sealed system between Old Testament and New Testament, Frye suddenly allows an even *newer* testament to intervene, the Qur'ān disrupting the mere 'doubleness' of biblical typology. Refashioned into a trialectic, Frye's dialectical model becomes instead a 'triple mirror' in which the Qur'ān supports, but also subtly opens up, the closed canon of biblical correspondence. Prompting Reckendorf to interrupt his sober annotations with a triad of surprised exclamations, this same 'identification' of 'Miriam and Mary' initiates a testamental triad that is both welcomed by Northrop Frye, and yet also obliquely interrupts his own view of the Bible's 'reflecting only itself to itself', with his 'Double Mirror' ironically envisioned via a third revelatory position.

Explicitly asserting the coherency and continuity of the biblical canon, while also implicitly appealing to a text that resists this same canon's completeness, the Qur'ān's recruitment by Frye solidifies his 'Double Mirror', but only through adding a surplus surface of reflection, this third mirror both fusing and diffusing the essential symmetry between the two testaments. For Frye, the Qur'ān's capacity to confirm typology in the biblical corpus is due, however, to yet another kind of surplus – indeed, to another superlative – which Frye associates with the Muslim scripture in his final phrases above. In a statement that challenges both scholarly norms and confessional conventions, Frye finds the Qur'ān as embodying a figurative supremacy, speaking from 'a totally typological and ahistorical point of view'. Even while teaching the closed typology of the Bible to his students, Frye undercuts the Bible's typological conclusiveness, discovering a climactic 'totality' represented instead by the Qur'ān. Although the New

Testament is understood by Frye as a complete fulfillment of the Old Testament, the Qur'ān is yet seen as advancing even further, no longer offering mere analogies between testaments, but asserting exact equivalences within a single *sūra*. For Frye, the Bible draws correspondences through nominal symmetries, with names and narratives echoing each other across differing books (Miriam/Mary; Exodus/Gospel); the Qur'ān, however, immediately *identifies* 'Miriam' and 'Mary', equating these figures in a unified chapter – an identification that culminates, yet resolves, the unfolding of sacred history, leading to the Qur'ān's 'ahistorical point of view'.[7]

First spoken informally in his 'Bible and Literature' lecture, Frye's recruitment of the Qur'ān to help fuse 'Exodus and the Gospel' would soon surface also in his formal writing, meriting mention in *The Great Code: The Bible and Literature*, published during the following year.[8] Broadening his audience, shifting from personal students to public readers, Frye also tightens up his characterisation of the Qur'ān's typology, treating the twinning of Moses and Christ in the following passage:

> The names Mary and Joseph recall the Miriam who was the sister of Moses and the Joseph who led the family of Israel into Egypt. The third sura of the Koran appears to be identifying Miriam and Mary; Christian commentators on the Koran naturally say that this is ridiculous, but from the purely typological point of view from which the Koran is speaking, the identification makes good sense.[9]

The core of Frye's 1981 teaching is reiterated here in his 1982 publication, the latter even providing additional detail that is merely glossed in the former; rather than a generic 'sura of the Koran' in his lecture, for example, Frye's *Great Code* clarifies that it is 'the third sura' (that is, Sūrat Āl ʿImrān) which is his source. It is what is missing from Frye's printed discussion that seems most significant, however. Instead of a Qur'ān 'that identifies the Miriam of the Exodus story with Mary of the Gospels', Frye presents in *The Great Code* merely a Qur'ān that '*appears* to be identifying Miriam and Mary' – a hedging that is complemented too by Frye's more hesitant claim regarding the Qur'ān's typology. For his 1982 readers, Frye writes of 'the purely typological point of view from which the Koran is speaking', while in his 1981 live lecture, Frye had categorically proclaimed that 'the Koran is speaking from a totally typological and ahistorical point of view' – a slightly grander, and more global, assertion. Complementing their differing content, the form of Frye's commentary on the Qur'ān also evolves from teaching to writing, his rich personality and presence muted in publication. In 1981, Frye emphatically included his oral audience in his Qur'ānic teachings; '*we* must remember', Frye had insisted, 'that the Qur'ān is speaking from a totally typological and ahistorical point of view'. A colloquial and common means of engagement, Frye's '*we* must remember' serves also to implicate his own students within a dichotomy of collective 'memory', contrasting himself and his undergraduates favourably against mere 'Christian commentators'. Instead of those who understand the Qur'ān's identification of 'Miriam' and 'Mary' to be 'ridiculous', Frye's own faction – '*we*', not only Frye, but his collegiate audience – must recall that this 'identification makes sense'.

It is, of course, entirely expected that such differences should emerge as Frye addresses divergent audiences, distinguishing readers of his scholarship from students in his college seminars. However, Frye's linguistic shifts also oddly reflect the very subject of his critical interest – the Qur'ān – a text that is urgently aware of its own reception and performance, anticipating those who both understand and misunderstand its message, while also balancing compositional dichotomies of orality and literacy. Even while lecturing on the Qur'ān's radical identity between Mary and Miriam, Frye reaches for a radical identity between himself and his audience ('we'); however, when Frye transitions to the printed page, his bold equation between Qur'ānic characters merely 'appears' to be operative, even while the equation between him and his audience ('we') is entirely edited out. Frye's initial and *totalising* approach to his live audience is also mirrored in his theory of total typology – a theory only advanced by Frye orally, even as he addresses Islam's originally oral revelation, shifting between you and we, while appealing to a scripture which itself features frequent lively shifts in person and pronoun, enriched by verbal acts of *iltifāt*. A bridge of 'identity' between biblical testaments, the Qur'ān surprisingly emerges – the present chapter suggests – as an index distinguishing Frye's own diverse efforts, surfacing both in his live teaching and literary texts, discretely interpreted with personal informality as well as published formality. Indeed, it is this supposedly 'ahistorical' text that ironically charts a history of Frye's own critical development, the Qur'ān plotting his progress towards celebrated publications, advancing from unedited acts of pedagogy to edited publication. Tracing orbits of Qur'ānic typology that encircle Frye's 1981 lecture initially quoted above, the final chapter of this study follows a 'centripetal' spiral that circles down to Frye's most intimate and central acts of reading 'the Koran', descending from Frye's spontaneous pedagogy, to his personal journals, even reaching his private and pencilled scribbles in Qur'ānic margins.[10]

II

'WORDS DESCENDING FROM HEAVEN AS RAIN'

Surfacing briefly in Frye's spoken lectures, the Muslim scripture is also to be found submerged in his own journals, the Qur'ān's role in Frye's classrooms anticipated by notebook entries he penned a full decade previous. Turning from Frye's oral teaching to his written journals, we naturally lose his live voice and physical presence. This shift in media also implies, however, a shift in readership; in his journals, Frye is both intentional author, and presumably, intended audience. Yet, as Frye's audience shrinks, his authorial freedom also seems to enlarge, his journals preserving a unique cache of more audacious and impulsive interpretations. A scattered source for his subsequent teaching and writing on the Qur'ān, Frye's journals contain kernels that will eventually mature into core concepts, including his interest in the 'third sura of the Koran', and its 'identifying Miriam and Mary'. Long before emerging in his 1981 'The Double Mirror', the Qur'ān forms the centre of a rich succession of entries in Frye's 'Notebook 11f' composed between 1969 and 1970. Ranging from denigration to celebration, Frye's reading of the Muslim scripture in 'Notebook 11f' culminates with the following reflection, offered as his Entry 81:

> [...] The dianoia is synchronic, the mythos diachronic. The diachronic sequence is given, & may be, as in the Koran or Ecclesiastes, given very much at random. Samuel Johnson has an excellent passage somewhere on the rationalizing Leibnitzian tendency of critics to demonstrate that a given sequence is the best of all possible sequences. But it isn't, necessarily. Anyway, we arrive at the synchronic dianoia through metaphorical identifications. In the Koran Mary *is* Miriam, Haman a contemporary of Pharaoh, Gideon & Saul & David's Goliath-killing all the same story. It isn't necessarily muddling, but synchronic identity, like Milton's 'blind fury'. (No doubt they were muddled in Mohammed's mind, but that's not the primary critical problem.)[11]

Balancing technical terminology and casual comment, this entry reflects Frye's critical polarities, spanning his profound expertise and his relaxed instruction. Infused with English colloquialism ('Anyway [...]'), Frye's entry nevertheless opens with a flurry of specialised Greek, juxtaposing '*dianoia*' (meaning) and '*mythos*' (narrative), as well as '*synchronic*' (time-unified) and '*diachronic*' (through time).[12] Here concerned with the most basic and broad categories of secular literature, Frye nevertheless sees the sacred as best exemplifying these categories, again appealing not only to the Bible, but to the Bible *and* the Qur'ān, pairing 'the Koran' and 'Ecclesiastes'. And in this pairing, it is again the Qur'ān that emerges as superlative, defined as the epitome of Frye's 'synchronic dianoia' – an argument that Frye advances through a series of 'metaphorical identifications', launching with the now-familiar merger of 'Mary' and 'Miriam'. However, it is Frye's entirely simple, yet urgently significant, means of fusing these two figures that distinguishes this private journal entry from his public teaching and writing. Promoting a 'synchronic identity' that collapses all difference between characters, Frye's language itself collapses, yielding merely an emphatic equation, asserting that 'In the Koran Mary *is* Miriam'. Precariously poised on his italicised '*is*', Frye asserts not mere allegorical analogy, but ontological unity. Rather than *The Great Code* (in which the Qur'ān 'appears to be identifying Miriam and Mary'), or even his Bible and Literature lecture (in which the Qur'ān 'identifies the Miriam of the Exodus story with Mary of the Gospels'), 'Notebook 11f' pronounces that Mary '*is*' Miriam in the Qur'ān, with Frye's own rhetoric reduced to immediate urgency, even as the relationship he describes is urgently immediate. Frye's Entry 81 is unique too in dilating his catalogue of Qur'ānic identifications, broadening the range of characters correlated in his reading of Muslim revelation. Flattening narrative time and distance, Frye discovers 'Haman' to be 'a contemporary of Pharaoh', even while 'Gideon & Saul & David's Goliath-killing' are synthesised within 'the same story'. Superseding the Bible yet again, the Qur'ān is portrayed as obviating Christian *mythos*, with Islamic *dianoia* nullifying the stages and sequences of 'story' itself.

In obviating biblical narrative, Frye's 'Koran' also threatens, however, to obviate the biblical critic too. In the culminating *dianoia* of the Qur'ān, no longer are clever readers required to draw typological relationships between testaments. Instead, correspondences between Old Testament and New Testament are not separated by disparate pages and periods, but are provided together in simultaneity, with an assured '*is*' anticipating our own critical insights into possible types and antitypes. The resulting ambivalent position of the literary critic in Frye's understanding of the Qur'ān is perhaps obliquely suggested in his entry's final sentences. Debating whether the powerful 'identifications' contained by the Qur'ān are sophisticated 'dianoia' or, instead, mere 'muddling', Frye raises the Prophet's own role in conveying – or, in his formulation, creating – the Qur'ānic text. Invoking a Miltonic allusion ('blind fury'), Frye defends the Qur'ān's 'identifications' even while parenthetically suggesting that they may indeed have been 'muddled within Mohammed's mind'. Clearing a space for subsequent interpreters, the 'muddling' here problematically associated with the Prophet, is not, Frye insists a 'primary critical problem'. And yet, it is precisely this 'muddling' that also allows for Frye's own critical cleansing of the Qur'ān's supposed confusion, requiring his own reading to help reveal the seemingly 'ridiculous' to be, in fact, authentically 'good sense'.[13]

The emphatic specificity of Frye's Entry 81, asserting 'Mary *is* Miriam', receives a more general and generic introduction in Frye's previous entry – Entry 80 of 'Notebook 11f' – which grounds the Qur'ān's 'metaphoric identifications' in the scripture's own performativity:

> To those accustomed to written books, a synchronic orally composed book like the Koran is intolerable. But Moslems wouldn't think of it

> diachronically, with unrepeated statements gaining the emphasis of repetition by being in dialectical sequence. They think of the Koran as words descending from heaven as rain descends from the sky, all over the place at once, and if you're looking for rain to break a drought, you don't complain that one raindrop is much like another.[14]

Reaching back to the rich dichotomy of 'written' versus 'oral', Frye juxtaposes *codex* and *al-Qur'ān*, contrasting common 'books' and '*the* recitation'.[15] The central concern of Entry 80 is not, however, literary form, but rather *our interpretation* of literary form, accenting reader response and reaction. Juxtaposing 'those accustomed to written books' with those accustomed to an 'orally composed book', Frye implicitly recalls his critique of 'Christian commentators' who fail to understand the Qur'ān's 'good sense'. Freshly significant in Entry 80, however, is Frye's explicit equation of his own understanding of the Muslim scripture with the 'understanding' of 'Moslems' themselves. The originality that Frye insightfully finds in the Qur'ān – its superlative 'synchronism' – is itself original to the Qur'ān's first audience, with Frye aligning himself with 'Moslems who wouldn't think of [the Koran] diachronically': an alignment that lends an oddly 'faithful' flavour to Frye's zealous defense of the Qur'ān's synchronism. Deepening Frye's domestication of the 'Moslem' perspective is the modulation of his own voice as Entry 80 unfolds. Although opening with a third-person externalisation of this religious viewpoint – asserting that 'Moslems' think or 'They think' – Frye soon slips into second person, adopting a universal 'you' by the conclusion of his entry ('if you're looking for rain…') even as he continues to exposit and endorse the 'Moslem' perspective.

This subtle shift in form occurs as Frye introduces perhaps the most vivid image which is featured in his Qur'ān entries in 'Notebook 11f', figuring the scripture itself as effusive bounty, 'as words descending from heaven as rain descends from the sky'. The Qur'ān is portrayed here not as identifying biblical figures, but rather as *self-identical*, serving as the natural nourishment in which each morsel 'is much like another'. Consistent with the Qur'ān's 'totalising' potential for Frye, this revelatory 'rain' aptly spans all space and time, spreading 'all over the place', and 'all […] at once', even while bridging all people, equally implying 'they' and 'you'. No longer interested in inter-testamental reflection, but rather intra-testamental unity, Frye's view of Islamic verses as identical 'raindrops' epitomises his interpretive approach to the Qur'ān, but also hints too at his critical ambivalences. Dropping everywhere in duplicate, the Qur'ān promises to 'break a drought', yet its relentless 'rain' may also threaten to yield more 'muddled' environs. An apt metaphor for Frye's 'personal view' of 'the Koran', this image of the showering scripture is nevertheless not personal to Frye, attributed instead to 'Moslems' themselves – an attribution which poses a problem: why does Frye believe that Muslims 'think of the Koran' in this way? What is the original source for this seemingly original metaphor?

III

'LEGIONS OF ANGELS THAT JESUS RELATED'

To find the literary home of Frye's image, it is necessary to return to Frye's literal home: the University of Toronto, and more particularly, Victoria College. Upon his death in 1991, the bulk of Frye's *nachlass* came to rest at Victoria, with the E. J. Pratt Library now housing not only generous holdings from Frye's personal papers, but also his personal library.[16] And catalogued among this key book collection is an item unassumingly labelled 'Frye annotated no. 1022' – a copy of *The Koran* – a copy 'annotated' by Frye himself, and first brought to scholarly attention by Todd Lawson.[17] Translated by John Meadows Rodwell, and first published as part of the Everyman's Library series in 1909, Frye's English translation of the Qur'ān features frequent marginalia, signalling passages that attracted his especial interest, including the following sequence from Sūrat al-Naḥl:

> [64] And we have sent down the Book to thee only, that thou mightest clear up to them the subject of their wranglings, and as a guidance and a mercy to those who believe.
>
> [65] And God sendeth down water from Heaven, and by it giveth life to the Earth after it hath been dead: verily, in this is a sign to those who hearken.[18]

Shifting from revelation to rain, these two verses embrace the precise polarities that inform Frye's Entry 80 in his 'Notebook 11f'. However, it is Frye's own annotations on these verses that make this echo unmistakable, scribbling in the narrow lefthand margins that surround this passage:

> descending word and its 'sign' of rain'[19]

Situating *āya* 65 as a 'sign' of *āya* 64, Frye discovers a shared 'descent' spanning Qur'ānic 'word' and 'rain', a 'sending down' that synthesises both 'Book' and 'water'. Recognising a verbal overlap in these verses, Frye's marginal tie between these *āyāt* is further tightened in his journal entry, however, where the two verses from Sūrat al-Naḥl are reformulated as one statement, 'the Koran' conceived simply as 'words descending from heaven as rain'.[20] Condensed into a single passage, these dual verses from Sūrat al-Naḥl also undergo a shift in perspective by the time Frye reaches his 'Notebook 11f'. While the Qur'ān here emphasises divine *author* – 'God', who sends down His revelation and rain – Frye's reading will ultimately accent human *audience*, highlighting in his Entry 80 those who receive rain and revelation from above. Evolving in structure, Frye's treatment of the twin verses does, however, echo the flexible form of his sacred source. While the Qur'ān transitions from 'We' to 'He' as it designates God between verses 64 and 65 – vacillating from first-personal plural to third-person singular – Frye too shifts grammatical person in designating humanity, transitioning from 'they' to 'you', comprising an instance of Frye's own *iltifāt* which ironically harmonises with the Qur'ān's essential stylistic shifts.

Scribbling in the margins of the translated Muslim scripture, it is especially fitting that Frye chooses these Qur'ānic *āyāt* of verbal 'descent' as a site for his own verbal descent into the Qur'ān, Frye's words landing beside verses that themselves herald the landing of divine 'words'. Sprinkling his ideas sporadically through Qur'ānic pages – allowing his annotations to surface 'all over the place at once', across the entire scripture – Frye deepens his intimacy with his Islamic source, fashioning his arguments on the Qur'ān immediately beside the Qur'ān's own arguments.[21] Publicly teaching that the Qur'ān fuses discrete sacred figures – Mary and Miriam, for instance – Frye's own private marginalia will fuse secular critic and sacred canon, merging Frye and the Qur'ān in conjoined speech. Marking the bottom of a spire of interiority, Frye's informal annotations serve too as fertile ground for his own formal cultivation, a site for his initial ideas on the Qur'ān which ultimately grow into notebook entries, live lectures, and finally, appear polished in his published scholarship. Finding the foundation for his Entry 80 in Frye's 'Notebook 11f', it is Frye's marginalia that also underlie his Entry 81 – the entry quoted above asserting the 'synchronic identity' of Islam's scripture. As seen in Figure 2, Frye includes a scribbled remark associating the Qur'ān with the 'synchronic' in his copy of Rodwell's *Koran* – a remark that itself intervenes between two Qur'ānic chapters, interrupting the sequence of *sūra*s even as Frye himself meditates on Qur'ānic 'sequence'.

Developing terminology here that will come to define Frye's concept of the Qur'ān – 'synchronic', 'no sense of history' – this annotation stands as an embryonic anticipation of Frye's mature thinking. While the ideas of this marginalia are repeated in later media, the context of Frye's comment lends more weight to its content. Advanced abstractly in later teaching and print, Frye's first definition of the Qur'ān as 'synchronic scripture' seen in Figure 2 is concretely embedded *within* his Qur'ānic reading as it unfolds. Standing not merely as Frye's critical judgement on the scripture, but as a critical justification for his own interpretations, Frye inscribes inside the Qur'ān itself a readiness to read its text 'synchronically'.

Featuring his declaration of hermeneutic principles, Frye's *Koran* also witnesses acts of practical criticism, with his marginalia unfolding a host

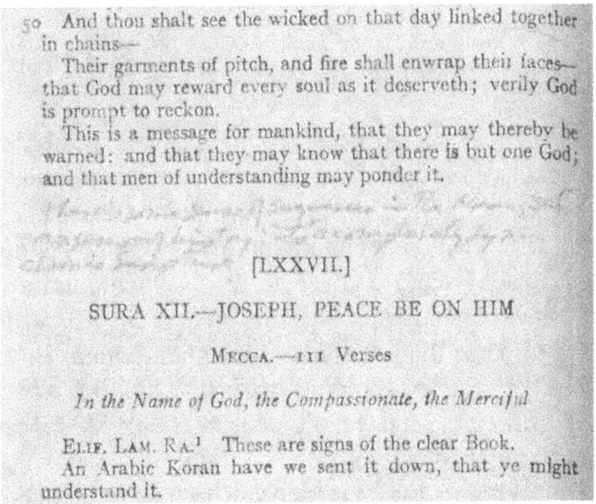
50 And thou shalt see the wicked on that day linked together in chains—
Their garments of pitch, and fire shall enwrap their faces—that God may reward every soul as it deserveth; verily God is prompt to reckon.
This is a message for mankind, that they may thereby be warned: and that they may know that there is but one God; and that men of understanding may ponder it.

[LXXVII.]

SURA XII.—JOSEPH, PEACE BE ON HIM

MECCA.—111 Verses

In the Name of God, the Compassionate, the Merciful

ELIF. LAM. RA.[1] These are signs of the clear Book.
An Arabic Koran have we sent it down, that ye might understand it.

Figure 2. Northrop Frye's pencilled inscription, included immediately after the end to Sūrat Ibrāhīm, and before the beginning to Sūrat Yūsuf, appearing on page 230 of Frye's copy of *The Koran*, trans. John Meadows Rodwell. Item held at, and image courtesy of, Victoria University Library, Toronto. Frye's marginalia, as pictured above, reads:

there's some sense of sequence in The Koran,
but no sense of history: it's a completely
synchronic scripture[22]

of imaginative interpretations sporadically inscribed throughout his English edition. While the Muslim scripture shapes Frye's rhetoric in his 'Notebook 11f', his own rhetoric envelopes the Muslim scripture, sketching fresh outlines for this sacred text. Reflecting his emphasis on the Qur'ān's 'ahistoricity', for instance, Frye divorces the scripture from conventional Islamic contexts, offering readings that are wholly unanchored from historical specificity. Especially eager to identify echoes of the Old Testament and New Testament, Frye consistently finds biblical threads in the Qur'ānic fabric, commenting on shared Abrahamic events. Adjacent to analogous episodes from the Bible, Frye pens phrases such as 'Babel' beside Qur'ān 16:26; 'burning bush' beside Qur'ān 20:10; and 'sacrifice of Isaac' beside Qur'ān 37:102.[23] However, it is the less obvious, and more inventive, biblical echoes that Frye identifies within the Qur'ān that best reflect his 'synchronic' theories. Reading once again Chapter 16 – Sūrat al-Naḥl – Frye is arrested by its verse 106, which Rodwell translates as:

> Whoso, after he hath believed in God denieth him, if he were forced to it and if his heart remain steadfast in the faith, *shall be guiltless*: but whoso openeth his breast to infidelity – on such shall be wrath from God, and a severe punishment awaiteth them.

To the immediate left of this printed passage, Frye scribbles in his own hand:

'Peter vs. Judas'.[24]

Complementing the Qur'ān's own contrast between fallible fidelity and intentional infidelity, Frye introduces his own contrast of faith, personifying Islamic precepts with biblical identities. Symptomatic of his Christian lens for reading the Qur'ān, Frye's annotation also suggests his desire to trace the 'diachronic' background to the Qur'ān's 'synchronic' surface, alluding to characters excerpted from New Testament *mythus*, with 'Peter' and 'Judas' helping to parse the polarities of Islamic *dianoia*. However, unlike the relationship between 'Mary' and 'Miriam' which Frye had found suggested in Sūrat Āl 'Imrān, the relationship between 'Peter' and 'Judas' is antinomous rather than synonymous ('*vs*'. rather than '*is*'), and also originates solely from Frye's own suggestion, with his biblical identities added to Qur'ānic margins, rather than extracted from between Qur'ānic lines.

Parsing Islamic principles with Christian names, Frye's annotation on this specific *āya* from Sūrat al-Naḥl suggests his broader program of 'christening' the Qur'ān, re-populating the Muslim scripture with biblical personages. A more complex example is found in Frye's compound reaction to a single verse in Sūrat Āl 'Imrān, whose 183rd *āya* is annotated on its righthand side by Frye. Table 6.1 represents this annotation.

Qur'ān 3:183	**Annotation**
To those who say, 'Verily, God hath enjoined us that we are	Elijah
not to credit an apostle until he present us a sacrifice which fire out of Heaven shall devour',	pattern
SAY: Already have apostles before me come to you with	Jesus'
miracles, and with that of which ye speak. Wherefore slew ye them? Tell me, if ye are men of truth.	argument

Table 6.1. A representation of Northrop Frye's marginal annotations of Qur'ān 3:183, as found in his personal edition of *The Koran*, trans. John Meadows Rodwell. Item held at, and quotation courtesy of, Victoria University Library, Toronto.

Similar to his supplying 'Peter vs. Judas' in Sūrat al-Naḥl, in Table 6.1 Frye provides biblical names to parse Qur'ānic proclamations. However, rather than a New Testament disagreement, Frye traces a development that unfolds from Old Testament to New, discovering 'Elijah' and 'Jesus' successively conjoined in a single verse of the Qur'ān. Although readers of the Bible will note that the episodes in 1 Kings 18 and Matthew 23, respectively, are divided by hundreds of pages and hundreds of years, Frye's synchronic Qur'ān fuses these figures in a lively oral dialogue.[25] Dramatising both typological challenge and typological fulfillment, Frye finds the Qur'ān casting 'Jesus' argument' as the fiery answer to the problem associated with the 'Elijah pattern', collapsing an incremental history of typology into immediate call and response.

For traditional students of the Qur'ān, Frye's annotations may seem most jarring not in their literary readings of the scripture, but in their erasure of literal settings. For instance, while normative exegesis of the Qur'ān would readily recognise the second half of verse 183 above to have been originally addressed to Muḥammad – opening with the characteristic imperative ('say'; '*qul*') – Frye instead finds this imperative as echoing New Testament 'argument', replacing historical Prophet with typological 'pattern'.[26] The tension of such testamental layering reaches a climax as Frye comments on Qur'ānic passages that are overtly grounded in historical circumstances. Earlier in Sūrat Āl 'Imrān, Frye had stopped to signal verse 13, which reads as follows in Rodwell's translation:

> Ye have already had a sign in the meeting of the two hosts. The one host fought in the cause of God, and the other was infidel. To their own eyesight, the infidels saw you twice as many as themselves: And God aided with His succour whom He would: and in this truly was a lesson for men endued with discernment.

This *āya* is exceptional, not merely in meriting Frye's interpretive attention, but in appearing to resist Frye's interpretive approach. Traditionally read as a reference to the Battle of Badr (624 CE), this verse opens with a direct address to the Qur'ān's original audience ('ye'), reminding the Prophet's early community of God's 'succour', epitomised by their surprising defeat of the 'infidel'.[27] Referencing a specific, temporal event – 'the meeting of the two hosts', in which the Meccans 'saw you [Muslims] twice as many as themselves' – this verse seems to evade Frye's assertion of an 'ahistorical' Qur'ān. However, rather than simply ignore this *āya*, Frye erases this *āya*'s traditional context. Altering the 'sign' heralded by verse 13 through adding his own unique signature, Frye re-centres this verse's meaning with a brief marginal comment:

> 'legions of angels that Jesus related'.[28]

Consistent with his defining Qur'ānic passages through biblical precedents, Frye finds Sūrat Āl 'Imrān anticipated by the Gospel of Matthew, with Qur'ān 3:13 recalling Jesus' query: 'Thinkest thou that I cannot now pray to my Father, and he shall presently give me more than twelve legions of angels?' (Matthew 26:53). An imaginative literary stretch – bridging the 'succour' delivered by Allah to the faithful, and the 'legions of angels' promised by Jesus – Frye's imaginative reach is also revolutionary in its religious implications. Again establishing an inter-denominational typology, the New Testament here serves not only as an implicit precedent for the Qur'ān, but is explicitly *fulfilled* by the Qur'ān. In the Gospel, Jesus speaks in the subjunctive, reaching forward to the future potential of angelic aid; in the Qur'ān, however, this aid is recently past, both completed and concluded, with divine support 'already' actualised and achieved. The New Testament – conventionally considered to be typological fulfillment of the Old Testament – is here displaced; the New Testament is itself transformed into an *older* testament, the 'sign' of this Qur'ānic verse from Sūrat Āl 'Imrān realising a Gospel intimation. Inverting its traditional status, Frye's marginalia implicitly denudes the New Testament of its role as fulfilling 'antitype', the Gospel receding merely to a precedent 'type', even while it looks ahead to the Qur'ān, this 'ahistorical' Islamic text ironically indexing a new history of biblical completion.[29]

IV

'M. DREW THE RELATION OF CHRIST & MOSES'

Reaching back to biblical precedents in the pages of his *Koran*, Frye also reaches forward to biblical poetics, discovering beloved authors – Dante, William Blake, John Milton, and S. T. Coleridge, for example – equally implied in the Muslim scripture. First suggested by his Entry 81, in which the Qur'ān's 'synchronic identity' is exemplified by Milton's 'blind fury', Frye conceives the Qur'ān as not only echoing the Christian sacred, but also anticipating the secular canon. For example, in the Qur'ānic account of creation, Frye discovers 'Miltonic uncomprehending angels' echoed in Sūrat al-Baqarah, penning this phrase beside the chapter's thirtieth verse, in which the angels question Allah's intention to establish humanity as *khalīfa*.[30] Earlier, inspired by the primordial universality proclaimed by Sūrat Yūnus, announcing that 'Men were of one religion only', Frye supplies beside this *āya* the brief comment 'everlasting gospel theme' – an allusion retreating back to Revelation 14:6 (the source for the phrase 'everlasting gospel'), as well as advancing forward to William Blake, who pens a poem of the same name beloved by Frye ('The Everlasting Gospel').[31] Assimilating the Qur'ān into the Bible's literary heritage, Frye also finds occasion to use this literary heritage to *distinguish* the Qur'ān from the Bible, with the Muslim scripture again superseding its Christian predecessor. For example, when reading Sūrat Maryam, Frye is intrigued by the positive portrait of Ishmael offered in this same *sūra*, whose fifty-fifth verse declares: 'And commemorate Ismael in "the Book"; for he was true to his promise, and was an Apostle, a Prophet' – a verse which Frye highlights in the margins, noting here simply 'not in Bible: cf. Melville'.[32] Alluding to the celebrated narrator of *Moby-Dick* – the 'Ishmael' of Herman Melville's 1851 masterpiece – Frye anchors this iconic American character within Qur'ānic characterisation, even while unmooring 'Ishmael' from his much less flattering genealogy first advanced in Genesis. Although regularly conceived as the most biblical of America's epics, Frye bends *Moby-Dick*'s trajectory of influence away from a pejorative Hebraic precedent ('not in Bible'), and towards the positive Arabic profile which is promoted in the Qur'ān.[33]

The Qur'ān's intervention between 'the Bible' and its 'Literature' recalls the Qur'ān's intervention within Frye's own 'Bible and Literature' lectures, surfacing in the midst of his 1981–82 classroom teaching. First appearing in his 'The Double Mirror: Exodus and the Gospel', it will be Frye's interest in literary influence and intertextuality that prompts the Qur'ān to resurface several programs later, mentioned once again in his 'Wisdom: The Proverb'.[34] Discussing the global parameters of biblical wisdom, Frye details the ubiquity of 'Ahikar' – an archetypal figure of antiquity, who surfaces not only in the Bible, but in a wide range of literary traditions, as Frye informs his students:

> And so we're not surprised to find that the story of Ahikar has embedded itself in all the literatures of the Near East. It is quoted in the Old Testament, and the Book of Tobit in the Apocrypha concerns a man who is said to be the nephew of Ahikar, thereby establishing a link with another popular tale. It is said to be echoed in the New Testament, though some scholars disagree with that. Ahikar found his way into Greek literature under the name of Aesop. And there is even a sura in the Koran which is...which bears his name, or at least another version of his name, although the Koran for the most part is even less interested in secular literature than the New Testament, which is saying a good deal.[35]

Beginning with 'the Old Testament', Frye's survey culminates with 'the Koran', the Muslim scripture capping this catalogue of 'all the literatures of the Near East'. Although just one text among many, the Qur'ān is also singled out by Frye, the scripture attracting his particular interest ironically due to its own *lack* of 'interest'. Superseding the 'New Testament', the Muslim sacred text is 'even less interested in secular literature' than the Christian canon – a comparison which seems consistent with Frye's previous celebration of the Qur'ān's 'totally typological' viewpoint. More surprising, however, is simply the Qur'ān's inclusion within this index of Ahikar's influence. Especially confounding to those familiar with the Qur'ān is Frye's halting assertion that 'there's even a sura in the Koran which is... which bears his name', particularly as 'Ahikar' is a 'name' that, of course, never appears in the Qur'ān, neither in its titles, nor throughout its text. Yet, as allowed by his conversational context, Frye is able to qualify his claim, adding quickly 'or at least another version of his name'. Referring here to 'Luqmān', the eponymous prophet of the Qur'ān's thirty-first chapter, Frye relies on scholarship that twins 'Ahikar' and 'Luqmān', viewing the latter as an Islamic iteration of the former.[36] It is not the accuracy of Frye's claim, however, but his audacious imperative to *re-name* a Qur'ānic character that seems most resonant. Even while distancing the Muslim scripture from all 'interest in secular literature', Frye brings the Muslim scripture near to 'all the literatures of the Near East' through a bold substitution of name, refiguring the Arabic 'Luqmān' as the universal 'Ahikar'.

This re-identification of a Qur'ānic character – Luqmān *is* Ahikar – seems yet 'another version' of Frye's most basic identification of Qur'ānic character: 'Mary *is* Miriam'. Holding the hermeneutic seeds for all his subsequent interpretations of the Qur'ān, this core equation aptly traces its own organic origins, however, to Frye's annotations in his copy of *The Koran*. Reading once again the Qur'ān's third chapter, Sūrat Āl 'Imrān, Frye is provoked by a footnote that was provided by his English translator – John Meadows Rodwell – who disparages this chapter's supposed 'confusion' between Miriam and Mary, asserting:

> It is difficult to avoid the conclusion that Muhammad is guilty of the anachronism of confounding Miriam with the Virgin Mary. On the other hand is the difficulty of conceiving that as the sequence of time and fact is observed with tolerable accuracy in regard to the main features of Jewish and Christian History, he should have fallen into so serious an error [...]

Immediately below this printed paratext, Frye provides a pencilled note, responding to Rodwell at the very bottom of the page, offering his own brief rebuke:

> 'M. drew the relation of Christ & Moses better than some Christians'.[37]

Several elements in this short statement now seem familiar. Resisting his translator, Frye again privileges the Qur'ān, conceiving the Islamic scripture to be superlative ('better'), exceeding the interpretive inadequacies of mere 'Christian commentators', such as the translator Rodwell himself.[38] Anticipating his later apology for the Qur'ān against 'Christian' readers in his 'Double Mirror' lecture, Frye's annotation also anticipates this lecture by dilating the 'Miriam and Mary' dichotomy into the much broader 'relation of Christ & Moses'. While Rodwell restricts himself to critiquing 'Muhammad' and his supposed 'confounding Miriam with the Virgin Mary', Frye transfers and expands the significance of these ancillary women, finding their identity to imply a more 'total typology', offering a *figura* that fuses Moses and Jesus; Exodus and the Gospel; Old Testament and New Testament.

Most familiar in Frye's comment on the Qur᾽ān here, however, is simply his *familiarity* with the Qur᾽ān itself, exemplifying Frye's informal and intimate approach to Muslim revelation. Recording his reading of the Qur᾽ān in relaxed style, buried at the bottom of his private page, Frye's familiarity is especially evident in the way he addresses the Muslim Prophet. While Rodwell rejects 'Muhammad' in his printed footnote, Frye's scrawl refers simply to 'M.', inscribing the Prophet's name as a personal abbreviation, pencilled as a single casual letter.[39] Culminating a cycle of nominal abbreviation that informs his entire campaign of Qur᾽ānic interpretation – interpretation which invariably (re)names and (re)identifies – Frye here names the Prophet anew in personal terms, even while seeking to identify with the Prophet's interpretive position. Rebuffing Rodwell's allegation of erroneous 'anachronism', Frye will instead defend the Qur᾽ān as meaningful 'synchronism'; however, more significant is the sympathy which Frye's marginal moment suggests, not only abbreviating Muḥammad's name, but endorsing the Muslim abbreviation of sacred history, collapsing all distinction between biblical Miriam and Mary. Spontaneously forging 'another version of his name', even while inscribing the scattered pages of the very *Koran* conveyed by the Prophet, Frye's pencilled comment becomes a personal 'sign' of his own private receptions, mirroring back identities in triplicate, with 'M.' serving as the abridged name that nevertheless bridges a fresh 'relation' between 'Christ & Moses'.

NOTES

1. Research and writing for this chapter was first encouraged by Todd Lawson, whose own ground-breaking scholarship on Frye is further mentioned below. I also gratefully acknowledge my earliest teachers at York University, Toronto, and especially John Willoughby, whose remembrances of Northrop Frye first prompted my viewing of 'The Bible and Literature' lecture series, and my reading of Frye's critical works in the late 1990s. See *Northrop Frye's Notebooks and Lectures on the Bible and Other Religious Texts*, ed. Robert D. Denham (Toronto: University of Toronto Press, 2003), pp. 415–607 for a transcript of Frye's 'The Bible and Literature' lectures (the passage quoted above appears on page 485). However, when quoting from *The Bible and Literature: A Personal View from Northrop Frye* I follow not this printed transcript, as it excises Frye's spontaneous missteps and stumbles, which are pivotal to my argument overall; transcripts are instead my own, taken directly from individual lectures as they were recorded (for full citation, see note 4, below).
2. For Reckendorf's shocked exclamation at the 'identification' between Miriam and Mary, see above, and Reckendorf (trans.), *al-Qōrān*, p. 175.

3. This assertion regarding Frye is cited in *The Qurʾān and Kerygma*'s Introduction above, and derives from *Educating the Imagination: Northrop Frye, Past, Present, and Future*, p. 3.
4. These lectures were recorded, and edited, as video episodes, and published as Northrop Frye, *The Bible and Literature: A Personal View from Northrop Frye* (Distributed by Information Commons, Media Distribution, University of Toronto, 1982). For these videos online, see <https://heritage.utoronto.ca/content/personal-view-northrop-frye-bible-and-literature-program-introduction>. Accessed 30 July 2019.
5. The chart drawn by Frye begins at minute 4 of his 'The Double Mirror: Exodus and the Gospel' program; see <https://heritage.utoronto.ca/content/video/bible-and-literature-personal-view-northrop-frye-program-12>. Accessed 30 July 2019.
6. This characterisation of the Bible as 'double mirror' is quoted from an article of the same name which Frye published even while delivering his 1981–82 lecture series; see Northrop Frye, 'The Double Mirror', *Bulletin of the American Academy of Arts and Sciences* 35:3 (1981): 32–41 (p. 34).
7. Frye's association of 'totally typological' with 'ahistorical' in his lecture may seem inconsistent with his definition of 'typology' in critical works such as *On the Bible and Human Culture*, where Frye suggests that 'What typology really is is a vision of history, or more accurately of historical process' (Northrop Frye, *Northrop Frye on Religion: Excluding* The Great Code *and* Words with Power, ed. Alvin A. Lee and Jean O'Grady (Toronto: University of Toronto Press, 2000), p. 72). However, see Todd Lawson's 'Typological Figuration and the Meaning of "Spiritual": The Qurʾānic Story of Joseph', *Journal of the American Oriental Society* 132:2 (2012): 221–244 – an article that represents a pioneering treatment of Qurʾānic typology through Frye's categories, and which reminds us that 'not only does typology move through time and transcend time (Frye's words), but, in fact, typology frequently erases or collapses time' (p. 224).
8. As mentioned above, *The Great Code* appeared in 1982. Frye's raw full lectures, which became the basis for *The Bible and Literature: A Personal View from Northrop Frye*, were delivered between September 1980 to March 1981 (see <https://heritage.utoronto.ca/frye/full-lectures>. Accessed 7 August 2019.).
9. Northrop Frye, *The Great Code: The Bible and Literature*, ed. Alvin A. Lee (Toronto: University of Toronto Press, 2006), p. 193.
10. My invocation of the 'centripetal' as a critical term echoes Frye himself, whose interest in this centre-seeking 'direction of the mind' is evidenced widely throughout his work, and surfaces explicitly within his '*Bible and Literature*' lectures (see, for example, Frye's Lecture 25, i.e., 'Conclusion: The Language of Love').
11. Frye, *Northrop Frye's Notebooks and Lectures on the Bible and Other Religious Texts*, p. 88. Introducing 'Notebook 11f' (which spans pages 72–139), Denham notes that '[i]nternal evidence reveals that this notebook dates from 1969–70' (p. 72); Denham also traces Frye's reference to Milton's 'blind fury' to *Lycidas*, l. 75. The core treatment of the Qurʾān in 'Notebook 11f' stretches over pages 83 to 90 in this published edition, with much extra-Qurʾānic material interspersed. Frye's appreciation of the Qurʾān also seems to evolve gradually through these pages; while the scripture is respected as 'synchronic dianoia' by Entry 81, Frye had disparaged the Qurʾān as a 'totally inadequate conception of a sacred book' and 'deadly dull' in his earlier entries (see entries 68 and 71 respectively).

12. In defining 'synchronic' and 'diachronic', I appeal here to their etymologies. However, Frye elsewhere helps to parse these terms by associating the former with 'imaginative vision', and the latter with 'teleological plot' in his 'Notebook 12' – a notebook which also repeats Frye's assertion that 'The Koran is a completely synchronic Scripture'; see *The 'Third Book' Notebooks of Northrop Frye 1964–1972*, ed. Michael Dolzani (Toronto: University of Toronto Press, 2002), pp. 217–218.
13. Frye recurrently traces the Qur'ān's composition to the Prophet himself; see, for instance, Frye's marginalia in his own copy of the Qur'ān, where he notes that Muḥammad 'seems to have' had access to 'only the Midrashim, not Genesis itself'. Quoted from 'Frye annotated no. 1022', Frye's own copy of *The Koran* (trans.), John Meadows Rodwell (London: J. M. Dent; New York: E. P. Dutton, 1909), p. 234 – an item detailed further in note 17 below. All quotations from 'Frye annotated no. 1022' are courtesy of Victoria University Library (Toronto). Frye's attribution of the Qur'ān to the Prophet does not, however, necessarily comprise a denigration in his own mind, noting, for instance, that 'Mohammed was a very great inspired poet' (see Frye, *Northrop Frye's Notebooks and Lectures on the Bible and Other Religious Texts*, p. 88).
14. Frye, *Northrop Frye's Notebooks and Lectures on the Bible and Other Religious Texts*, p. 88. This passage – appreciating 'the Koran' as 'descending from heaven' – recalls another Frye appraisal included a few pages earlier, where he portrays the Qur'ān's later *sūra*s as 'a shower of lyrical apocalyptic sparks, charms, riddles, curses, etc.' (see Frye, *Northrop Frye's Notebooks and Lectures on the Bible and Other Religious Texts*, p. 85). Frye's discussion of what 'Moslems' would and 'wouldn't think' is also reminiscent of a latter passage in which he asserts that the 'repetitiousness of the Koran would drive a reader out of his mind if he were reading it as he would read any other book. But for a Mohammedan, brought up from infancy to learn it by heart, to attach the greatest possible reverence & weight to what it says, it does exactly the job it should do' (see Frye, *Northrop Frye's Notebooks and Lectures on the Bible and Other Religious Texts*, p. 195 and below).
15. With '*the* recitation', I gesture to the etymology of '*al-qur'ān*' (القرآن) itself.
16. For Frye's papers and personal books at the Victoria University Library (E. J. Pratt Library), see the Northrop Frye materials as described in the library's online Special Collections catalogue: <http://library.vicu.utoronto.ca/collections/special_collections/f11_northrop_frye>. Accessed 30 July 2019.
17. I am indebted to Todd Lawson for first bringing to my attention this item – i.e., 'Frye annotated no. 1022' – and its valuable marginalia. My following discussion would not have been possible if not for Lawson's 'Frye's Qur'ān' (a paper presented at the 2011 Conference on the Qur'ān, hosted by the Centre of Islamic Studies, SOAS, London), and his subsequent efforts to encourage study of Frye and Islam among fellow scholars. I am also very grateful to Roma Kali at the Victoria University Library, who facilitated my research on Frye's Qur'ānic marginalia during the summers of 2013 and 2017, and the Victoria University Library for their permission both to quote from 'Frye annotated no. 1022', as well as include an image from this item (see note 22 below). The Victoria University Library also possesses another copy of the Qur'ān owned by Frye; designated 'Frye annotated no. 1466', and comprising *The Koran: Commonly called the Alkoran of Mohammed*, trans. George Sale (London: F. Warne 1887), this item features only sporadic annotations on Sale's 'Preliminary Discourse', with no marginalia inscribed through the body of the translation itself.

18. 'Frye annotated no. 1022', p. 204. For the sake of clarity, I supply the standard numbers (64, 65) for these *āyāt*, which are not provided in Rodwell's edition; while his translation does include numbers for every tenth verse (10, 20, 30 etc.), these do not necessarily align with standard numbering conventions.
19. 'Frye annotated no. 1022', p. 204.
20. Although Frye was not familiar with Arabic, Rodwell's English translation over these two *āyāt* allows Frye to recognise that verse 64 and verse 65 share the same verb (in Arabic, أنزل ; *anzala*); compare 'And we have sent down (*anzalnā*) the Book to thee only' in verse 64, with 'And God sendeth down (*anzala*) water from Heaven' in verse 65.
21. Frye's annotations span the entirety of Rodwell's translation, from its contents list (Frye annotated no. 1022, p. xiv) – where Frye pencils a tick beside each one of the listed *sūra*s, presumably to mark that he has read each one – to 'Frye annotated no. 1022', p. 499, which comprises one of the final pages in this edition.
22. 'Frye annotated no. 1022', p. 230; image courtesy of Victoria University Library (Toronto). Frye's focus on 'sequence in the Koran' as he annotates Rodwell's translation acquires a fresh urgency due to Rodwell's decision to re-order the *sūra*s of the Qur'ān according to the supposed order of their revelation; thus, Rodwell's translation begins with Sūrat al-ʿAlaq (Sūra 96) rather than Sūrat al-Fātiḥa (Sūra 1). Frye is well-aware of Rodwell's radical revision of the Qur'ān's normative chapter order, as Rodwell himself mounts an apology for his choice in his 'Preface', and also includes the conventional numbering for each sūra before its translation (e.g., the Chapter of 'Joseph' pictured above features the normative number 'XII' immediately before its title, despite appearing as Chapter LXXVII in Rodwell's translation).
23. 'Frye annotated no. 1022', pp. 210, 94 and 82 respectively.
24. 'Frye annotated no. 1022', p. 208.
25. For Frye's marginalia on Qur'ān 3:183, see 'Frye annotated no. 1022', p. 403. Frye seems to align the first half of the *āya* with Elijah's contest with the priests of Baal (1 Kings 18:21–40), and the *āya*'s second half with Jesus's rebuke of 'hypocrites', who are associated with the killing of prophets (Matthew 23:29–30).
26. For the Qur'ānic imperative '*qul*' as understood to be commonly addressed to the Prophet Muḥammad, see Rosaline Ward Gwyne, *Logic, Rhetoric, and Legal Reasoning in the Qur'ān: God's Arguments* (London: RoutledgeCurzon 2004), pp. 81–82.
27. For the thirteenth *āya* of Sūrat Āl ʿImrān as a 'rare historical aside' which refers to 'the victory at Badr', see Francis E. Peters, *Mecca: A Literary History of the Muslim Holy Land* (Princeton, NJ: Princeton University Press, 1994), p. 71.
28. 'Frye annotated no. 1022', p. 386. Although Frye's 'legions of angels that Jesus' is entirely unmistakable in his handwriting, the final word of Frye's comment ('related') spills over the line, and is somewhat unclear.
29. Frye offers his typological reading of Qur'ān 3:13 although he is certainly aware of this verse's ostensible reference to a historical event. Rodwell himself supplies a footnote to this same verse, parsing the 'sign' which 'Ye have already had' by noting that 'In the battle of Bedr, Muhammad, with 319 followers routed 1000 Meccans, A. H. 2'.
30. 'Frye annotated no. 1022', p. 341. For Dante and Coleridge in Frye's *Koran* marginalia, see also 'Frye annotated no. 1022', pp. 298 and 166 respectively. In the former, beside Rodwell's 'and on *the walls* AL ARAF', Frye writes 'Dante's wall of love'. In the latter, Frye scribbles beside a verse in Sūra 17 that begins 'And

every man's fate have We fastened about his neck' an annotation that reads 'bird: cf. A.M'., most likely implying the 'A[ncient] M[ariner]' – Coleridge's celebrated 1798 poem which does indeed concern a 'bird' that is 'fastened about [the] neck'.

31. 'Frye annotated no. 1022', p. 276. For Frye's appeal to Blake's 'Everlasting Gospel', see *Northrop Frye's Notebooks and Lectures on the Bible and Other Religious Texts*, p. 227.
32. 'Frye annotated no. 1022', p. 121.
33. The dual genealogy implied by Ishmael in Melville's *Moby-Dick* – biblical and Qurʾānic – which Frye here intuits is treated in my *Nineteenth-Century U. S. Literature in Middle Eastern Languages* (Edinburgh: Edinburgh University Press, 2013), pp. 110–112.
34. 'Wisdom: The Proverb' comprises Program 20 in the thirty-episode *The Bible and Literature: A Personal View from Northrop Frye*, while 'The Double Mirror: Exodus and the Gospel' represents Program 12.
35. This selection begins near the twenty-first minute of Frye's 'Wisdom: The Proverb' program; an edited version of this quote appears in Frye, *Northrop Frye's Notebooks and Lectures on the Bible and Other Religious Texts*, p. 545.
36. For this link between Luqmān and Ahikar, Frye seems to have relied on Robert Henry Charles, *The Apocrypha and Pseudepigrapha of the Old Testament*, 2 vols. (Oxford: Clarendon Press, 1913); see 'Frye annotated no. 1022', p. 267, where Frye responds to a footnote by Rodwell (who cites the opinion that 'Lokman' is 'Æsop'), by instead writing 'not Aesop: Ahikar. See Charles's ed. of The Pseudepigrapha'. For another contemporaneous source addressing the similarities between 'Aḥiḳar' and 'Loḳman', however, see *The Story of Aḥiḳar from the Aramaic, Syriac, Arabic, Armenian, Ethiopic, Old Turkish, Greek and Slavonic Versions*, ed. F. C. Conybeare, J. Rendel Harris and Agnes Smith Lewis (Cambridge: Cambridge University Press, 2nd ed., 1913), esp. pp. lxxv–lxxvii.
37. 'Frye annotated no. 1022', p. 385. Similar to the situation described in note 28 above, Frye again splits the final word of his annotation over the line, rendering it less legible, and thus not included in my transcription. The most likely candidate for this final word is 'previously', which would render Frye's full statement: 'M. drew the relation of Christ & Moses better than some Christians previously'.
38. Regarding the supposed 'anachronism of confounding Miriam with the Virgin Mary', Rodwell offers a later footnote to Sūrat Maryam that suggests that such an 'anachronism is probably only apparent' (see 'Frye annotated no. 1022', p. 119). However, Frye also voices a defense of the Qurʾān against Rodwell in other *loci* as well. See, for example, 'Frye annotated no. 1022', p. 346, where Frye responds to a Rodwell footnote which claims that 'Muhammad either knowingly rejected the divinity of the Holy Ghost, or confounded Gabriel announcing the conception with the Holy Spirit that overshadowed Mary'; disparaging Rodwell's critique, Frye scribbles at the bottom of this page that 'all spirits are the one Spirit, Gabriel. There's no "confusion": this man [i.e., Rodwell] is an idiot'.
39. Frye's abbreviated reference to Muḥammad as 'M', here in Sūrat Āl ʿImrān, is not unique but parallels other annotations in his *Koran*. See, for example, 'Frye annotated no. 1022', p. 145, where he notes 'Milton's treatment of Enoch & Noah is a little like M's'.

CODA: 'SYNTHESIS OF THE WORD'

On the morning of 17 May 1949, Northrop Frye supervised exams at the University of Toronto, invigilating the undergraduate final for 'English 2b' – a course covering British poetry from 'Dryden to Keats'.[1] After testing his students on their poetry readings, Frye went off to write his own prose, before finally breaking for the day to buy some books. In his diary, Frye described his day as follows:

> Finished 2b exams & in the afternoon I slobbered another bibful of deathless prose for the benefit of *Here & Now* on criticism & book-reviewing. Then on an impulse I bought two Everymans, the Koran & George Macdonald's *Phantastes*, & a rather dubious Jungian book. The Koran still baffles me: I can't figure out why the hell anybody went for that book. It probably makes a lot more sense in Arabic as a prose-poetry synthesis of the Word in which rhetorical & dialectic aspects are indistinguishable.[2]

Wearied by his academic duties – overseeing 'exams' and 'slobber[ing]' barely passable 'prose' – Frye makes a few 'impulse' purchases in the afternoon. In addition to a 'dubious Jungian' volume, Frye also brings home 'two Everymans', buying not only a Christian 'fantasy', but also a copy of 'the Koran'. Together with *Phantastes* – a fictional 'romance' by apologist and pastor, George Macdonald – Frye acquires the Muslim scripture, picking up the precise edition that he will later annotate, scribbling marginalia in this same copy bought spontaneously on 17 May 1949.[3]

Even before reading his Everyman 'Koran', however, Frye records this above written response, his diary entry assessing the Muslim scripture in advance of glossing its pages. Rather than admire his acquisition, Frye is initially puzzled and perplexed, questioning the Qur'ān's own canonicity. In the morning, Frye had supervised his students as they grappled with English poetry; by evening, it is Islam's own poetic scripture that successfully 'baffles' Frye, Canada's leading critic 'still' unsure why 'anybody went for that book'. And yet, no sooner than he had voiced this uncertainty, Frye interrupts his own incomprehension, suddenly shifting from pejorative confusion to positive conjecture. Not content to stop at perplexity, Frye spontaneously begins to speculate, guessing that the Muslim scripture 'probably makes a lot more sense in Arabic' – a statement that opens Frye up to fresh possibilities, associating the Qur'ān with the very same ideas and ideals that catalyse his entire career. Anticipating his later label, calling the Qur'ān 'totally typological', Frye here suspects the Muslim scripture to be a superlative 'synthesis', a textual marriage where modes of speech are seamlessly merged. Fusing 'prose' and 'poetry', the Qur'ān equally conjoins the 'rhetorical & dialectic', unifying these 'aspects' so completely that they become 'indistinguishable'. The centre of a literary 'synthesis', the Muslim scripture is ultimately framed by Frye as logocentric, characterised by a capitalised 'the Word': a definite phrase with decidedly Christian resonance. Inciting first his infernal confusion – with Frye asking 'why the hell anybody went for that book' – the Qur'ān suddenly rises in his estimation, ascending to the highest kerygmatic category of 'the Word' itself.

Invoking 'the Koran' as absolute 'synthesis', Frye's diary entry merges in miniature the same processes and polarities which are also mapped macrocosmically by the present study. As with each of the authors addressed in *The Qur'ān and Kerygma*, Frye combines conscious rejection with creative recuperation, initially unsympathetic to 'the Koran', yet ultimately integrating the scripture within his critical enterprise. Straddling imaginative potential and the problematics of intent, Frye's 'impulsive' purchase is framed by initial historical scepticism, and yet leads to linguistic speculation, supposing the scripture's authentic 'sense' to be 'probably' embedded in its 'Arabic'. Recalling this study's opening chapters on al-Qūṭī and al-Ghazzī, it is the Qur'ān's original language that overcomes Christian resistance, with 'Arabic' propelling Frye's imaginative pivot from 'bafflement' to belief in the Qur'ān's potential. Shifting from dialect to 'dialectic', Frye mentally translates the Muslim scripture, rendering its original language into a literary 'synthesis' – a speculative process that is paralleled by the actual translation acts addressed in *The Qur'ān and Kerygma*. Bridging Qur'ānic verses and Christian versifying in Chapters 1 and 2, it is Arabic that intersects more multilingual environs in Chapters 3 and 4, before becoming submerged under later biblical renditions and annotations in Chapters 5 and 6. Variable in their Arabic literacy – from al-Qūṭī's fluency to Frye's unfamiliarity – it is a shared willingness to re-imagine and integrate Qur'ānic idioms that ties together the biblical authors covered in the present study. Dissolving strict divisions, the Qur'ān is framed by Frye as hyphenated in genre – 'poetry-prose' – as well as conjoined in form and content, with its 'rhetorical & dialectic aspects' equated. The source of 'synthesis', the Qur'ān itself, however, serves as catalyst for later acts of literary synthesis, its 'rhetorical' power successfully piercing religious 'dialectic' and difference, with authors from discrete traditions – Orthodox and Catholic, Chalcedonian and Miaphysite, Protestant and Jewish – merged in their 'indistinguishable' blending of biblical commitments with Islamic idioms.

Opening its introduction by quoting Frye's 'last big book', the present study began by citing his 1990 *Words with Power*, finding the Muslim scripture surface in Frye's final major publication. The present epilogue ends this study by returning four decades earlier, reading Frye's personal reflections from 1949, recording his 'impulsive' purchase of *The Koran* in an entry from one of his 'earliest extant' diaries.[4] Locating the Qur'ān at alternate edges of a Christian life – spanning public and private writings, as well as forty years of a career – *The Qur'ān and Kerygma* is thus itself enveloped by a broad structural echo, its epilogue amplifying the 1949 source for its introductory quotations from 1990. Reversing chronology to find such repetitions in content, it is a 'Coda' therefore, and not a 'Conclusion', that closes this study, finishing with a finale that reverberates forward, rather than merely recurring to the past. Unearthing Qur'ānic echoes in each of its six chapters – reaching back more than a millennium, from the ninth to the twentieth century – this study also aspires to preface the rich biblical receptions of the Qur'ān that are no doubt still to emerge in the new millennium. Indeed, in Frye's early and ambivalent diary entry from 1949, it is just such a fruitful future of Qur'ānic prospects across traditions that seems imaginatively implied. First asking 'why' the Muslim faithful '*went* for that book', Frye voices scepticism in the past tense; however, as he projects the kerygmatic potential of the Qur'ān, Frye yet speculates on what is 'probably' true, while also advancing to speak in the grammatical present. Supposing that the Muslim scripture likely '*makes* a lot more sense in Arabic', Frye's verbs catch up to the contemporary, suggesting finally that the Qur'ān so completely incorporates literary types that they '*are* indistinguishable', ending his diary entry with a sudden shift forward in tense that serves to make the 'synthesis of the Word' seem ever more 'Here & Now'.

NOTES

1. For a description of this 'English 2b' course, see page 12 of the sixteen-page pamphlet *University of Toronto, Department of University Extension, Pass Course for Teachers Calendar Summer Session, 1949* (University of Toronto, 1949). In this quotation, I have added italicisation to clarify the titles of texts (i.e., *Here & Now*, *Phantastes*).
2. Northrop Frye, *The Diaries of Northrop Frye, 1942–1955*, ed. Robert D. Denham (Toronto: University of Toronto Press, 2001), p. 207.
3. The term 'romance' derives from the subtitle of George Macdonald's 1858 novel, i.e., *Phantastes: A Faerie Romance for Men and Women* (London: Smith, Elder & Co.). Although Frye owned two copies of the Qur'ān (see Chapter 6, note 17 above), it is clear that the copy which was purchased on 17 May 1949 was indeed 'Frye annotated no. 1022', as this Rodwell translation comprises an 'Everyman'

edition, unlike Frye's other Qur'ān edition – 'Frye annotated no. 1466' – which was instead published by Warne as one of the 'Chandos Classics'.

4. See the 'Introduction' to Frye, *The Diaries of Northrop Frye, 1942–1955*, p. xix, which notes that while Frye's 'earliest extant diary is from 1942', the 'next one that has survived' was 'written in 1949'.

BIBLIOGRAPHY

Abdel Haleem, M. A. S., 'Grammatical shifts for rhetorical purposes: "Iltifat" and related features in the Qur'ān'. *Bulletin of the School of Oriental and African Studies* 55:3 (1992): 407–432.

—— (trans.), *The Qur'an: A New Translation*, Oxford: Oxford University Press, 2011.

Adawi, Subhi Ali (trans.), *ha-Qōrān: bəLashōn Aḥer*. Haifa: Gasṭliṭ, 2015.

Akkach, Samer, *Intimate Invocations: Al-Ghazzi's Biography of Abd al-Ghani al-Nabulusi (1641–1731)*. Leiden: Brill, 2012.

Ali, Yusuf (trans.), *Koran: An English Interpretation of the Holy Quran with Full Arabic Text*. Lahore: Muhammad Ashraf, 1992.

Allies, Thomas W., *The Throne of the Fisherman: The Root, the Bond, and the Crown of Christendom*. London: Burns & Oates, 1887.

Arberry, A. J. (trans.), *The Koran Interpreted*. New York: George Allen & Unwin Ltd, 1955.

Assaf, David, *Untold Tales of the Hasidim: Crisis & Discontent in the History of Hasidism*. Waltham, MA: Brandeis University Press, 2011.

Ayoub, Mahmoud M., 'Literary Exegesis of the Qur'ān: The Case of al-Sharīf al-Raḍī'. In *Literary Structures of Religious Meaning in the Qur'ān*, ed. Issa J. Boullata. Richmond: Curzon Press, 2000, pp. 292–309.

Bakhos, Carol, *Ishmael on the Border: Rabbinic Portrayals of the First Arab*. Albany, NY: State University of New York Press, 2006.

Bar Hebraeus, *Le Candélabre du Sanctuaire de Grégoire Abou'lfaradj dit Barhebraeus. Quatrième base, De l'Incarnation*, ed. and trans. Joseph Khoury, in *Patrologia Orientalis*, vol. 31. Paris: Firmin-Didot, 1966.

—— *Historia Compendiosa Dynastiarum*, ed. Edward Pococke, 2 vols. Oxford: H. Hall, 1663.

—— *Specimen Historiae Arabum, Sive, Gregorii Abul Farajii Malatiensis*, ed. Edward Pococke. Oxford: Humphrey Robinson, 1650.

—— *Specimen Historiae Arabum*, ed. Edward Pococke. Oxford: Clarendon Press, 1806.

Bewell, Alan, Neil ten Kortenaar and Germaine Warkentin (eds.), *Educating the Imagination: Northrop Frye, Past, Present, and Future*. Montreal and Kingston: McGill-Queen's University Press, 2015.

Bringhurst, Robert, 'Reading between the Books: Northrop Frye and the Cartography of Literature'. In *Educating the Imagination: Northrop Frye, Past, Present, and Future*, ed. Alan Bewell, Neil ten Kortenaar, Germaine Warkentin. Montreal and Kingston: McGill-Queen's University Press, 2015.

Burman, Thomas E., *Reading the Qur'ān* in Latin Christendom, *1140–1560*. Philadelphia: University of Pennsylvania Press, 2009.

Burnett, Charles, 'The Translating Activity in Medieval Spain'. In *The Legacy of Muslim Spain*, ed. Salma Khadra Jayyusi. Leiden & New York: E. J. Brill, 1992, pp. 1036–1058.

Carter, Michael, 'Foreign Vocabulary'. In *The Blackwell Companion to the Qur'ān*, ed. Andrew Rippin. Oxford: Blackwell, 2006, pp. 120–139.

Casewit, Yousef, 'A Muslim Scholar of the Bible: Prooftexts from Genesis and Matthew in the Qur'an Commentary of Ibn Barrajān of Seville (d. 536/1141)'. *Journal of Qur'anic Studies* 18:1 (2016): 1–48.

Casiday, Augustine, '"The Sweetest Music That Falls Upon the Ear": Translating and Interpreting the Psalter in Christian Andalucia'. In *Meditations of the Heart: The Psalms in Christian Thought and Practice: Essays in Honour of Andrew Louth*, ed. Andreas Andreopoulos, A. M. Casiday, Carol Harrison, and Andrew Louth. Turnhout: Brepols, 2011, pp. 225–242.

Charles, Robert Henry, *The Apocrypha and Pseudepigrapha of the Old Testament*, 2 vols. Oxford: Clarendon Press, 1913.

Charlesworth, James H., 'Jesus and the Temple'. In *Jesus and Temple: Textual and Archaeological Explorations*, ed. James H. Charlesworth. Minneapolis, MN: Fortress Press, 2014, pp. 145–81.

Chittick, William C., *The Sufi Path of Knowledge: Ibn al-'Arabi's Metaphysics of Imagination*. Albany, NY: State University of New York, 2009.

Conybeare, F. C., J. Rendel Harris, and Agnes Smith Lewis, *The Story of Aḥiḳar from the Aramaic, Syriac, Arabic, Armenian, Ethiopic, Old Turkish, Greek and Slavonic Versions*. Cambridge: Cambridge University Press, 2nd ed., 1913.

Dalman, Gustaf, *Jesus-Jeshua: Studies in the Gospels* (trans.), Paul P. Levertoff. London: S.P.C.K.; New York: Macmillan, 1929.

Davis, Stephen J., *Coptic Christology in Practice: Incarnation and Divine Participation in Late Antique and Medieval Egypt*. Oxford: Oxford University Press, 2008.

Demiri, Lejla, *Muslim Exegesis of the Bible in Medieval Cairo: Najm al-Dīn al-Ṭūfī*'s (d. *716* = 1316*) Commentary on the Christian Scriptures*; *a Critical Edition and Annotated Translation with an Introduction*. Leiden: Brill, 2013.

Department of University Extension, *Pass Course for Teachers Calendar Summer Session, 1949*. University of Toronto, 1949.

D'Israeli, Isaac, *Calamities of Authors*; *Including some Inquiries respecting their Moral and Literary Characters*, 2 vols. John Murray: London, 1812.

Doiṭsh, Ya'aḳov and Michael Meerson (eds. and trans.), *Toledot Yeshu: The Life Story of Jesus; Two Volumes and Database*. Tübingen: Mohr Siebeck, 2014.

Dunlop, D. M., 'Ḥafṣ B. Albar – the Last of the Goths?' *Journal of the Royal Asiatic Society of Great Britain & Ireland* 86 (1954): 137–151.

Edgar, Swift and Angela M. Kinney (eds.), *The Vulgate Bible*. Cambridge: Harvard University Press, 2010.

Einboden, Jeffrey, 'The Genesis of *Weltliteratur*: Goethe's *West-Ostlicher Divan* and Kerygmatic Pluralism'. *Literature and Theology* 19:3 (2005): 238–250.

—— *Islam and Romanticism: Muslim Currents from Goethe to Emerson*. London: Oneworld, 2014.

—— *The Islamic Lineage of American Literary Culture: Muslim Sources from the Revolution to Reconstruction*. New York: Oxford Univeristy Press, 2016.

—— *Nineteenth-Century US Literature in Middle Eastern Languages*. Edinburgh: Edinburgh University Press, 2013.

Efron, John M., *German Jewry and the Allure of the Sephardic*. Princeton, NJ: Princeton University Press, 2016.

Elmarsafy, Ziad, *The Enlightenment Qur'an: The Politics of Translation and the Construction of Islam*. New York: Oneworld Publications, 2014.

al-Falimbant, 'Abd aṣ-Ṣamad, *Sayr as-Sālikīn fī Ṭarīqat as-Sādāt aṣ-Ṣufiyya*, 2 vols. Singapore: Pustaka Nasional, 1953.

Fenton, Paul B., 'Moritz Steinschneider's Contribution to Judaeo-Arabic Studies'. In *Studies on Steinschneider: Moritz Steinschneider and the Emergence of the Science of Judaism in Nineteenth-Century Germany*, ed. Reimund Leicht and Gad Freudenthal. Leiden: Brill, 2012, pp. 363–382.

Fernández-Morera, Darío, *The Myth of the Andalusian Paradise: Muslims, Christians, and Jews Under Islamic Rule in Medieval Spain*. Wilmington, Delaware: ISI Books, 2016.

Förstel, Karl, *Schriften zum Islam von Arethas und Euthymios Zigabenos und Fragmente der Griechischen Koranübersetzung*: Griechisch-Deutsche Textausgabe. Wiesbaden: Harrassowitz Verlag, 2009.

Fox, Michael V., *Proverbs 10–31: A New Translation with Introduction and Commentary*. New Haven: Yale University Press, 2010.

Frye, Northrop, *The Bible and Literature: A Personal View from Northrop Frye*. Distributed by Information Commons, Media Distribution, University of Toronto, 1982.

—— *The Diaries of Northrop Frye, 1942–1955*, ed. Robert D. Denham. Toronto: University of Toronto Press, 2001.

—— 'The Double Mirror', *Bulletin of the American Academy of Arts and Sciences* 35:3 (1981): 32–41.

—— 'Frye annotated no. 1022', Victoria University Library.

—— *The Great Code: The Bible and Literature*, ed. Alvin A. Lee. Toronto: University of Toronto Press, 2006.

—— *Northrop Frye on Religion: Excluding* The Great Code *and* Words with Power, ed. Alvin A. Lee and Jean O'Grady. Toronto: University of Toronto Press, 2000.

—— *Northrop Frye's Notebooks and Lectures on the Bible and Other Religious Texts*, ed. Robert D. Denham. Toronto: University of Toronto Press, 2003.

—— *The 'Third Book' Notebooks of Northrop Frye 1964–1972*, ed. Michael Dolzani. Toronto: University of Toronto Press, 2002.

—— *Words with Power: Being a Second Study of 'the Bible and Literature'*, ed. Michael Dolzani. Toronto: University of Toronto Press, 2016.

Gacek, Adam. *Arabic Manuscripts: A Vademecum for Readers*. Leiden: Brill, 2012.

al-Ghazzī, Sulaymān, *Sulaymān* Al-*Ghazzī*: *Shā'ir* wa-*Kātib Masīḥī Malakī*, ed. Neophytos Edelby, 3 vols. Jūniya, Lebanon: al-Maktabat al-Būlusiyya, 1984–1986.

Glassman, Bernard, *Benjamin Disraeli: The Fabricated Jew in Myth and Memory*. Lanham, MD: University Press of America, 2003.

Goitein, S. D., *Studies in Islamic History and Institutions*. Leiden: E. J. Brill, 1968.

Good, Deirdre J., 'The Miriamic Secret'. In *Mariam, the Magdalen, and the Mother*, ed. Deirdre

Good. Bloomington: Indiana University Press, 2005, pp. 3–26.

Griffith, Sidney H., 'Christian Lore and the Arabic Qur'ān: The "Companions of the Cave" in *Sūrat al-Kahf* and in Syriac Christian Tradition'. In *The Qur'ān in its Historical Context*, ed. Gabriel S. Reynolds. London: Routledge, 2008, pp. 124–37.

—— *The Church in the Shadow of the Mosque: Christians and Muslims in the World of Islam*. Princeton, NJ: Princeton University Press, 2010.

—— 'Disputes with Muslims in Syriac Christian Texts: From Patriarch John (d. 648) to Bar Hebraeus (d. 1286)'. In *Religionsgespräche im Mittelalter*, ed. Bernard Lewis and Friedrich Niewöhner. Wiesbaden: Harrassowitz, 1992, pp. 251–273.

—— 'The *Kitab Misbah al-Aql* of Severus Ibn al-Muqaffa': A Profile of the Christian

Creed in Arabic in Tenth Century Egypt'. *Medieval Encounters* 2 (1996): 15–42.
—— '"Melkites", "Jacobites" and the Christological Controversies in Arabic in Third/ Ninth-Century Syria'. In *Syrian Christians under Islam: The First Thousand Years*, ed. David Thomas. Leiden: Brill, 2001, pp. 9–55.
—— 'Al-Naṣārā in the Qur'ān: A Hermeneutical Reflection'. In *New Perspectives on the Qur'ān: The Qur'ān in its Historical Context 2*. London: Routledge, 2011, pp. 301–332.

Grillmeier, Alois and Theresia Hainthaler, *Christ in Christian Tradition: Vol. 2, Part 4*, trans. O. C. Dean. London: Mowbray, 1996.

Gwyne, Rosaline Ward, *Logic, Rhetoric, and Legal Reasoning in the Qur'ān: God's Arguments*. London: RoutledgeCurzon, 2004.

Haivry, Ofir, *John Selden and the Western Political Tradition*. Cambridge: Cambridge University Press, 2017.

Hallaq, Wael, *Sharī'a*: Theory, *Practice, Transformations*. Cambridge: Cambridge University Press, 2012.

Hamilton, Alastair, *Europe and the Arab World: Five Centuries of Books by European Scholars and Travellers from the Libraries of the Arcadian Group*. Dublin: Arcadian Group, 1994.

Hamori, Esther J., *When Gods Were Men: The Embodied God in Biblical and Near Eastern Literature*. Berlin: Walter De Gruyter, 2008.

Hamza, Feras, 'Temporary Hellfire Punishment and the Making of Sunni Orthodoxy'. In *Roads to Paradise: Eschatology and Concepts of the Hereafter in Islam*, ed. Sebastian Günther, Todd Lawson, and Christian Mauder, 2 vols. Leiden: Brill, 2016, pp. 371–406.

Hobart, John H., *A Charge to the Clergy of the Protestant Episcopal Church in the State of New-York*. New York: T. and J. Swords, 1815.

Hoffmann, Thomas, *The Poetic Qur'ān: Studies on Qur'ānic* Poeticity. Wiesbaden: Harrassowitz, 2007.

Holladay, William L., *The Psalms through Three Thousand Years: Prayerbook of a Cloud of Witnesses*. Minneapolis: Fortress Press, 2000.

Holt, P. M., *Studies in the History of the Near East*. London: Frank Cass, 1973.

Hugi, Jacky, 'Reading the Quran in Hebrew'. *Al-Monitor*, 29 December 2015. <http://www.al-monitor.com/pulse/tr/contents/articles/originals/2015/12/quran-translation-hebrew-galilee-israeli-arab-muslim.html>. Accessed 11 July 2019.

Ibn Baṭrīq, Sa'īd, *Contextio Gemmarum, sive, Eutychii Patriarchæ Alexandrini Annales*, ed. and trans. Edward Pococke, 2 vols. Oxford: Humphrey Robinson, 1658–59.
—— *Eutychii Ægyptii, Patriarchæ Orthodoxorum Alexandrini*, ed. John Selden. London: Excudebat Richardus Bishopus, 1642.
—— *Eutychii Patriarchae Alexandrini Annales*, ed. L. Cheikho, B. Carra de Vaux, and H. Zayyat. Paris: C. Poussielgue, 1906.

Ibn al-Muqaffa', *Histoire des Conciles (Second Livre)*, ed. and trans. L. Leroy in *Patrologia Orientalis*, vol. 6. Paris: Librairie de Paris, 1911, pp. 465–600.
—— *Réfutation de Sa'īd ibn Batriq (d'Eutychius) (Le Livre des Conciles)*, ed. and trans. P. Chebli in *Patrologia Orientalis*, vol. 3. Paris: Librairie de Paris, 1909, pp. 121–242.

Jager, Eric, *The Tempter's Voice: Language and the Fall in Medieval Literature*. Ithaca: Cornell University Press, 1993.

James, David, *Early Islamic Spain: The History of Ibn al-Qūṭīya*. London: Routledge, 2011.

Johnson, George W., *Memoirs of John Selden and Notices of the Political Context during his Time*. London: Orr and Smith, 1835.
Kalmar, Ivan, *Early Orientalism: Imagined Islam and the Notion of Sublime Power*. London: Routledge, 2012.
Lawrence, Bruce, *The Koran in English: A Biography*. Princeton, NJ: Princeton University Press, 2017.
Lawson, Todd, 'Typological Figuration and the Meaning of "Spiritual": The Qur'ānic Story of Joseph'. *Journal of the American Oriental Society* 132:2 (2012): 221–244.
Lewis, Agnes (ed.), *Acta Mythologica Apostolorum: Transcribed from an Arabic Ms. in the Convent of Deyr-Es-Suriani, Egypt, and from Mss in the Convent of St. Catherine, on Mount Sinai*. London: Clay, 1904.
Lindley, Keith, *The English Civil War and Revolution: A Sourcebook*. London: Routledge, 1998.
Luxenberg, Christoph, '*Al-Najm* (Q 53), Chapter of the Star: A New Syro-Aramaic Reading of Verses 1–18'. In *New Perspectives on the Qur'ān*: The *Qur'ān* in its Historical Context 2, ed. Gabriel S. Reynolds. London: Routledge, 2011, pp. 279–297.
Macdonald, George, *Phantastes: A Faerie Romance for Men and Women*. London: Smith, Elder & Co., 1858.
Maimonides, Moses, *Moreh Nevukhim*, ed. Profiat Duran, vol. 1. Ṿarsha: Bi-defus Y. Goldman, 1872.
Marracci, Ludovico (trans.), *Alcorani Textus Universus Ex Correctioribus Arabum*, 2 vols. Padua: Ex Typographia Seminarii, 1698.
Mathisen, R. W., 'Barbarian "Arian" Clergy, Church Organization, and Church Practices'. In *Arianism: Roman Heresy and Barbarian Creed*, ed. Guido M. Berndt and Roland Steinacher. London: Routledge, 2016, pp. 145–192.
Matthews, Nancy L., *William Sheppard, Cromwell's Law Reformer*. Cambridge: Cambridge University Press, 1984.
Mauder, Christian, 'Al-Suyūṭī's Stance toward Worldly Power: A Reexamination based on Unpublished and Understudied Sources'. In *Al-Suyūṭī, a Polymath of the Mamlūk Period: Proceedings of the Themed Day of the First Conference of the School of Mamlūk Studies*, ed. Antonella Ghersetti. Leiden: Brill, 2017, pp. 81–97.
McGaughey, Douglas R., *Strangers and Pilgrims: On the Role of Aporiai in Theology*. Berlin: Walter De Gruyter, 1997.
Meinardus, Otto F. A., *Christians in Egypt: Orthodox, Catholic, and Protestant Communities Past and Present*. Cairo: The American University in Cairo Press, 2007.
Meisami, Julie S. and Paul Starkey (eds.), *Encyclopedia of Arabic Literature: Volume 1*. London Routledge, 1998.
Miller, Michael L., 'European Judaism and Islam: The Contribution of Jewish Orientalists'. In *A History of Jewish–Muslim Relations: From the Origins to the Present Day*, ed. Abdelwahab Meddeb and Benjamin Stora. Princeton, NJ: Princeton University Press, 2013, pp. 828–836.
Mir, Mustansir, 'Language'. In *The Blackwell Companion to the Qur'ān*, ed. Andrew Rippin. Malden, MA: Blackwell Publishing 2008, pp. 88–106.
Moazzen, Maryam, 'A Garden beyond the Garden: ʿAyn al-Quḍāt Hamadānī's Perspective on Paradise'. In *Roads to Paradise: Eschatology and Concepts of the Hereafter in Islam*, ed. Sebastian Günther, Todd Lawson, and Christian Mauder, 2 vols. Leiden: Brill, 2016, pp. 566–578.

Moreman, Christopher M., *Beyond the Threshold: Afterlife Beliefs and Experience in World Religions*. Lanham, MD: Rowman & Littlefield, 2010.

Moussa, Mohammed, *Politics of the Islamic Tradition: The Thought of Muhammad al-Ghazali*. London: Routledge, 2016.

Nallino, C. A., 'Le fonti arabe manoscritte di Ludovico Marracci sul Corano'. In the *Rendiconti della R. Accademia nazionale dei Lincei, Cl. di scienze morali, storiche e filologiche*, 6th series, vol. 7 (1932): 303–349.

Nanquette, Laetitia, *Orientalism versus Occidentalism: Literary and Cultural Imaging between France and Iran since the Islamic Revolution*. London: I. B. Tauris, 2016.

Netton, Ian (ed.), *Encyclopedia of Islamic Civilization and Religion*, Abingdon, UK: Routledge, 2008.

Nielsen, Jørgen S. and Samir Khalil Samir (eds.), *Christian Arabic Apologetics during the Abbasid Period, 750–1258*. Leiden: E. J. Brill, 1993.

Noble, Samuel, 'Prose theological treatises', in *Christian–Muslim Relations 600–1500*, ed. David Thomas. <http://dx.doi.org/10.1163/1877-8054_cmri_COM_25140>. Accessed 7 August 2019.

—— 'Sulaymān al-Ghazzī' in *Christian–Muslim Relations 600–1500*, ed. David Thomas. <http://dx.doi.org/10.1163/1877-8054_cmri_COM_25138>. Accessed 7 August 2019.

Noble, Samuel and Alexander Treiger (eds.), *The Orthodox Church in the Arab World: 700–1700; An Anthology of Sources*. DeKalb, IL: Northern Illinois University Press, 2014.

O'Collins, Gerald, *Jesus Our Redeemer: A Christian Approach to Salvation*. Oxford: University Press, 2010.

Osborne, T. et al. (eds.), *A New and General Biographical Dictionary: Containing an Historical and Critical Account of the Lives and Writings of the Most Eminent Persons in Every Nation; Particularly the British and Irish*, 12 vols. London, 1761–1767.

Patrick, Simon, *A Commentary upon the First Book of Moses called Genesis*. London: Ri. Chiswell, 1704.

Peacey, Jason, '"Printers to the University" 1584–1658'. In *History of Oxford University Press, Volume I, Beginnings to 1780*, ed. Ian Gadd. Oxford: Oxford University Press, 2014, pp. 51–78.

Peters, Francis E., *Mecca: A Literary History of the Muslim Holy Land*. Princeton, NJ: Princeton University Press, 1994.

π, 'Review of Hermann Reckendorf (trans.), *al-Qōrān ō ha-Miqrā*'. *Monatsschrift für Geschichte und Wissenschaft des Judentums*, vol. 6 (1857): 357–359.

al-Qushayrī, Muslim ibn al-Ḥajjāj, *Mukhtaṣar Saḥīḥ Muslim*, ed. ʿAbd al-ʿAẓīm ibn ʿAbd al-Qawī al-Mundhirī. Beirut: Dār wa-Maktabat Hilāl, 1987.

al-Qūṭī, Ḥafṣ, *Le Psautier Mozarabe de Hafs le Goth*, ed. and trans. Marie-Thérèse Urvoy. Toulouse: Presses Universitaires du Mirail, 1994.

Ramadan, Tariq, *Islam: The Essentials*, trans. Fred Reed. London: Pelican, 2017.

Raphael, Ray, *A People's History of the American Revolution: How Common People Shaped the Fight for Independence*. New York: The New Press, 2016.

Reckendorf, Hermann, *Die Geheimnisse der Juden*, 5 vols. Leipzig: Wolfgang Gerhard, 1856–57.

—— (trans.), *al-Qōrān ō ha-Miqrā*. Leipzig: Wolfgang Gerhard, 1857.

Reckendorf Jr., Hermann, *Arabische Syntax*. Heidelberg: Carl Winter Universitätsverlag, 1921.

—— *Mohammed und die Seinen*. Leipzig: Quelle & Meyer, 1907.

Reynolds, Gabriel S., 'The Quran and the Apostles of Jesus'. *Bulletin of the School of Oriental and African Studies* 76:2 (2013): 209–227.

—— *The Qur'ān and its Biblical Subtext*. London: Routledge, 2010.

Robinson, Gnana, *Let us be Like the Nations: A Commentary on the Books of 1 and 2 Samuel*. Grand Rapids: Eerdmans, 1993.

Rodwell, John Meadows (trans.), *The Koran*. London: J. M. Dent; New York: E. P. Dutton, 1909.

al-Sa'dī, 'Abd al-Raḥmān ibn Nāṣir, *Taysīr al-Karīm al-Raḥmān fī Tafsīr Kalām al-Mannān*. Riyadh: Obeikan, 2013.

Sacra Congregatio de Propaganda Fide, *Biblia Sacra Arabica Sacrae Congregationis De Propaganda Fide Jussu Edita, Ad Usum Ecclesiarum Orientalium*, 3 vols. Rome, 1671.

Sadan, Arik, 'The Mood of the Verb following Ḥattā, according to Medieval Arab Grammarians'. In *The Foundations of Arabic Linguistics: Sībawayhi and early Arabic Grammatical Theory*, ed. Amal E. Marogy and M. G. Carter. Leiden: Brill, 2012, pp. 173–185.

Safran, Janina M., *Defining Boundaries in Al-Andalus: Muslims, Christians, and Jews in Islamic Iberia*. Ithaca: Cornell University Press, 2015.

Saint-Laurent, Jeanne-Nicole M., *Missionary Stories and the Formation of the Syriac Churches*. Oakland: University of California Press, 2015.

Sale, George (trans.), *A Comprehensive Commentary on the Qurán: Comprising Sale's Translation and Preliminary Discourse*, ed. E. M. Wherry, 4 vols. Boston: Houghton, 1882–1886.

—— (trans.), *The Koran: Commonly called the Alcoran of Mohammed*. London: C. Ackers, 1734.

—— (trans.), *The Koran: With Explanatory Notes from the Most Approved Commentators*. London: Warne, 1909.

Sale, George and Sulaymān ibn Ya'qūb al-Ṣāliḥānī (eds.), *al-'Ahd al-Jadīd*. London: S.P.C.K., 1727.

Santoyo, Julio-César, 'Revisiting the History of Medieval Translation in the Iberian Peninsula'. In *The Routledge Companion to Iberian Studies*, ed. Javier Munoz-Basols, Morales M. Delgado, and Laura Lonsdale. Florence: Taylor and Francis, 2017, pp. 93–104.

Schippers, Arie, 'Medieval Opinions on the Difficulty of Translating the Psalms: Some Remarks on Ḥafṣ al-Qūṭī's Psalms in Arabic *Rajaz* Metre'. In *Give Ear to My Words: Psalms and Other Poetry in and around the Hebrew Bible*, ed. Janet Dyk and Nico A. Uchelen. Amsterdam: Societas Hebraica Amstelodamensis, 1996, pp. 219–226.

Seifrid, Mark, *The Second Letter to the Corinthians*. Grand Rapids: Eerdmans, 2014.

Selden, John, *Opera Omnia*, ed. David Wilkins, 3 vols. in 6 vols. London, 1726.

Shotter, David, *Nero Caesar Augustus: Emperor of Rome*. London: Routledge, 2014.

Singer, Isidore (ed.), *The Jewish Encyclopedia: A Descriptive Record of the History, Religion, Literature, and Customs of the Jewish People from the Earliest Times to the Present Day, Volume X*. New York: Funk and Wagnalls, 1909.

Singerman, Robert, *Jewish Translation History: A Bibliography of Bibliographies and Studies*. Amsterdam: John Benjamins Publishing Company, 2002.

Simonsohn, Uriel, 'Motifs of a South-Melkite Affiliation in the *Annales* of Sa'īd ibn Baṭrīq'. In *Cultures in Contact: Transfer of Knowledge in the Mediterranean*

Context: Selected Papers, ed. Tovar S. Torallas and J. P. Monferrer-Sala. Córdoba: CNERU, 2013, pp. 243–254.

—— 'Sa'īd Ibn Baṭrīq'. In *Christian–Muslim Relations: A Bibliographical History; Volume 2, 900–1050*, ed. David Thomas, Alexander Mallett, and Barbara Roggema. Leiden: Brill, 2011, pp. 224–233.

Smith, Jeremy L., *Verse and Voice in Byrd's Song Collections of 1588 and 1589*. Woodbridge, UK: Boydell Press, 2016.

Spevack, Aaron, *The Archetypal Sunnī* Scholar: Law, *Theology, and Mysticism in the Synthesis of al-Bājūrī*. Albany, NY: State University of New York Press, 2014.

Spicq, Ceslaus, *Agape in the New Testament. Vol. II, Agape in the Epistle of St. Paul, the Acts of the Apostles and the Epistles of St. James, St. Peter and St. Jude*. St. Louis: Herder, 1965.

Steinschneider, Moritz, *Die Arabische Literatur der Juden: ein Beitrag zur Literaturgeschichte der Araber grossenteils aus handschriftlichen Quellen*. Frankfurt am Main: Kauffmann, 1902.

Sviri, Sara, 'Words of Power and the Power of Words: Mystical Linguistics in the Works of al-Hakim al-Tirmidhi'. *Jerusalem Studies in Arabic and Islam* 27 (2002): 204–244.

Swanson, Mark N., *The Coptic Papacy in Islamic Egypt (641–1517)*. Cairo: American University in Cairo Press, 2010.

al-Ṭabarī, *Daqāiq Lughat al-Qur'ān fī Tafsīr Ibn Jarīr al-Ṭabarī*, ed. 'Abd al-Raḥmān 'Umayrah. Beirut: 'Ālam al-Kutub, 1992.

Takahashi, Hidemi, *Barhebraeus: A Bio-Bibliography*. Piscataway, NJ: Gorgias Press, 2013.

—— 'Barhebraeus und seine islamischen Quellen. Têgrat têgrātā (Tractatus tractatuum) und Ġazālīs Maqāṣid al-falāsifa'. In *Syriaca: Zur Geschichte, Theologie, Liturgie und Gegenwartslage der Syrischen Kirchen; 2*. Münster: LIT Verlag, 2002, pp. 147–175.

—— 'Reception of Islamic Theology among Syriac Christians in the Thirteenth Century: The Use of Fakhr al-Dīn al-Rāzī in Barhebraeus' Candelabrum of the Sanctuary'. *Intellectual History of the Islamicate World*, 2:1–2 (2014): 170–192.

Teule, Herman, 'The Crusaders in Barhebraeus' Syriac and Arabic Secular Chronicles. A Different Approach'. In *East and West in the Crusader States. Context-Contacts-Confrontations*, ed. Krijnie Ciggar, Adelbert Davids, and Herman Teule. Leuven: Peeters, 1996, pp. 39–49.

Tieszen, Charles L., *Christian Identity amid Islam in Medieval Spain*. Leiden: Brill, 2013.

Toomer, G. J., *Eastern Wisedome and Learning: The Study of Arabic in Seventeenth-Century England*. Oxford: Clarendon Press, 2007.

Tottoli, Roberto, 'New light on the translation of the Qur'ān of Ludovico Marracci from his manuscripts recently discovered at the Order of the Mother of God in Rome'. In *Books and Written Culture of the Islamic World: Studies Presented to Claude Gilliot on the Occasion of his 75th Birthday*, ed. Andrew Rippin and Roberto Tottoli. Leiden: Brill, 2015, pp. 91–130.

Townley, James, *Illustrations of Biblical Literature: Exhibiting the History and Fate of the Sacred Writings, from the Earliest Period to the Present Century*, 3 vols. London: Longman, Hurst, Rees, Orme, and Brown, 1821.

Twells, Leonard, Zachary Pearce, Thomas Newton and Samuel Burdy, *The Lives of Dr. Edward Pocock, the Celebrated Orientalist by Dr. Twells; of Dr. Zachary Pearce,*

Bishop of Rochester, and of Dr. Thomas Newton, Bishop of Bristol, by Themselves; and of the Rev. Philip Skelton, by Mr. Burdy, 2 vols. London: Rivington, 1816.

Ullmann, Manfred, *Wörterbuch der klassischen arabischen Sprache, Vol. II/1*. Wiesbaden: Otto Harrassowitz Verlag, 1983.

Versteegh, Kees, *The Arabic Language*. Edinburgh: Edinburgh University Press, 2014.

Vinokur, Val, *The Trace of Judaism: Dostoevsky, Babel, Mandelstam, Levinas*. Evanston, IL: Northwestern University Press, 2008.

Waardenburg, Jacques, 'Towards a Periodization of Earliest Islam according to its Relations with Other Religions'. In *The Qur'an: Style and Contents*, ed. Andrew Rippin. Farnham, UK: Ashgate, 2011.

Wansbrough, John, *The Sectarian Milieu: Content and Composition of Islamic Salvation History*. New York: Prometheus, 2006.

Wehr, Hans, *A Dictionary of Modern Written Arabic*, ed. J. Milton Cowan. Wiesbaden: Otto Harrassowitz, 1961.

Werbner, Pnina, '*Du'a*: Popular Culture and Powerful Blessing at the 'Urs'. In *South Asian Sufis: Devotion, Deviation, and Destiny*, ed. Clinton Bennett and Charles M. Ramsey. London: Bloomsbury, 2013, pp. 83–94.

Wilde, Clare, *Approaches to the Qur'ān in Early Christian Arabic Texts (750–1258 C.E.)*. Bethesda, MD: Academica Press, 2014.

—— 'Early Christian Arabic Texts: Evidence for Non-ʿUthmānic Qur'ān Codices, or Early Approaches to the Qur'ān?' In *New Perspectives on the Qur'ān*: The *Qur'ān* in *its Historical Context 2*, ed. Gabriel S. Reynolds. London: Routledge, 2011, pp. 358–371.

Woodward, Mark R., *Java, Indonesia and Islam*. Dordrecht: Springer, 2011.

INDEX

Aaron, 115–116
Abraham, 50, 103, 116
Aesop, 137
Ahikar, 137–8
Alexandria, 56–8, 65, 67
Ammonius, 56–7, 64
Antonomasia, 83–6
Arabic, 3–5, 9–55, 56–8, 60–2, 65–73, 81–96, 103–4,106–115, 117, 137–8, 144–6
Arianism, 10
Armenian, 6
Ashmunein, 60
al-asmāʾ al-ḥusnā, 14–16, 23, 37–40, 89–91

Babel, 133
Bar Hebraeus, Gregory, 4, 70–3, 81–2
  Chronicon Ecclesiasticum, 70
  Mukhtaṣar Taʾrīkh al-Duwal, 70
Barqa, 65
basmala, 14–15, 72, 92, 107–8
Battle of Badr, 135
Bible
  Book of Tobit, 137
  Hebrew Bible
    1 Kings, 108–9, 134
    2 Samuel, 111–112
    Deuteronomy, 114
    Ecclesiastes, 128
    Exodus, 41–2, 95, 116, 124–6, 129, 137, 139
    Genesis, 59–60, 63, 86, 117–118, 137
    Numbers, 112
    Psalms, 110–112
      Psalm 1, 6, 9–12, 84, 87–8, 93
      Psalm 9, 90–1
      Psalm 10, 20
      Psalm 23, 91
      Psalm 30, 20–1
      Psalm 33, 16–17
      Psalm 46, 15–16
      Psalm 50, 22–4
      Psalm 55, 16
      Psalm 72, 114
      Psalm 85, 89, 93
      Psalm 87, 93–4
      Psalm 90, 21–2
      Psalm 92, 110
      Psalm 94, 91–2
      Psalm 103, 85–6
      Psalm 105, 24
      Psalm 106, 114
      Psalm 109, 22
      Psalm 113, 110
      Psalm 114, 17–18, 92
      Psalm 117, 27–8, 35–6
      Psalm 118, 18–19, 24–7, 90
      Psalm 127, 88–9
      Psalm 150, 110
      Zabūr, 12–13, 111
  New Testament
    Gospels, 1, 43, 115–116, 118, 124–6, 129, 136–7, 139
      John, 49
      Mark, 65, 67–8
      Matthew, 35, 135–6
      Sermon on the Mount, 1
    Revelation, 136
  translations
    Biblia Sacra Arabica, 4, 83, 86–95
    Septuagint, 96
    Vulgate, 4, 11, 20, 83, 85–7, 94, 96
Blake, William, 136
Buddha, 1
  Deer Park Sermon, 1
Burman, Thomas, 82

Canada, 1, 5, 144

Catholicism, 4, 57, 81–4, 90
Chalcedonianism, 4, 57–8, 60, 63, 70, 146
Charles II, 70–1
Civil War (England), 4, 58, 65–7, 69–70, 73
Claudius Caesar, 65, 67
Coleridge, S. T., 136
Convivencia, 10
Coptic, 6, 57, 60, 63, 65
Córdoba, 10

Dante Alighieri, 136
David, 13, 21–2, 106, 111–112, 128–9
Davis, Stephen J., 60
Demetrius, 56
devil, 21–2, 43–4, 59–63, 93, 113–114
Diocletian, 63–4, 72
disciples, 28, 63–6, 68
Disraeli, Benjamin, 102
D'Israeli, Isaac, 102, 104–105
  Calamities of Authors, 102
Domitian, 72–3
Dryden, John, 144

Ecumenical Councils, 60, 63–4
Edelby, Neophytos, 41–2
Egypt, 4, 41, 56–8, 60–1, 64–8, 124–6
Elijah, 134–5
Elmarsafy, Ziad, 82, 96
England, 4, 58, 65–7, 69–72, 105

fiqh, 10
France, 70
Frye, Northrop, 1–3, 5–6, 124–139, 144–6
  'The Bible and Literature' lectures, 124–6, 128–9, 137–8
  The Great Code, 1–2, 126, 129
  journals, 127–131
  Koran marginalia, 5, 131–6, 139, 144
  Words with Power, 1–2, 5, 146

Gabriel, 105
al-Ghazzī, Sulaymān, 3–4, 35–58, 145
  Dīwān
    poetic prayer, 37–8
    Qaṣīda 1, 43
    Qaṣīda 2, 41–2
    Qaṣīda 8, 40
    Qaṣīda 12, 43–4
    Qaṣīda 13, 48
    Qaṣīda 26, 49
    Qaṣīda 31, 46–8
    Qaṣīda 65, 44
    Qaṣīda 67, 38–9
    Qaṣīda 71, 45
    Qaṣīda 78, 39
    Qaṣīda 79, 35, 37, 50
Gideon, 128–9
Goethe, J. W., 3
Goliath, 128–9
Great Schism, 57
Greek, 1, 10, 12, 56, 83–4, 124, 128, 137
Griffith, Sidney H., 3, 36, 57, 72

ḥadīth, 14, 59, 71
ḥāfiẓ, 26–7, 90
Halle, 106
Haman, 128–9
heaven, 37, 39, 45–7, 59, 61–2, 84–7, 91–2, 96, 130–131, 134
Heidelberg, 106
hell, 20–21, 45, 93–4
Heracles, 56, 64
Here & Now, 144, 146
Holt, P. M., 82
ḥūr, 46–7

Ibn Baṭrīq, Sa'īd, 4, 56–62, 64–70, 72–3
Ibn al-Muqaffa', Severus, 4, 60–5, 72–3
iltifāt, 39, 127, 132
Ireland, 70
Isaac, 133
Isaiah, 61
Ishmael, 102–5, 107, 116, 118, 136–7
Israel, 41, 108–9, 111–112, 124, 126

Jacob, 112
Jerome, St., 11–13, 87–8
Jesse, 112
Jesus, 22–3, 28, 35–7, 43–4, 46–50, 95, 115–118, 124–5, 134–6, 139
jinn, 21–2, 43, 113–114
Johnson, Samuel, 128
Joseph, 124, 126
Judas, 134

Kaʿba, 104
Keats, John, 144
kerygma, 1–2, 6, 85, 145–6

Latin, 4, 10–12, 14, 65–7, 69–70, 81–9, 94–6, 110
Lawson, Todd, 131
Lazarus, 48–9
Leipzig, 5, 104, 106, 115
London, 4, 58, 65, 69, 94–6, 102
Luqmān, 138

Macdonald, George, 144
  Phantastes, 144
Marracci, Ludovico, 4, 81–97, 103, 107, 110
  Alcorani Textus Universus, 4, 81–4, 94, 103
  Biblia Sacra Arabica, 4, 83, 86–95
Martha, 49
Mary, 22, 115–118, 124–9, 132, 134, 136, 138–9
Mary Magdalene, 40, 43
Maximian, 63–4
Mecca, 28, 39, 104, 135
Melville, Herman, 137
  Moby-Dick, 137
Miaphysitism, 57, 60, 63, 70–1, 146
miḥrāb, 27–8, 35–6
Milton, John, 128–9, 136
Miriam, 116, 124–9, 132, 134, 138–9
Modad, 103
Moses, 41–2, 49–50, 138–9
Mozarabic, 10
Muḥammad (Prophet), 24, 66, 106, 129, 135, 138–9

Nallino, C. A., 82
Nero, 65, 67–68, 72
New England, 68
Noble, Samuel, 3, 37

Padua, 81, 95
Palestine, 3, 36, 56
Peter, 65–68, 134
Pharaoh, 128–9
Pococke, Edward, 4, 69–73, 81–2, 103–104
Pope Innocent XI, 81, 95

Qurʾān
  Sūra 1, 25, 87
  Sūra 2, 17, 25, 61–2, 87, 136
  Sūra 3, 17, 22, 66, 126, 134–6, 138
  Sūra 4, 47, 112
  Sūra 5, 66
  Sūra 6, 14, 50, 89
  Sūra 10, 91, 136
  Sūra 11, 17, 132
  Sūra 12, 132
  Sūra 15, 88
  Sūra 16, 131, 133–4
  Sūra 17, 50
  Sūra 18, 19
  Sūra 19, 115–117, 124, 136–7
  Sūra 20, 16, 41–2, 60, 133
  Sūra 22, 45, 69
  Sūra 23, 46
  Sūra 28, 42
  Sūra 30, 46, 49
  Sūra 35, 87
  Sūra 37, 46, 133
  Sūra 40, 37–9
  Sūra 42, 82
  Sūra 54, 19
  Sūra 55, 15–16, 45, 62–3
  Sūra 59, 16, 38
  Sūra 61, 66
  Sūra 71, 38
  Sūra 72, 21, 113–114
  Sūra 74, 21
  Sūra 77, 46
  Sūra 81, 84–6, 96
  Sūra 87, 9, 110–111
  Sūra 89, 18, 92
  Sūra 90, 109–110
  Sūra 94, 26
  Sūra 95, 94
  Sūra 110, 73
  Sūra 113, 62
  Sūra 114, 22
Quraysh, 103–4
al-Qūṭī, Ḥafṣ ibn Albar, 3, 5–6, 9–28, 35–7, 43, 84, 87, 90, 92, 110, 145 (see also Bible, Hebrew Bible, Psalms)

Reckendorf, Hermann, 5, 105–118, 124–5

Die Geheimnisse der Juden, 106
al-Qōrān ō ha-Miqrā, 5, 105–118, 124–5
Reckendorf, Shlomo, 106–7
Reckendorf Jr., Hermann, 106
Mohammed und die Seinen, 106
Restoration (England), 69–70
Revolution (American), 4, 58, 67–8
Reynolds, Gabriel Said, 64
Robert of Ketton, 66–7
Rodwell, John Meadows, 131–5, 138–9
Rome, 64–5, 67, 82, 86, 89, 95–6

Sacra Congregatio de Propaganda Fide, 83, 86
Saint-Laurent, Jeanne, 63
saja', 37
Sale, George, 4–5, 95–7, 102–107
Arabic New Testament, 94–5
Koran, 4–5, 95–7, 102–107
Universal History, 102
Samir, Fr Samir Khalil, 3
Saul, 128–9
Scotland, 70
Selden, John, 65–70
Shahrastānī, 81
sharī'a, 35–7, 49–51, 56–7, 89–90
Society for Promoting Christian Knowledge, 94
Spain, 3, 9–10, 16, 28, 36
Steinschneide, Moritz, 106
Stiles, Ezra, 67–8
Sufism, 3, 13, 89
Syriac, 6, 70

tafsīr, 13–14, 41, 89,
Takahashi, Hidemi, 72
ta'wīl, 13
tawḥīd, 40, 51, 82, 89
temple, 27–8
Ten Commandments, 95
tetragrammaton, 11, 117
Toomer G. J., 66
Treiger, Alexander, 3
Trinity, 10, 23, 40, 51, 81–2, 84
typology, 42, 124–7, 129, 135–7, 139, 145

United Church, 5
University of Toronto, 1, 5, 131–2, 134, 144
Urvoy, Marie-Thérèse, 10

Vatican, 83, 86, 96

Weil, Gustav, 106
Mohammed der Prophet, 106

Yale University, 67–8

www.ingramcontent.com/pod-product-compliance
Lightning Source LLC
Chambersburg PA
CBHW052100230426
43662CB00036B/1717
* 9 7 8 1 7 8 1 7 9 4 1 1 1 *